The Order of Genocide

The Order of Genocide

Race, Power, and War in Rwanda

SCOTT STRAUS

Cornell University Press Ithaca and London

First published 2006 by Cornell University Press
First printing, Cornell Paperbacks, 2008

Printed in the United States of America

Library of Congress Cataloging-in-Publication Data
Straus, Scott, 1970–
    The order of genocide : race, power, and war in Rwanda / Scott Straus.
        p. cm.
    Includes bibliographical references and index.
    ISBN-13: 978-0-8014-7492-7 (pbk. : alk. paper)
    1. Genocide—Rwanda.   2. Rwanda—History—Civil War, 1994—Atrocities.
3. Rwanda—Ethnic relation.   I. Title.
    DT450.435S765 2006
    967.57104′31—dc22   2006019352

Cornell University Press strives to use environmentally responsible suppliers and materials to the fullest extent possible in the publishing of its books. Such materials include vegetable-based, low-VOC inks and acid-free papers that are recycled, totally chlorine-free, or partly composed of nonwood fibers. For further information, visit our website at www.cornellpress.cornell.edu.

Paperback printing   10 9 8 7 6 5 4 3

For Sara

Contents

Preface and Acknowledgments

The Order of Genocide is a book that I did not intend to write—for three reasons. First, I never expected to write about Rwanda or about genocide. I was a journalist before becoming an academic, and in 1995 when I established myself as a freelance reporter in Nairobi I had no interest in conflict or in Africa's Great Lakes region. I wanted to cover the less gory aspects of African politics and society: elections, political change, health issues, statecraft, and the like. That vision lasted only a year.

I first encountered ethnic violence in Burundi in 1996. My editors wanted me to cover the undoing of the fragile Hutu-led government there, and I did. That was in July. Three months later, I was in Somalia, and my editor from the *Houston Chronicle* called, urging me to cover a brewing war in eastern Zaire. The story was shaping up to be a major one, he said, and the paper wanted me to cover it exclusively. Exclusive coverage was a break, and I seized it. I returned to Nairobi, packed a light bag, including the one book on the Rwandan genocide I owned (but had not yet read), and flew to Kigali. From the capital, I took a taxi to the Zairean border in northwest Rwanda.

I covered the war in Zaire for the next seven months, and it was in Zaire where my fascination with Rwanda began. The war involved a complex mix of players, but in the early days the conflict was primarily a Rwandan one. Two years earlier, there had been civil war and genocide in Rwanda. The regime that committed the genocide lost the war, and many former government soldiers, members of militia, and

politicians—as well as more than a million Hutu refugees—fled to
Zaire as the Tutsi-led rebel forces consolidated control of Rwanda.
Two years later, the one-time rebels (who then controlled the Rwandan
state) attacked Zaire, trying to finish off their rivals.

The days of November 1996 would be fateful ones. The Tutsi forces
were victorious. The rump-defeated government and military fled
deeper into Zaire. The refugee population split. Some followed their
former leaders into Zaire. Others marched home to Rwanda to face
their fate there. I covered these often dramatic events. I also covered
scenes of horror. One night, a mortar bomb exploded near my hotel,
blowing up a boy. Another day, I came upon a mass grave of freshly
macheted women and children. These experiences had a profound effect on me. The rush of war, the massive refugee flows, and the massacre shocked and captivated me at the same time. The events were
outside my frame of reference, and I could not make any sense of them.

I date the origins of *The Order of Genocide* to that month. I never
expected to be in Zaire or Rwanda or to cover raw violence, but once
I witnessed such events, I could not let go of them easily. Eventually
my trauma—that is, I believe, what I experienced—formulated itself
as an intellectual question: why does violence of this magnitude happen? And the more I thought about that question, the more I was
drawn to what I considered the root event in the region: the Rwandan
genocide of 1994, in which at least half a million civilians were systematically slaughtered. How could I make sense of violence of this
scale and character? That question is the foundation for *The Order of
Genocide.*

The second reason I did not intend to write this book concerns
methodology. In 1998, I traded my reporter's notebooks for graduate
school, and I quickly gravitated to theories of mass violence and African politics. I devoured books, wanting to understand how genocide
happens and wanting to understand the politics I had reported but understood only superficially. Political science methods courses held little appeal, at least initially.

However, the more I learned about Rwanda and genocide, the more
I saw that the theory had outpaced the evidence. Observers had formulated numerous hypotheses about why genocide happens, but the
supporting evidence was thin. What evidence did exist was often anecdotal or superficial. Journalists (like me) had quoted a couple Rwandans, and those quotations in turn became the basis for theories.
Human rights activists showed that particular leaders planned the violence. Historians showed the deep roots of identity. Propaganda was

a fascination. But how specifically did all this relate to the actual violence? Why did people kill? Was it because of the leaders' manipulation? Was it because of poverty? Was it because of obedience? Was it because of indoctrination? And why was the violence on such a large scale? Not only were the existing answers to these questions unsatisfactory, but the actual dynamics of violence were also poorly understood. They were a black box.

My questions thus shifted. The issue became not just why genocide happens, but also how that question can be answered and what exactly did happen. I soon realized that these were questions of evidence and interpretation, and questions of evidence and interpretation are ultimately methodological in nature. And so I became convinced of the need to collect information systematically and in particular of the need to collect evidence that would allow me to test various theories. I did not want to generalize from anecdotes. I wanted representative evidence, and I wanted evidence appropriate to the explanations that already existed. Moreover, I wanted to analyze that evidence systematically using a variety of methods.

Why does all this matter? *The Order of Genocide* is fundamentally about explaining genocide in Rwanda, but methodology is critical to that endeavor, and I use a range of methods to collect and analyze evidence. I mention all of this because I want the book to interest readers who care about genocide but do not necessarily care about social science. (I hope for the reverse as well: I hope the book interests social scientists who care about methods but not necessarily about genocide.) But from the reader who may balk at statistics or at the combination of statistics and genocide, I request perseverance. Methods matter. Theory matters. What distinguishes the book—and what often distinguishes scholarship from journalism—is the systematic collection and analysis of evidence.

The third reason this book is not one I expected to write concerns scope. This too is a methodological issue. When I began to research Rwanda, I anticipated conducting a broad comparative analysis of genocide. I planned to examine the Armenian genocide, the Holocaust, Cambodia under the Khmer Rouge, and the Balkan wars of the 1990s. I would search for commonalities among those cases and the Rwandan one in order to understand the determinants of genocide. However, I encountered two major problems with the approach. First, the comparison was too broad. The cases were too varied historically, politically, and empirically. Political scientists often seek generalizations and use comparison to achieve their goal. But while scholars may reasonably characterize the above cases as "genocide," the patterns and levels of violence in each varied considerably. The cases spanned three continents, the countries had quite different levels of economic development, and the violence occurred in different historical periods. There were, in short, too many moving parts for meaningful comparison—at least for my taste.

I decided against cross-national comparison for another important reason. The more I investigated the Rwandan genocide, the more I discovered a yawning gap of information about the micro-dynamics of violence. Yet many theories of genocide in general and Rwanda in particular seek to explain individual-level behavior. Moreover, although scholars had offered many explanations of the Rwandan genocide, there were very few empirical tests of the theories. Hence—given the problems with cross-regional comparisons of genocide and with the poor match between theory and evidence for Rwanda—I decided the best way forward would be a single-country study, but one that would incorporate temporal, regional, and local variation and seek to test general theories.

One final but important point: writing about genocide is not to be taken lightly. I have witnessed two common flaws. First, authors sometimes trade on horror. Second, because the violence is so awful, many have a hard time examining it closely, which in turn leads to quick generalizations and abstractions. In the eight years that I have spent researching and writing about genocide, I have tried to avoid these pitfalls. I have tried to be sensitive to evidence, to avoid sensationalizing the violence, and to stop short of making unnecessarily provocative statements. In the book, my tone is occasionally muted, but this choice reflects an ethics of presentation.

The book does not include a bibliography. Readers wishing to view or download a list of the sources used in this book may do so at www.polisci.wisc.edu/users/straus/research.html.

During the course of this project, I benefited enormously from the kindness and generosity of many people and organizations. The National Science Foundation, the Social Science Research Council, the United States Institute of Peace, the Center for African Studies at the University of California, Berkeley, and the Graduate School and African Studies Program at the University of Wisconsin–Madison, all provided critical financial support and encouragement, often at key moments.

Generosity also has come in the form of friendship, information, suggestions, criticism, and invitations to speak. I thank in particular Mark Beissinger, Bob Bates, Thierry Cruvellier, Lynn Eden, Michel Feher, Ed Friedman, Nelson Kasfir, Heinz Klug, Danielle de Lame, René Lemarchand, Steven Miller, Tamir Moustafa, Catharine Newbury, David Newbury, Rita Parhad, Leigh Payne, Victor Peskin, Jon Pevehouse, Dan Posner, Filip Reyntjens, Geoffrey Robinson, Jamie Rosen, Ted Ruel, Lara Santoro, Michael Schatzberg, David Schoenbrun, Gay Seidman, Steve Stedman, Sarah Stein, Laura Stoker, Aili Tripp, Henry Turner, Peter Uvin, Philip Verwimp, and Rebecca Walkowitz. In addition, Michael Barnett, Alison Des Forges, Stathis Kalyvas, Ben Valentino, Libby Wood, and Crawford Young all read the manuscript in its entirety and made invaluable suggestions. Joe Soss helped me put together the graphs and provided sound advice. Scott Gehlbach and Alice Kang as well as members of the Comparative Politics Research Colloquium in Madison provided terrific comments on the last stages of the manuscript. Emily Fischer, Michael Holloway, and Alice Kang supplied excellent research assistance. Heather Francisco of the University of Wisconsin–Madison Cartography Lab designed and executed the maps in the book. I pursued Cornell University Press to publish this book, in part, because of Roger Haydon's reputation for editorial acumen. I have not been disappointed: he has been an outstanding editor. Karen Laun and Martin Schneider also provided many smart and sound editorial suggestions.

Conducting research in Rwanda depended on the permission of the Rwandan government, in particular the Ministries of Interior and Local Administration as well as the Prosecutor's Office. For this I thank them. My stay in Rwanda was at times trying. I cannot imagine what the research there would have been like without the unstinting and superb companionship of Lars Waldorf, Ben Siddle, and Eithne Brennan. Lars later read the entire manuscript and made some terrific suggestions. I also owe an enormous debt to Théogène Rwabahizi, my principal assistant in Rwanda, with whom I worked closely. Aloys Habimana was a source of knowledge and assistance in Kigali—as he is now in Madison.

My advisers at the University of California, Berkeley, deserve enormous credit for their insight, suggestions, and criticisms as my interest in the Rwandan genocide developed. In particular, I thank David Leonard who was as ethical, astute, and helpful an adviser as any student could have. Michael Watts was a source of inspiration and prescient advice from the day I arrived on campus. David Collier, Michael

Mann, and Hanna Pitkin all provided outstanding and detailed comments. Bob Price was a source of sanity. Mike Rogin was one of the most incisive and extraordinary men I have ever known, and he was extremely influential in the early stages of this project. Mike died unexpectedly the day I started to conduct research abroad. I wish he were here to see the final product.

Finally, an enormous thank you to my parents (all four), who offered unwavering support and encouragement throughout. And to Sara Guyer, who endured the nightmares, anxiety, doubt, excitement, distance, and stubbornness that a project like this requires (or that I required of it). By her intelligence, Sara has taught me how to see the unobvious and, by her example, to appreciate judgment. The book and I would be half of what we are without her.

The usual caveats apply. Though I have benefited greatly from others, the mistakes and views herein are my own.

The Order of Genocide

Introduction

In 1994, a small group of hardliners within Rwanda's ruling party and military organized the twentieth century's most rapid extermination campaign. In the midst of a civil war and right after a presidential assassination, the hardliners consolidated control of the Rwandan state, eliminated their main political opponents, formed an interim government, and declared war on "the Tutsi enemy." The hardliners ultimately deployed loyal army units and militia, mobilized the civilian administration, and urged every able man to join the fight. The instructions were the same everywhere: eliminate the Tutsis.

One hundred days later, the hardliners lost the civil war, but by then the violence they had unleashed had claimed at least half a million civilian lives. Tens of thousands were Hutus, but the violence's defining characteristic—its organizing principle—was the systematic annihilation of Rwanda's Tutsi minority.[1] The violence was low-tech: many perpetrators used ordinary farm tools, such as machetes, clubs, and hoes, to kill. The violence was public, face-to-face, crowd-enforced, and neighbor sometimes killed neighbor. But the episode's central feature was a deliberate, systematic, state-led campaign to eliminate a racially defined social group. The violence was genocide. The aim of

---

1. Estimates for the total number of civilians who were killed during the genocide vary from 500,000 to more than a million. The estimates that I cite here come from Alison Des Forges, *Leave None to Tell the Story: Genocide in Rwanda* (New York: Human Rights Watch, 1999), 15–16. The numbers killed—of both Tutsi and Hutu—are discussed in greater detail in chapter 2.

this book is to use social science to understand how and why genocide happened.

The task presents distinct challenges. Genocide is about extraordinary human violence, about violence of a character and level that is rare, and about violence that represents a mind-numbing transgression of the normal respect for human life. Genocide is ultimately about how ordinary people come to see fellow citizens, neighbors, friends, loved ones, and even children as "enemies" who must be killed. Genocide is, moreover, a massively complex social phenomenon. Genocide involves a range of social institutions, from the state and the military to the church and the media. And in the Rwandan case, genocide included the participation of hundreds of thousands of individuals, of whom the majority had no prior history of committing lethal violence.

Key Questions

The central question that frames this book is: how and why did genocide happen? That question in fact aggregates several others: Why did Rwanda's hardliners choose genocide as a strategy to keep power? What factors led them to order violence against civilians and ultimately to order extermination? But then why did they succeed? Why did genocidal violence take root across the country and why did it spread so quickly? What drove tens of thousands of ordinary Rwandans to commit genocide?

In the past decade, a great deal has been written and said about the Rwandan genocide. Much of that research seeks to dispel the notion that the genocide resulted from tribal chaos and "ancient hatred." Rwanda, many have argued—properly in my view—is a case of modern genocide. Elites planned it. They used the state to implement their plan. They drew on a specific nationalist ideology. And the violence was a systematic campaign to destroy a named population group. The violence was not just tribalism run amok. It was genocide.

The current consensus offers a far more accurate picture of events than does the tribal hatred model. But the current consensus also contains important analytical and empirical gaps. Most existing research on Rwanda is descriptive and focuses on the top—on Rwandan history and on the ruling elite's responsibility in the genocide. Considerably less is known about the middle and the bottom—that is, how and why elite decisions led to widespread exterminatory violence. And considerably less is known about *why* the elites took the decisions they did.

It is not enough to say that Hutu hardliners planned genocide, that they used the state, and that they drew on a nationalist ideology. Rather, we need to explain why the elites succeeded—why so many complied with the orders to kill—and what probable factors drove the elites to make the fateful decisions that they did. This book addresses these gaps in knowledge and understanding and in so doing seeks to explain precisely how and why genocide happened in Rwanda.

A major focus of this book is an examination of the genocide's local dynamics. In order to answer the above questions—what drove the killing, why so many participated—it is crucial to investigate carefully how the violence started and spread in local areas across the country. Rwanda is overwhelmingly rural, and most of the killing happened in the countryside. Yet how violence spread to these rural areas—and spread so quickly and intensively—is not well understood. What were the patterns of violence in rural areas? Who mobilized whom? Who were the perpetrators? Did violence start at the same time across the country or were there important regional differences? These and other questions need to be investigated in order to understand how and why genocide happened in Rwanda.

A second major focus of the book is an evaluation of explanations. Theories that purport to explain genocide and aspects of genocide are not in short supply. Some authors focus on macro-level factors such as ideologies of nationalism or utopia, periods of social upheaval, widespread deprivation, modernity, and the strategic calculations of leaders. Other authors focus on why perpetrators commit genocide. Here scholars variously emphasize ethnic antipathy, ideological beliefs, the desire for material wealth, frustration caused by deprivation, peer pressure, obedience to authority, and indoctrination through propaganda. The list of plausible explanations is, in fact, fairly long. The problem is a lack of evidence and using what evidence does exist to test hypotheses. Thus, a principal objective of the book is to generate evidence systematically and to use that data to evaluate which factors drove the violence.

A third major focus of the book is to develop a theory of genocide in Rwanda—one that can account for what was happening at both the national and local levels. Genocide is by definition an aggregate event. In reality, genocide consists of thousands of specific instances of violence that have a similar character and purpose. In that sense, genocide is comparable to social revolution: genocide is a large, macro-social process that scholars shoehorn into a single category. A comprehensive explanation of genocide needs to account for not just one or two instances of violence and not just for violence at a particular level. Rather, a comprehensive theory should seek to bridge the various levels. That task is all the more challenging because while the Rwandan genocide was analytically neat in one sense—the violence did have a similar character and purpose (extermination)—the dynamics were often kaleidoscopic. This book aims to account theoretically for both the outcome of genocide and the complex reality of the violence.

Throughout, the focus is Rwanda, but the theories and ideas that frame the book are intended to be general. The Rwandan genocide is a critical case study for scholars, policymakers, and students who are interested in ethnic conflict and genocide. By the same token, many interpretations of the Rwandan genocide derive from studies of other genocides and other episodes of ethnic violence. Thus, the purpose of the book is not only to evaluate and develop explanations of the Rwandan genocide, but also to treat Rwanda as a test case for general theories of ethnic conflict and genocide. Any general macro-level or micro-level theory of genocide should find application in Rwanda. At the same time, my arguments about the Rwandan genocide should offer insight into the dynamics driving other episodes of ethnic violence and genocide.

Research Methods and Design

Research design and methods are critical to this book. A major problem with the existing literature—whether on Rwanda as a single case or in a comparative context—is that authors often make speculative claims on the basis of limited and not systematically collected information. This book tries to correct that tilt. As I noted in the preface, some readers may bristle at the focus on methodology, and others may find methodological discussions dry. But methodology is important for getting to the next stage of understanding about why this genocide happened and for deepening our understanding of why genocide happens more generally.

Most of the evidence in this book comes from research I conducted in Rwanda in 2002. The research project had three stages. First, I conducted a nationwide survey of convicted perpetrators in Rwandan prisons who had pled guilty to their crimes. Most respondents were randomly sampled. Convicted perpetrators, or *génocidaires*, have their biases, and I discuss them later. The main reason for this approach is that I wanted information about the dynamics of mobilization and participation, and these perpetrators directly took part in and observed the killing. Despite the problems of interviewing perpetrators, the method is one of the very few ways to evaluate hypotheses about why individuals participate in genocide. Moreover, the approach is not uncommon to studies of the Holocaust, and my method in part derives from that literature.[2]

In total, I interviewed 210 respondents in fifteen prisons during the survey portion of my research. In the interviews, I sought information about who the perpetrators were (in terms of their ages, professions, education levels, and the like), I asked them questions about their belief systems before the genocide, I asked them a series of questions about how they were mobilized into the genocide and what happened during the violence, and I asked them why they committed violence, often against people they knew. These interviews form the evidentiary backbone of this book.

The second research stage was a micro-comparative study of genocidal dynamics in five Rwandan locations. Violence broke out in all but one commune under government control in Rwanda. (A commune is an administrative unit equivalent to a town or district.) What I discovered through interviewing perpetrators is that genocide happened differently in different areas. In some areas, soldiers initiated the killing; in other areas, civilian authorities did; in still other areas, ordinary civilians led the charge. In some areas, violence started very quickly after the president's assassination, while in others local Hutus actively resisted for two weeks before being overwhelmed. And in one commune under government control genocide did not happen at all.

Political scientists who study violence have made rewarding use of the micro-comparative method.[3] The approach yields insight because it can hold many variables constant while focusing on variation. Rwanda differs from the modal case of violence because, with the exception of one commune, killing ultimately happened in all areas under government control. Moreover, there do not appear to be significantly different levels of violence countrywide, as I discuss in chapter 2. Thus, my primary axis of comparison is not level of vio-

2. Particularly influential for me were Hannah Arendt, *Eichmann in Jerusalem: A Report on the Banality of Evil*, rev. ed. (New York: Penguin Books, 1965); and, especially, Christopher Browning, *Ordinary Men: Reserve Police Battalion 101 and the Final Solution in Poland* (New York: HarperCollins, 1992).

3. Stathis Kalyvas, *The Logic of Violence in Civil War* (New York: Cambridge University Press, 2006); Ashutosh Varshney, *Ethnic Conflict and Civic Life: Hindus and Muslims in India* (New Haven: Yale University Press, 2002); and Steven Wilkinson, *Votes and Violence: Electoral Competition and Ethnic Riots in India* (New York: Cambridge University Press, 2004).

lence but pattern of mobilization. Of the five locations I studied, four typified different patterns of mobilization, and one was the commune where genocide did not happen. In each, I interviewed a cross section of Rwandans, including survivors, perpetrators, current and former officials, and other local leaders. I learned a great deal from this study. The principal findings are in chapter 3, but the insights from the microcomparative study infuse the entire book.

The third research stage entailed return trips to the Rwandan prisons. In this stage, I selected particular respondents to interview, rather than sampling randomly. Those I chose to interview had been identified in the previous two research phases as leaders of the killing or as particularly aggressive killers. I interviewed these prisoners principally in order to double-check the evidence that I had collected. Because many of these perpetrators were recalcitrant or denied the crimes of which others accused them or for which they had been found guilty, the interviews were often frustrating and yielded few, though occasionally important, details. In total, I interviewed nineteen respondents during this research stage, bringing the total number of perpetrators I interviewed to roughly 230.

To the original research that I conducted, I have added as much secondary material as I could find. This material includes evidence from international court cases, human rights reports, journalist's accounts, and works written by other scholars who have studied Rwanda's genocide. I also conducted archival research in Belgium, Rwanda's former colonial ruler.

Each research stage and source of data will be discussed in greater detail in the chapters that follow. Alone, each source has strengths and weaknesses. Taken together, they offer a multifaceted evidentiary basis from which I evaluate and develop arguments. Again, methodology matters in interpretation. The Rwandan genocide was traumatic, interpretations are deeply politicized both inside and outside the country, and the killings are the subject of both domestic and international criminal prosecution. Finding unbiased data in that environment is extremely difficult, if not impossible. Thus, a central principle of my interpretation of the evidence I collected is triangulation. I take the position that no one swath of data or method of analysis is sufficient on its own. In the chapters that follow, I examine dynamics at national, regional, commune, and individual levels, and I analyze the findings using both quantitative and qualitative techniques.

The Argument

I find that the Rwandan genocide happened in the following way. After President Juvénal Habyarimana was assassinated on April 6, 1994, and in the midst of a defensive civil war against Tutsi-led rebels, Hutu hardliners declared all Tutsis to be "the enemy." In a context of intense crisis and war, the declaration that Tutsis were the enemy functioned as a de facto policy—in effect, an authoritative order and a basis for authority—around which coalitions of actors could mobilize to take control of their communities. Once local actors who subscribed to the hardliners' position had secured enough power, they made killing Tutsis the new order of the day and demanded compliance from the Hutu civilian population. In the Rwandan context, where state institutions are dense at the local level, where civilian mobilization is a common state practice, where the idea of state power is resonant, and where geography provides little opportunity for exit, large-scale civilian mobilization to kill was rapid, and the violence was extraordinarily intense and devastating.

I argue that three main factors drove this process. The first of these is the war: without a war in Rwanda, genocide would not have happened. (By war, I mean here the civil war that began on April 7, 1994, after the president was assassinated and which the hardliners were losing.) War matters for several reasons. First, war provided the essential rationale for mass killing: security. The logic of Rwanda's genocide was predicated on eliminating a threat, on self-protection and the reestablishment of order. War was critical to that logic. Second, war legitimized killing. In war, parties to the conflict sought to physically destroy their opponents. Third, the war that took place during the genocide was intense and defensive. The war thus created a climate of acute uncertainty and insecurity. That context was critical to why some individuals fomented violence; to why those who fomented violence gained the upper hand; and to why many individuals agreed to take part in the killing. Fourth, war—in this case civil war—led to the involvement of specialists in violence: soldiers, gendarmes, and militias. Specialists in violence in turn facilitated killing. In short, war underpinned the logic of genocide, war legitimized killing, war empowered hardliners, and war led specialists in violence to engage the domestic political arena.

The assassination of Rwanda's president was part of this dynamic. The assassination ruptured Rwanda's political order and created a temporary gap in authority. The president's death caused anger, lead-

ing to calls for violent revenge; the assassination augmented the anxiety, fear, and confusion of the war; the rupture in political order also
set the stage for local power struggles. The latter is particularly important. After the president's death, Hutu hardliners succeeded in
gaining control of the state and urged war against the Tutsi "enemy."
That idea—war against the Tutsis—then became the terms around
which power was contested around the country. The hardliners and
those who adhered to the program of genocide ultimately won the upper hand in almost all areas not yet lost to the rebels. Genocide became the order of the day. But it would not likely have happened
outside a context of war, including the rupture caused by the president's assassination.

The second main factor is the nature of Rwandan state institutions.
The Rwandan state matters for a number of reasons. First, the state in
Rwanda has unusual depth and resonance at the local level, which
meant that, by controlling the state, the hardliners had the capacity
to enforce their decisions countrywide. Second, control of the state allowed the hardliners to associate killing Tutsis with authority, thus
equating violence with de facto policy. Third, Rwanda has a long history of obligatory labor, and expectations derived from that history
contributed to large-scale civilian mobilization during the genocide.
The potency of the Rwandan state cannot be taken for granted, because most African states are weak, especially in rural areas. Thus, in
addition to demonstrating the importance of the state to the outcome
of genocide, this book also explains why Rwanda's state is so effective
at civilian mobilization.

Related to Rwanda's state is the country's geography. Rwanda is the
most densely populated country in Africa and one of the most densely
populated countries in the world. Rwanda also is a land of rolling, cultivated hills. There is very little open, undeveloped space in the country. As a result, the country's population is very visible and vulnerable,
particularly in rural areas, and there is very little physical room for escape. The shortage of "exit" options is part of the reason that the
killing was so rapid and intensive, and it also helps explain why so
many Rwandans complied with the state's orders to kill. Rwanda's
geography amplifies, and is ultimately inseparable from, the state's capacity for social control and mobilization. In short, the speed, intensity, and participatory character of the violence during the genocide
cannot be divorced either from Rwanda's state institutions or from the
country's geography.

Third, ethnicity mattered, but in surprising ways. Overall, I find that the mechanisms driving individuals to kill were not primarily about ethnic prejudice, preexisting ethnic antipathy, manipulation from racist propaganda, or nationalist commitments. On balance, Hutus did not kill Tutsis because they hated Tutsis in some constant fashion, because they believed Tutsis were no longer human, or because they were deeply committed ideologically to Hutu nationalism or to ethnic utopia. These dimensions of motivation mattered for some perpetrators, but not for the majority.

That said, the logic of extermination in Rwanda depended on the idea that Tutsis are fundamentally alike. The genocidal mandate from the hardliners was to equate "enemy" with "Tutsi" and to declare that Rwanda's "enemies" had to be eliminated. The hardliners did not invent ethnic categories in Rwanda. Those categories preexisted the genocide. Yet awareness of ethnic difference in and of itself was not the cause of the violence. Before the genocide, most ordinary Hutus and Tutsis in the countryside lived next door to each other without conflict. Many intermarried, and in my interviews with Hutus and Tutsis alike I found strong evidence of interethnic cooperation before the genocide.

Yet something changed. During the genocide, Tutsis were labeled the enemy, and many Hutus, most of whom had no apparent history of antipathy toward Tutsis, accepted the claim. The mechanism that allowed that process to happen is collective ethnic categorization. In case after case, as we shall see, when justifying killing civilians, perpetrators substituted the Tutsi category for the individuals they were attacking. A perpetrator will say something like, "There was a war. The authorities told us to kill the Tutsi enemy, and we did." Perpetrators will say this even when pushed to recognize that the people they were killing were individuals whom they knew not to be involved in the war. This idea of "Tutsi = enemy" is impossible without some preexisting, society-wide, and resonant notion of ethnic categories. The categories matter.

But what caused the shift from awareness of ethnic categories to collective categorization and violence? On the whole, my findings do not support ideational factors such as ideological beliefs or preexisting ethnic antipathy. Rather, the principal mechanisms, I argue, were (1) wartime uncertainty and fear; (2) social pressure; and (3) opportunity. In the aggregate, Hutus killed because they wanted to protect themselves during a war and during a period of intense uncertainty, because they felt that complying with those who told them to kill would be less costly than not complying, and because they opportunistically used the period of confusion and violence to obtain power and property. Not all individuals committed violence for each of these reasons. The mechanisms appeared to varying degrees in different people, but in the aggregate these were the primary mechanisms driving the collective ethnic categorization and the violence.

Implications

There are a number of ways to read this book. For readers who wish to understand the Rwandan genocide better, the book offers a new interpretation and considerable information about local-level dynamics. For readers who wish to understand ethnic conflict and genocide—of which Rwanda is a textbook example—the book offers a detailed, empirical study of a critical case. For readers interested in how and why ordinary human beings participate in extraordinary violence, the book offers much evidence and theory to answer those questions. For readers interested in political mobilization, the book documents and explains how a society rapidly shifts from quiescence to mass participatory violence. Finally, for readers who are curious about how to study mass violence and ethnic conflict, the book offers a series of concrete methods that can be used to collect and analyze evidence for other cases.

The book's arguments also have theoretical implications that extend beyond Rwanda. For example, my findings support "ordinary men" theories of genocide perpetrators. I find that the profile of Rwanda's perpetrators strongly resembles the profile of adult men in the country. Rwanda's perpetrators were not especially mad, sadistic, hateful, poor, uneducated, ideologically committed, or young.[4] There are some exceptions, of course. I find in each location a core group of extremely violent men, and they tended to be younger and to have fewer preexisting ties with Tutsis than other perpetrators. On the whole, however, Rwanda's killers were ordinary men—farmers, fathers, and sons—with fairly few distinctive characteristics.

My findings point also to the critical importance of self-protection as a mechanism that can lead to violence. Many Rwandans became perpetrators because they feared advancing rebels and because they feared the negative consequences of disobeying. The specific nature of

---

4. Arendt, *Eichmann in Jerusalem*; Browning, *Ordinary Men*; and James Waller, *Becoming Evil: How Ordinary People Commit Genocide and Mass Killing* (Oxford: Oxford University Press, 2002).

Rwanda's war and state mattered for the calculations Rwandans made. But the broader implication is that ordinary men will choose, in particular circumstances, to commit violence in order to safeguard themselves and their families.

At a more macro level, scholars of genocide emphasize utopic ideologies and authoritarian regimes.[5] I find little evidence of these factors in the Rwandan case. On the first point, the leaders who instigated genocide did so primarily to win a civil war, not to radically restructure society. On the second point, the Rwandan state capacity to enforce decisions and mobilize the citizenry was critical to the outcome, but an authoritarian regime was not. Rather, the compromised and fractured power of the hardliners drove the violence. In particular, multipartyism and a peace accord before the genocide eroded the power of previously dominant elites, which in turn led them to pursue irregular and extreme tactics to keep power. Those tactics grew into genocide after the president's assassination and in the context of an intense and defensive war. Absolute power did not drive the radical measures; rather, new constraints, fractured power, and a defensive civil war did.

My findings confirm that genocide emerges from top-down instrumental decisions, but they also help clarify under what conditions leaders choose mass violence as a strategy.[6] In particular, the decision to foment violence was intimately connected to war and, more specifically, to fighting a defensive war from a position of eroded power. The relationship between war and genocide is one that scholars of genocide increasingly emphasize.[7] My research shows how and why war

5. On utopia, see Eric Weitz, *A Century of Genocide: Utopias of Race and Nation* (Princeton: Princeton University Press, 2003); on dictatorships and authoritarianism, see Rudolph Rummel, *Death by Government* (New Brunswick: Transaction Books, 1994); and Irving Louis Horowitz, *Taking Lives: Genocide and State Power* (New Brunswick: Transaction Books, 1997).

6. The "instrumental" origin of ethnic violence—meaning that elites promote violence for their own instrumental gain—is a common argument in the literature on ethnic conflict. Such a view also underpins much writing on the Rwandan genocide, including, for example, Des Forges, *Leave None*. The strategic origins of genocide are emphasized in Benjamin Valentino, *Final Solutions: Mass Killing and Genocide in the Twentieth Century* (Ithaca: Cornell University Press, 2004).

7. The relationship between war and genocide is emphasized in new scholarship on the comparative study of genocide. See, in particular, Manus Midlarsky, *The Killing Trap: Genocide in the Twentieth Century* (Cambridge: Cambridge University Press, 2005); Martin Shaw, *War and Genocide: Organized Killing in Modern Society* (Oxford: Polity, 2003); and Benjamin Valentino, Paul Huth, and Dyland Balch-Lindsay, "Draining the Sea: Mass Killing, Guerrilla Warfare," *International Organization* 58, no. 2 (2004), 375–407.

mattered. Ethnic nationalism also played a role.[8] While I do not find that strong nationalist commitments drove low-level participation, the prominence of elite-level ethnic ideologies shaped the decision of leaders to choose genocide as a strategy to win the war and to keep power.

The evidence also challenges a static model of genocide. I argue that Rwanda's genocide was not necessarily "meticulously planned" well in advance, as is often said. Rather, I argue that a dynamic of escalation was critical to the hardliners' choice of genocide. The more the hardliners felt that they were losing power and the more they felt that their armed enemy was not playing by the rules, the more the hardliners radicalized. After the president was assassinated and the rebels began advancing, the hardliners let loose. They chose genocide as an extreme, vengeful, and desperate strategy to win a war that they were losing. Events and contingency mattered.

The literature on the Holocaust provides an imperfect but instructive analogy. One model of the Holocaust sees Hitler and key Nazi officials as having planned the Jews' extermination well in advance of World War II. This "intentionalist" model views the genocide as a top-down implementation of the core Nazi vision of eliminating the Jews. Another model emphasizes "cumulative radicalization" in that the Nazis consistently ratcheted up the intensity of violence in response to various (mostly external) factors, chiefly the war against the Soviet Union and the 1941 entry of the United States. The latter model sees racial ideology as a core Nazi belief that established a normative context in which lower level officials competed and improvised. In this reading, genocide was a contingent policy, one that developed over time. New comparative research on genocide supports the same conclusion. Genocide is not usually the first choice of leaders, but the outcome of a process of escalation—a "final solution," as Benjamin Valentino argues.[9]

Rwanda was not Germany, and Rwanda's genocide was not exactly like Germany's. But to the extent that comparison is possible, my evidence supports a cumulative radicalization model. In Rwanda, the shift to multipartyism mattered, the 1990–93 civil war mattered, the

---

8. The connection between organic nationalism and genocide is a central theme in Michael Mann, *The Dark Side of Democracy: Explaining Ethnic Cleansing* (New York: Cambridge University Press, 2005).

9. Valentino, *Final Solutions.* The idea that genocide is not the first response of leaders to threat, but rather a choice taken after other decisions fail, also is emphasized in Mann, *The Dark Side of Democracy.*

assassination of the president mattered, and so did the 1994 civil war that ultimately unseated the hardliners. Without these events—but chiefly the last two—the leaders would not likely have chosen genocide and the dynamics of genocide would not likely have succeeded.

The arguments in this book have a number of policy implications as well. The world's inaction in the face of genocide in Rwanda has received a great deal of attention since 1994.[10] However, there is some debate about whether an outside military intervention could have succeeded in halting the genocide. My analysis suggests that an intervention would have been effective, but to be effective in saving hundreds of thousands of lives it would have had to materialize quickly.

An outside intervention would have changed the dynamics for a number of reasons. An intervention would have stabilized Rwanda. Stabilization would have short-circuited the uncertainty and fear that drove the violence and underpinned the hardliners' ability to carry the day (in areas not yet lost to the rebels). An outside intervention also would have strengthened the hand of Hutu moderates, who initially fought against the killing but were ultimately overwhelmed. My evidence also suggests that most Hutu men were not pre-programmed to kill. Had the moderates controlled the balance of power in various local areas, most Rwandans would probably have accepted a moderate position. In other words, my findings indicate that all other things being equal, most Hutu men would have just as easily complied with orders for peace as with orders for violence.

For an intervention to succeed, the international community would have had to act quickly. My findings show that once hardliners gained the upper hand in a particular location, the killings rapidly spiked. The Rwandan genocide is often described as a hundred-day event, and some analysts extrapolate a daily rate of killing based on the genocide's duration. But, as we shall see, once the killing started, it had extraordinary momentum. There is one region of Rwanda for which detailed information about killing is available, and my analysis of that study shows that roughly three-quarters of the total observed murders happened in a nine-day period. There was nothing inevitable about this outcome, and the dynamic could have tipped in the other direction. But once the violence started, it was extremely rapid and intense.

10. Michael Barnett, *Eyewitness to a Genocide: The United Nations and Rwanda* (Ithaca: Cornell University Press, 2003); Alan Kuperman, *The Limits of Humanitarian Intervention: Genocide in Rwanda* (Washington, D.C.: Brookings Institution, 2001); and Linda Melvern, *A People Betrayed: The Role of the West in Rwanda's Genocide* (London: Zed Books, 2000).

My arguments also have consequences for social and political life after genocide. Situational factors were critical to widespread participation in the genocide. Hutus did not kill primarily because there is a culture of hatred against Tutsis or deep anti-Tutsi prejudice in the society. To the contrary, Hutus and Tutsis lived side by side, intermarried, and cooperated together at most times in recent Rwandan history. Most Rwandans chose to commit violence only in the context of an intense civil war and only when genocide became the order of the day decreed from above. Rwandans are easy to mobilize, both then and now, but committing violence against Tutsis is not ingrained in Rwandan culture. Indeed, once the war ended and the Tutsi rebels decisively took power, Hutu violence against Tutsis in Rwanda effectively stopped.

These points matter because Rwanda's new authorities have ruled repressively since taking power after the genocide. They have banned ethnicity from public discourse, shut down independent media outlets, squelched civil society, and effectively criminalized any serious political opposition. The authorities have done so in the name of combating "divisionism" and what many Tutsis perceive as hardwired ethnic hatred. Many fear that given the chance, Hutus would rise up again and commit genocide. If my model is correct, then repression is not necessary to prevent future violence. Rwandans are particularly vulnerable to coercive mobilization, and a future rupture in political order and acute insecurity could again produce civilian-perpetrated violence. But Hutus are not predisposed to hating Tutsis, despite the large-scale civilian participation that characterizes the Rwandan genocide.

The Layout

The rest of the book will present evidence to support and explicate these arguments. The chapters are organized in the following way. Chapter 1 is a background chapter. I discuss the main competing interpretations of the Rwandan genocide as well as Rwandan history. For those unfamiliar with that history, the chapter should be a useful introduction. Toward the end of the chapter, I also discuss the central hypotheses that frame the empirical chapters to follow. Chapter 2 examines the genocide at the national and regional levels. I discuss the fateful days when the hardliners set Rwanda down a path of genocide, broad patterns of violence during the genocide, and regional variation in the level and timing of violence. I also document the extraordinary rapidity of the killing. Chapter 3 moves to the local level. In particular, I present findings from my micro-comparative study and use that discussion to model how violence spread.

Chapters 4, 5, and 6 focus on individual perpetrators. In chapter 4, I discuss perpetrator characteristics—age, education level, number of children, and the like—and I compare my sample's profile to that of Rwanda's national population. I also detail the composition of typical attacks during the genocide and estimate how many genocide perpetrators there were. Chapter 5 shifts to perpetrators' attitudes. I focus on ethnic relations before the genocide as well as on the extent of ideological indoctrination. The chapter also analyzes perpetrators' self-identified motivations. As in chapter 4, I also try to determine why some perpetrators were more violent than others during the genocide. Chapter 6 is more qualitative in nature. In the chapter, I am chiefly concerned with how perpetrators explain the overall logic of genocide. According to them, what was the general rationale for attacking unarmed Tutsi civilians and what was the rationale for extermination? How did perpetrators perceive what was happening around them? What did they think the goals of the violence were? In this chapter, the focus is on the logic of genocide, not the specific reasons why individuals say they participated. In contrast to chapters 4 and 5, where I present mostly summary findings, chapter 6 reproduces excerpts from interviews.

Chapters 7 and 8 take a historical turn. Chapter 7 examines periods of violence in Rwandan history prior to the genocide. In particular I discuss whether the conditions in which violence happened in the 1950s, 1960s, 1970s, and early 1990s resemble the conditions of 1994. The methodological principle is comparative historical analysis, but rather than comparing different countries I look at different time periods within the same country. Chapter 8 examines the Rwandan state and the country's history of institutionalized mobilization to account for the clear importance of the dynamics of power and authority that recur in the evidence I collect. In that chapter, I also provide an account for why the Rwandan state is more powerful at the local level than in most other African countries.

In the conclusion, I summarize my findings, but I focus on the theoretical and policy implications in greater detail than I do here. In particular, I situate my findings and arguments in the broader literature on genocide and mass violence. I also show how the arguments would extend to other major cases, such as the Armenian genocide, the Holocaust, Cambodia under the Khmer Rouge, and the Balkans. Taken together, the book offers a multi-level, multi-method, triangulated analysis of one of the most important political events of the second half of the twentieth century.

1 Background to the Genocide

The Rwandan genocide was a world-historical event that happened in a country with a tiny international presence. That alone says something about changing international norms. In the late twentieth and early twenty-first centuries, the gravest violations of human rights generate intense international concern even in small landlocked countries in Central Africa. It also helps explain why powerful international actors chose not to intervene militarily to stop the genocide. Rwanda did not command enough economic or strategic interest to justify the risks of troop deployment.

But the importance of the crime of genocide and Rwanda's previously limited visibility have also shaped how many have understood the genocide. Initial commentary labeled Rwanda an extreme case of a common African problem, namely "tribalism." That idea remains pervasive in nonspecialist audiences today. But the notion that ancient tribal hatred drove the Rwandan genocide is deeply misleading, and a range of informed commentators—scholars, high-level international commissioners, human rights advocates, and international courts—have spent great deal of energy debunking the notion.

The result is a new consensus on the Rwandan genocide, one that emphasizes the colonial manipulation of ethnicity in Rwanda, the planning and organization of the genocide before it happened, and the responsibility of specific Rwandans in fomenting the genocide. The new consensus has undone the shallow initial commentary that played up "tribal" hatred. The new consensus has also produced some very important gains in understanding the genocide. However, the new consensus, I will argue, has created its own lacunae and misconceptions.

In this chapter, I trace the trajectory of commentary on the Rwandan genocide and identify the questions that remain unanswered. Much of the chapter is about Rwandan political history from the colonial period to the early 1990s. This history is necessary to show the limitations of the tribal hatred model, but I hope that the history also will help readers unfamiliar with Rwanda who want to know more about the background to the genocide. In my discussion, I dwell on the 1990–93 period when the hardliners set the stage for the genocidal violence that engulfed the country in April 1994. Toward the end of the chapter, I identify the key questions about the genocide that the new consensus leaves unanswered. History now overdetermines the genocide, I argue. Such a teleological view is a major improvement from an ahistorical account of "ancient" hatreds, but the new consensus also eclipses the specific dynamics that drove the genocide. In closing, I identify and discuss the main hypotheses about why the genocide happened and why so many participated in it.

"Ancient Tribal Hatred" and Its Discontents

Tribe offers understanding without history. Tribe can explain Africa in a way that disregards how countries were put together, how leaders and parties have governed, and how economics and institutions shape behavior. Tribe is usually a pre-political category. African political history, both recent and distant, has never commanded great international attention, and thus tribe for many is the essential unit of analysis for explaining outcomes on the continent.

Rwanda is no exception to the rule, and when the genocide broke, "tribalism" overwhelmingly framed the debate. Two additional factors contributed to the reflex. First, Rwanda's killers often murdered in the most rudimentary and horrifying ways. They used machetes, tree limbs, clubs, knives, and sometimes rifles: most perpetrators employed whatever they had or whatever they could improvise. Such techniques made the violence look elemental and primitive. The killers also massacred in churches, schools, and government offices—wherever Tutsis victims had fled for safety—and they often left the bodies there and on the sides of roads. Knowing little of African history and seeing such shocking images, many outside observers leapt to the conclusion that "tribal hatred" must have sparked and sustained such horrifying violence.

Second, various political leaders who sought to diminish their own responsibility peddled a tribal version of events. In particular, the Hutu hardliners who orchestrated the violence claimed that they played no such role. The situation was chaotic, they claimed, a war of all against all. They, the leaders, had no control, so the international criticism levied against them was misguided.[1] Some Western leaders and scholars also unwittingly adopted a similar view, equating genocide with state "failure" or state "collapse."[2] These factors—ignorance about Rwandan history, the genocide's horror, and the efforts of government leaders to downplay their responsibility—all contributed to the use of "ancient tribal hatred" as the initial explanation for the Rwandan genocide.[3]

Since the genocide, the notion of "ancient tribal hatred" has stuck in public discourse and, as a result, framed expert commentary on the genocide. A variety of writers—scholars, human rights experts, and essayists—have tried, in effect, to dislodge the notion that "ancient tribal hatred" drove Rwanda's genocide. There are four major themes that run through this commentary.

First, tribe is the wrong register for describing Rwanda's ethnic categories. Rwanda has three commonly recognized ethnic groups—Hutus, Tutsis, and Twas. Many debate the exact proportion of each, but the Hutus comprised 84–90 percent of Rwanda's population before the genocide, Tutsis were 9–15 percent, and Twas were 1 percent. Rwanda's ethnic categories are the subject of a deep and careful scholarship, some of which I discuss below. But however scholars understand the categories' origins, the groups are most certainly not "tribal." Hutus and Tutsis speak the same language (Kinyarwanda);

1. For examples, see Jean-Marie Aboganena, "Bagosora s'explique," *Africa International* 296 (August 1996), 18–21; and Alison Des Forges, *Leave None to Tell the Story: Genocide in Rwanda* (New York: Human Rights Watch, 1999), 285.

2. For example, see Eliane Sciolino, "For West, Rwanda Is Not Worth the Political Candle," *New York Times*, April 15, 1994; I. William Zartman, "Introduction: Posing the Problem of State Collapse," in *Collapsed States: The Disintegration and Restoration of Legitimate Authority*, ed. I. William Zartman (Boulder, CO: Lynne Rienner, 1995), 4; and "Rwanda" in *Africa South of the Sahara 2003*, 32nd ed. (London and New York: Europa Publications, 2004), 824.

3. See, for example, William Schmidt, " Terror Convulses Rwandan Capital as Tribes Battle," *New York Times*, April 9, 1994, 1; and the dialogue quoted in Samantha Power, *"A Problem from Hell": America and the Age of Genocide* (New York: PublicAffairs, 2003), 355–56.

they belong to the same clans; they live in the same regions and, in most areas, the same neighborhoods; they have the same cultural practices and myths; and they have the same religions. Many also intermarry.

Second, the idea of "ancient tribes" suggests that the categories are stable across time; tribe here functions as an ahistorical concept. Such is clearly not the case for Rwanda: the salience and meaning of Rwanda's ethnic categories have changed over time. Precolonial Rwanda was a monarchical political system, and Rwanda had one of the most powerful and sophisticated kingships in Eastern Africa. In Rwanda—as throughout the Great Lakes region of Africa—a central social and economic distinction was between farming and animal husbandry. Of the two, animal husbandry had greater status and power. The terms *Hutu* and *Tutsi* appear to have their origins in this distinction. In general, Hutus were farmers of lower social status, while Tutsis were pastoralists of higher social status. Tutsis also controlled the monarchy. Not all Tutsis were royal aristocrats, and not all Hutus were poor farmers; there was variation within the categories. The terms also belonged to the lexicon of the precolonial Rwandan monarchy. As the monarchy spread, so too did the categories and their relevance. Moreover, the categories were not fixed. After acquiring enough cattle, a Hutu could become Tutsi.[4]

European rule did not invent the terms *Hutu* and *Tutsi*, but the colonial intervention changed what the categories meant and how they mattered. When Europeans began exploring the Great Lakes region in the late nineteenth century, they were impressed with Rwanda's comparatively hierarchical, orderly, and sophisticated system of rule. In the Rwandan Tutsis, the European explorers and missionaries believed that they had found a "superior" "race" of "natural-born rulers." Europeans wrote that Tutsis had migrated with their cattle from northern Africa at some earlier time and had come to dominate the more lowly Hutus, which the Europeans considered an inferior "race" of Bantu "negroids." This conception of Rwandan society reflected the anthropological ideas of the day, in particular the so-called

---

4. The literature on the nature of the terms *Hutu* and *Tutsi* is vast and complex, drawing on archeology, palynology, lexical analysis, and oral history. For the best analyses, see Jan Vansina, *Le Rwanda ancien: le royaume Nyiginya* (Paris: Karthala, 2001), 23–60; Jean-Pierre Chrétien, *The Great Lakes of Africa: Two Thousand Years of History*, trans. Scott Straus (New York: Zone Books, 2003), chs. 2–3; Catharine Newbury, "Ethnicity in Rwanda: The Case of Kinyaga," *Africa* 48, no. 1 (1978), 17–29; and Catharine Newbury, *The Cohesion of Oppression: Clientship and Ethnicity in Rwanda, 1860–1960* (New York: Columbia University Press, 1988).

"Hamitic Hypothesis," which saw civilization in Africa as the product of "Caucasoid" (white-like) Hamitic peoples.[5]

However strange such a way of seeing the world strikes the contemporary reader, the colonial period was rife with such theories. Colonial-era documents consistently describe Hutus as short, stocky, dark-skinned, and wide-nosed. By contrast, the Tutsis are presented as tall, elegant, light-skinned, and thin-nosed. Under Belgian colonialism, anthropologists even "scientifically" measured the differences between Hutus and Tutsis. And, critically, in the 1930s Belgian colonial officers introduced identity cards that labeled Rwandans according to their ethnicity. European race thinking also became the basis for allocating power in the colonial system. The Europeans practiced indirect rule, in so doing reinforcing Tutsi dominance and increasing the arbitrariness and repression of local rule. In short, under colonial rule, "race" became the central determinant of power; as a consequence, "race" became a symbol of oppression.[6]

Major changes in the Belgian administration began after World War II. Under pressure from the newly established United Nations, Belgium introduced reforms that increased Hutu political representation. Some Catholic missionaries also took up the cause of the oppressed Hutu masses, and a new Hutu political class emerged. From the mid-1950s until independence in 1962, Rwandan politics cascaded in a complex series of events. In brief, the old-guard Tutsi elite whose interests were at stake resisted reform, but their measures to reassert control backfired, hardening Belgian commitments to change and radicalizing the emergent Hutu counter-elite.

The result was the "Hutu Revolution." The revolution was a mix of events, most importantly a Belgian-supported overthrow of the Tutsi monarchy, the installation of a Hutu president and Hutu-dominated government, the purging of Tutsis from positions of local authority, and widespread anti-Tutsi violence. The shifts in the meaning of ethnic identity now came full circle: race thinking that had once hardened identity categories and benefited the Tutsi minority now gave rise to ethnic nationalism. Rwanda's new Hutu leaders claimed

5. On the Hamitic Hypothesis and the racialization of Rwanda's social categories, see Chrétien, *The Great Lakes of Africa*, ch. 2; and Mahmood Mamdani, *When Victims Become Killers: Colonialism, Nativism, and the Genocide in Rwanda* (Princeton: Princeton University Press, 2001).

6. On the Belgian impact, see Chrétien, *The Great Lakes of Africa*, ch. 4; Newbury, *The Cohesion of Oppression*; Filip Reyntjens, *Pouvoir et droit au Rwanda* (Tervuren, Belgium: Musée Royale de l'Afrique Centrale, 1985); and Jean Rumiya, *Le Rwanda sous le mandat belge (1916–1931)* (Paris: L'Harmattan, 1992).

independence in the name of the previously-oppressed Hutu majority. Democracy meant Hutu rule.[7]

This history is condensed (I address the entire period, in particular the anti-Tutsi violence, more fully in chapter 7). Yet I hope at least one central point comes through clearly: seen in historical context, the categories "Hutu" and "Tutsi" are not stable. Colonialism changed their meaning (from status and economic activity to race), institutionalized and stabilized categories that had been more fluid (through identity cards and race measurements), and intensified the connection between race and power. Under colonialism, in short, race overshadowed the organization of society; race became the country's central political idiom. The "ancient tribal hatred" model of the genocide misses this history. To claim that Hutus and Tutsis have hated each other for centuries and that this age-old hatred fueled the genocide are gross oversimplifications.

The third major problem with the "ancient tribal hatred" model is that it obfuscates the importance of particular officials in the genocide and the way they used the state to execute their plans. We may not know exactly when certain influential hardliners decided on a path of genocide or exactly why they chose mass violence. However, there is little question that the military and political hardliners who controlled Rwanda's state during the genocide instructed subordinates and the population to destroy the Tutsi population. This top-down, intentional, state-driven dimension to the violence is central to why scholars, international jurists, and human rights experts almost universally recognize the violence as an unambiguous case of genocide.

By contrast, the ancient hatred model suggests the genocide was an anarchic period of all against all, the product of tribal warfare. This is an error. The Rwandan state played a critical role in how and why the violence happened in the way that it did. The leaders who controlled the state ordered the killing, and they deployed the resources they had at their disposal—loyal military units, government spokesmen, militias, and radio broadcasts—to spread the message of violence. And the killing of Tutsis was deliberate and systematic. The notion of anar-

---

7. The best accounts of this period are René Lemarchand, *Rwanda and Burundi* (London: Pall Mall, 1970); Ian Linden, *Church and Revolution in Rwanda* (Manchester: Manchester University Press, 1977); Jacques J. Maquet and Marcel d'Hertefelt, *Élections en société féodale: Une étude sur l'introduction du vote populaire au Ruanda-Urundi* (Brussels: Académie royale des Sciences coloniales, 1959), 16–32; and Reynjtens, *Pouvoir et droit*, 185–97.

chy—of the absence of state direction during the violence—is thus quite misleading.

Pre-Genocide Rwanda

The fourth major thread of analysis focuses on the period immediately before the genocide. The events of this period are complex, and I will do my best to summarize, synthesize, and highlight the main points. But the details are critical to understanding the genocide, so I urge readers to be patient with the multifaceted complexity of the 1990 to early 1994 period. To understand that period, however, I need to begin, briefly, with the pre-1990 period.

Two major political trends dominated post-independence Rwanda. First, the principles of the Hutu Revolution guided official policy, which meant that Hutus dominated the government and military, often to the exclusion of Tutsis. Rwanda's first president, Grégoire Kayibanda, who ruled from 1962 to 1973, was more discriminatory towards Tutsis than his successor. Under Kayibanda, there was a series of anti-Tutsi massacres in the early 1960s and in 1973 (as with the revolution period, these episodes are discussed in greater detail in chapter 7). Rwanda's second president, Juvénal Habyarimana, who ruled from 1973 to 1994, diminished anti-Tutsi discrimination. Even so, Habyarimana maintained strong limits on Tutsi advancement through a system of regional and ethnic quotas.[8]

Second, regionalism shaped significant political conflict *among* Hutus. Kayibanda came from Gitarama Prefecture in the south-central region of the country. His rule largely benefited Hutus from his home region. Habyarimana, by contrast, came from Gisenyi Prefecture, and his rule largely benefited northerners, in particular those from the northwest. By 1990, northwesterners held a near-total monopoly on key posts in the government, in the army, and in state-run companies known as parastatals.[9]

8. On the treatment of Tutsis under Habyarimana, see Colette Braeckman, *Histoire d'un génocide* (Paris: Fayard, 1994), 82–83; Valens Kajeguhakwa, *Rwanda: De la terre de paix à la terre de sange et après?* (Paris: Éditions Reme Perrin, 2001), 155–64; Filip Reyntjens, *L'Afrique des grands lacs en crise: Rwanda, Burundi: 1988–1994* (Paris: Karthala, 1994), 27, 32–36; James Gasana, *Rwanda: Du parti-état à l'état-garnison* (Paris: L'Harmattan, 2002), 27–35; and Catharine Newbury, "Rwanda: Recent Debates over Governance and Rural Development," in *Governance and Politics in Africa*, ed. Goran Hyden and Michael Bratton (Boulder, CO: Lynne Rienner, 1992), 198–99.

9. Reyntjens, *L'Afrique des grands lacs*, 33–34

In the early 1990s, these two axes of Rwandan political history collided. In October 1990, Tutsi exiles under the banner of the Rwandan Patriotic Front (RPF) attacked Rwanda from southern Uganda. The rebels were primarily descendants of Tutsi families who had fled Rwanda after the Hutu Revolution. That was the first major change: civil war between the Hutu-dominated government and Tutsi-dominated rebels. The civil war lasted, at least nominally, until government and rebel delegations signed a peace accord in 1993.

The second major change was political. Like most other African states, Rwanda was a single-party state for almost the entire postcolonial period. However, the end of the cold war changed the political status quo on the continent. With the fall of communism in Europe, Western donor countries and many African elites no longer accepted single-party dictatorships, and Rwanda was no exception. In 1991, under pressure from France, which was then Rwanda's principal international backer, President Habyarimana formally ended the exclusive rule of his party, the Mouvement révolutionnaire national pour le développement (MRND). Immediately thereafter, a vigorous, largely Hutu opposition quickly arose to challenge the president and his party. The Hutu opposition was strongest in the southern, southwestern, and south central regions. The largest opposition party was the Mouvement démocratique républicain (MDR).[10]

Facing twin challenges to power from rebels and political opponents, the ruling elite's hold on power began to erode. In April 1992, under domestic and international pressure, President Habyarimana formed a coalition government with the political opposition. That government in turn began peace negotiations with the RPF rebels. After numerous rounds of negotiations, the two sides reached an agreement in August 1993. Known as the Arusha Accords (because the talks were held in Arusha, Tanzania), the agreement was broadly favorable to the rebels, who were awarded 50 percent of the officer corps in the Rwandan armed forces and 40 of regular personnel. Politically, the agreement called for a transitional, broad-based government, which was to be followed by multi-party elections. Under the agreement, the ruling MRND party only received only a third of the government posts in the transitional government. There was one other, key component of the Arusha Accords: they called for a ceasefire and for an international peacekeeping force to monitor the ceasefire and to secure

10. On the multiparty process in Rwanda, see Jordane Bertrand, *Rwanda, le piège de l'histoire: l'opposition démocrate avant le genocide 1990–1994* (Paris: Karthala, 2000).

Rwanda during its period of transition.[11] The United Nations tipped General Roméo Dallaire of Canada to lead the peacekeeping force, and he began deploying troops to Rwanda in late 1993.[12]

These were the formal changes that took place between 1990 and 1993, ones that compromised the ruling elite's previous lock on power. But the formal changes also triggered a series of informal and irregular measures that in turn laid the groundwork for genocide. In particular, Rwanda's ruling elite—MRND stalwarts and Habyarimana's inner circle—maneuvered to keep power during and after the political transition. The ruling elite had profited under Habyarimana, and most had little intention of relinquishing their power without a fight. And it would be the ruling elite's responses to the whipsawing threat of Tutsi military challenge and the domestic Hutu opposition that would have huge consequences for Rwanda. Below I identify six major hardliner responses, each of which ultimately played a role in the genocide.

First, the hardliners explicitly linked the Tutsi-dominated RPF to the resident Tutsi population living in Rwanda. Senior officers and Habyarimana himself made the connection immediately following the RPF's 1990 invasion when they labeled Tutsi civilians as rebel "accomplices." The government subsequently arrested as many as 13,000 civilians, most of them Tutsis.[13] A little more than a year later, a military commission made the connection between the RPF and the resident Tutsi population explicit. In December 1991, the commission released a memo that identified the country's "principal enemy" as "Tutsi inside or outside the country, who are extremist and nostalgic for power and who have never recognized and still do not recognize the realities of the 1959 Social Revolution and who want to take power by any means necessary, including arms."[14] Many observers, includ-

11. For a detailed account of the Arusha negotiations, see Bruce Jones, *Peacemaking in Rwanda: The Dynamics of Failure* (Boulder, CO: Lynne Rienner, 2001).

12. His autobiography is well worth reading. Roméo Dallaire with Brent Beardsley, *Shake Hands with the Devil: The Failure of Humanity in Rwanda* (Toronto: Random House Canada, 2003).

13. Estimates of the number arrested vary. Article 19 estimates 6,000–7,000, of whom 90 percent were Tutsi: Article 19, *Broadcasting Genocide: Censorship, Propaganda, and State-Sponsored Violence in Rwanda, 1990–1994* (London: Article 19, 1996), 26. The figure of 13,000 is provided in Des Forges, *Leave None*, 49.

14. My translation comes from the French in FIDH et al., *Rapport de la commission internationale d'enquête sur les violations des droits de l'homme au Rwanda depuis le 1er octobre 1990 (7–21 janvier 1993)*, March 1993, 63–66. The chief of staff, Colonel Déogratias Nsabimana, allegedly distributed this secret memorandum to his commanders in September 1992 after a round of negotiations in Arusha. Des Forges, *Leave None*, 62.

ing the international prosecutors who subsequently tried the genocide's high criminals, claim that the document is evidence of a pre-1994 plan to commit genocide. Colonel Théoneste Bagosora, who many consider the principal architect of the genocide, headed the ten-member commission.

Second, the Rwandan army both expanded dramatically and launched a civilian defense program.[15] The civilian defense program began in 1990 and had several components. Neighborhood civilian patrols were one. Each patrol consisted of ten adult men who carried traditional weapons and established roadblocks in their neighborhoods.[16] Another component of civilian defense was the distribution of firearms to civilian administrators and to army reservists; the army also trained some civilian authorities in firearms use.[17] The central idea behind the civilian defense program was that to combat the rebel threat, which purportedly had clandestine internal support, the government would arm its civilian administration. In so doing, however, the government incorporated civilians into war—which, again, set the stage for civilian participation in the genocide.

Third, hardliner politicians and military officers funded and trained a youth militia in 1992 and 1993. Most militiamen were members of the "*interahamwe.*" The *interahamwe* began as the MRND "youth wing." In general, youth wings were organizations of young or unmarried men who did a political party's bidding in a local community. Youth wings marched in support of a party, held rallies, flew party flags, and the like. Almost every political party had a youth wing, including the opposition political parties. What distinguished the *interahamwe* was that hardliners within the military and MRND party hierarchy siphoned off some youth and trained them militarily. In this sense, some *interahamwe* became militias—military-trained young

15. From 1990 to 1994, the Rwandan Armed Forces more than quadrupled, from 7,000 to 31,000 men, and purchased weaponry. On the army size, see a U.S. Defense Intelligence Agency report written on May 9, 1994. The report is now declassified and available, as "Document 11," at www.gwu.edu/~nsarchiv/NSAEBB/NSAEBB53/index2.html.

16. I base this claim on the interviews I conducted with perpetrators in the survey portion of my field research. Some respondents said they began the nightly patrols immediately after the first RPF attack in 1990.

17. I base this claim on interviews conducted in Rwanda and on research conducted by Alison Des Forges. I interviewed several sector heads who were trained in late 1993 and early 1994. In *Leave None,* Des Forges reproduces pages from Colonel Bagosora's 1993 diary that indicate plans to train sector heads (*conseillers*), communal police, and army reservists (see unnumbered pages between 106 and 107 in *Leave None*).

men as opposed to political party toughs. When exactly military training of *interahamwe* began is unclear,[18] as is the exact number, but by
early 1994, there appear to have been at least several thousand militias in different parts of Rwanda.[19]

Some commentators now claim—incorrectly as I show in later
chapters—that most genocide perpetrators were military-trained *interahamwe*. (The confusion stems from the fact that during and after
the genocide, the term *interahamwe* became synonymous with genocide perpetrator.) Nonetheless, *interahamwe* militias did play an important role in the genocide. In many locations, as we shall see, they
tipped the balance of power toward killing Tutsis, and they spearheaded many of the attacks. The question is whether the hardliners
initially established the militia in order to commit genocide.

A crucial piece of evidence in this debate concerns what an informant told a member of the UN peacekeeping force in January 1994.
According to Dallaire, the commander of the UN force, the informant
was an officer of the government's elite Presidential Guard fighting
force. In 1993, the informant left the army to train *interahamwe*. According to the informant, the program was initially part of the civil defense program to combat the RPF. MRND Party President Mathieu
Ngirumpatse ran the program. However, the informant worried because there were instructions to create lists of Tutsis, which would allow the militiamen to "exterminate" Tutsi civilians. In fact, the
informant estimated that the militiamen could murder as many as a
thousand Tutsis in twenty minutes.[20] Alarmed, Dallaire cabled to UN

18. Des Forges cites a source who witnessed the training in January 1993. James
Gasana, the former minister of defense, claims that training did not begin until the end
of 1993. Linda Melvern cites witnesses who claim training began in 1992: Des Forges,
Leave None, 101; Gasana, *Rwanda*, 214; and Linda Melvern, *Conspiracy to Murder: The
Rwandan Genocide* (London: Verso, 2004), 25.

19. Des Forges estimates 2,000 trained militia in and around Kigali as of April 1994
(*Leave None*, 180). The May 1994 U.S. DIA report cited above claims that there were
8,000 paramilitary forces in Rwanda, but what "paramilitary" means is unclear and
whether all such paramilitary forces existed before the genocide started is also unclear.
In January 1994, an informant told Dallaire that 1,700 youths had been trained since October 1993 and were stationed in Kigali (see below). James Gasana estimates three con-
tingents of 600 persons each were trained at the end of 1993 (Gasana, *Rwanda*, 226). In
the reproduced pages of Bagosora's diary quoted above, he refers to 2,000 recruits. In
terms of locations, existing documentation and my field research suggest that militia
existed in Byumba Prefecture, in Bicumbi Commune in Kigali-Rural, in Gisenyi Prefecture, in Ruhengeri Prefecture, in Kigali-City, and outside Cyangugu town (see Des
Forges, *Leave None*, 101, 106–7, 144, 150–51).

20. This account is drawn from Dallaire, *Shake Hands*, 142.

headquarters in New York, advising that he wanted to raid weapons caches that the informant had revealed.[21] However, the "genocide fax" backfired. Officials at UN headquarters in New York told Dallaire to inform the president of what the Canadian had learned—a decision that many observers, including Dallaire, in hindsight believe was a missed opportunity to stop a genocide in the making.[22]

The informant's claims are not conclusive evidence that the hardliners planned, before April 1994, the genocide that would take place. Dallaire's cable indicated that the *interahamwe* numbered 1,700 persons and were stationed in Kigali.[23] At a minimum, however, the cable shows that before April 1994 hardliners within the MRND party and the military were developing plans to massacre Tutsi civilians—and these were not the only extreme tactics on hand. According to several reports, the hardliners developed lists of RPF supporters and leading Hutu opponents in Kigali. Some scholars label the lists "death lists" because during the first days of the genocide, hardliners systematically assassinated leading Hutu opposition figures and RPF supporters. By February 1994, the lists allegedly consisted of some 1,500 names.[24] There are also allegations that hardliners within the military established "death squads" and secret organizations beyond the *interahamwe*.[25] Some observers link the death squads to a series of anti-Tutsi massacres between 1990 and 1993 (discussed in greater detail in chapter 7). All these developments—the militia training, the "death lists," the "death squads," and the massacres—show at a minimum that the hardliners most threatened by the changes during the early 1990s had radicalized by early 1994. They pursued irregular tactics to keep power and were prepared to use lethal violence against civilians if need be.

21. A copy of the fax is available at www.gwu.edu/~nsarchiv/NSAEBB/NSAEBB53/index2.html, "Document One."

22. Dallaire, *Shake Hands*, 145–47.

23. See www.gwu.edu/~nsarchiv/NSAEBB/NSAEBB53/index2.html.

24. See Gérard Prunier, *The Rwanda Crisis: History of a Genocide* (New York: Columbia University Press, 1995), 222n22; and Gasana, *Rwanda*, 243. Both claims are based on testimony from Jean Birara, former Central Bank governor, who, according to Prunier, was a relation of Nsabimana's. The 1,500 names were Kigali residents, according to Prunier, who refers to the documents as "death lists."

25. On "death squads," see Prunier, *The Rwanda Crisis*, 168; Filip Reyntjens, "Akazu, 'Escadrons de la Mort,' et autres 'Réseau zero'': Un historique des résistances au changement politique depuis 1990," in *Les crises politiques*, ed. Guichaoua; and Melvern, *Conspiracy to Murder*, 27–32. In his memoir, Dallaire refers to a "shadow force" and a "well-organized conspiracy inside the country, dedicated to destroying the Arusha Peace Agreement by any means necessary" (*Shake Hands*, 150–51).

Fifth, MRND supporters funded and distributed a barrage of racist propaganda. The propaganda was a mix of fear-mongering about the ruthlessness of the RPF (the rebels were routinely accused of committing atrocities against Hutu civilians), ethnic nationalism (Tutsis were labeled as "Hamitic" foreigners, a minority, and a danger to the Hutu majority), chauvinism (Hutus had to unite and be vigilant against the enemy), and ethnic stereotyping (Tutsis were often called RPF "accomplices").[26] The propaganda appeared in the print media, on the radio, and at political rallies. The most illustrative and infamous examples come from the weekly magazine *Kangura* and the private radio station called Radio Télévision Libre des Mille Collines (RTLM).

As with militia training, eroding official control fueled private propaganda. For example, hardliners formed the private RTLM station in mid-1993 after an opposition member became minister of information (the ministry controlled state-run Radio Rwanda). Whatever the initial intent, the content of much of the private media was highly inflammatory. In 1990, *Kangura* published the "Hutu Ten Commandments," instructing Hutus to sever ties with Tutsis and to protect the gains of the Hutu Revolution.[27] Song was another important medium. In one famous ditty, Simon Bikindi, a MRND propagandist and singer, called on the "great majority" (*rubanda nyamwishi*) to be vigilant against Rwanda's enemies.[28] I return to these ideas later.

A final development was the creation of a political alliance known as "Hutu Power." To understand the origins of Hutu Power, a short but important detour is necessary—to neighboring Burundi. Burundi shares the same ethnic makeup as Rwanda, but there Tutsis controlled the state after independence. As part of Africa's wave of democratization, Burundi ended one-party rule, and in June 1993 voters elected Melchior Ndadaye president. He was Burundi's first Hutu president. A peaceful transition followed and was hailed as a democratic success

26. For details, see the decision in the "media trial" in which three Rwandan journalists were found guilty of genocide: International Criminal Tribunal for Rwanda, "The Prosecutor v. Ferdinand Nahimana, Jean-Bosco Barayagwiza, and Hassan Ngeze," ICTR Case No. 99–52-T, Judgment and Decision, December 3, 2003.

27. For a list in French of the commandments, see Jean-Pierre Chrétien et al., *Rwanda: Les medias du génocide* (Paris: Karthala, 1995), 141–42; for an English translation, see African Rights, *Rwanda: Death, Despair, and Defiance*, rev. ed. (London: African Rights, 1995), 42–43. Repeated articles in *Kangura* stressed that Hutus and Tutsis were different "races," made nativist Hutu claims against "Hamitic" Tutsis, and presented the armed conflict as a race war. See Chrétien et al., *Les médias*, 95–99, 110–11.

28. Donald McNeil Jr., "Killer Songs," *New York Times Magazine*, March 17, 2002, 58.

story in Africa. However, on October 21, 1993, Tutsi military officers captured and assassinated Ndadaye. The assassination reverberated in Rwandan political circles. Hardliners in Rwanda seized on the events to claim that Tutsis never would share power and sought only domination of Hutus.[29]

At a rally in November 1993—after both the signing of the Arusha Accords and Ndadaye's assassination—an MDR faction leader, Frouald Karamira, baptized his party wing *"Pawa,"* a variation on the English word "power." Karamira proceeded to attach *"Pawa"* to other political parties, with time for the crowd to chant *"Pawa"* after him. He ended with a call to "Hutu United *Pawa."*[30] The phrase captures a strategic and ideological shift in domestic Rwandan politics that occurred in late 1993. At least for some Hutu politicians, the response to the RPF battlefield gains, to the Arusha Accords, to events in Burundi, and to the mainstream domestic Hutu opposition was a call for Hutu unity. The shift to Hutu Power is another indication of radicalization along nationalist lines: to respond to whipsawing threats, some Hutus elites openly embraced exclusivist nationalism that in turn framed Tutsis as a common enemy.

The escalation was not one-sided. As Hutu hardliners developed irregular and radical tactics, RPF leaders clandestinely prepared for combat. Less is known comparatively about the actions and intentions of the RPF leadership during this period, in particular after the Arusha Accords were signed but before the genocide began. Under the terms of the peace agreement, the RPF stationed a battalion at the parliament building in Kigali. However, according to several reports, the rebel leadership stealthily shipped hardware and other military supplies to troops there.[31] The RPF also maintained a network of cells around the country and, according to at least one former RPF officer who has since broken ranks, the RPF leadership sought to destabilize the Habyarimana regime through political assassinations, the laying of landmines, and killing of civilians.[32]

In sum, between 1990 and early 1994, Rwanda was in a deep, multifaceted, and escalating crisis. Three years of civil war and violent

29. James Gasana claims that the assassination "panicked" the Hutu domestic political class. See Gasana, *Rwanda,* 226.

30. Gasana, *Rwanda,* 223; Bertrand, *Rwanda,* 245.

31. Des Forges, *Leave None,* 180; and confidential interview, Kigali, January 16, 2002.

32. For the account by the former RPF official, see Abdul Ruzibiza, *Rwanda: L'histoire secrète* (Paris: Éditions du Panama, 2005); on the network of cells, see Des Forges, *Leave None,* 180–81; and for evidence about the RPF's preparing for war, see Dallaire, *Shake Hands,* 156.

multiparty politics had brutalized the country. Hundreds of thousands of Rwandans were internally displaced in the north, and there were tens of thousands of Burundian refugees in the south.[33] A nominal coalition government existed, with the opposition holding key posts, but in reality there was a major political impasse.[34] A peace agreement was in place, but both government forces and the RPF were rearming and preparing for war.[35] Crucially, the hardliners who once dominated Rwanda's state and economy pursued irregular means to keep power. The hardliners trained militias, circulated weapons, developed assassination plans, and funded racist propaganda.

The New Consensus

I am now in a position to summarize the current consensus, which weaves together these various elements into three major themes. First, authors focus on ethnicity, nationalism, and propaganda. The main points are that (a) Rwanda has a specific, colonially inflected history of racialized ethnicity; (b) Rwanda's colonial history and independence gave rise to a form of ethnic nationalism, which in turn became Rwanda's official postcolonial ideology; and (c) prior to the genocide, Hutu hardliners disseminated virulent, racist propaganda that was based on the country's history of racialized ethnicity and nationalism.[36]

Second, the new consensus holds that specific Hutu hardliners are responsible for the genocide. These include, principally, military officers, government officials, political party leaders, and journalists responsible for broadcasting or publishing racist propaganda before and during the genocide. Authors sometimes refer to the group as "the *akazu*," which means "little house" in Kinyarwanda and was the

33. Although in early 1993, an estimated 900,000 Rwandans were displaced, less than 300,000 remained so by the end of that year—the last publicly available date for which an estimate has been made. See World Bank, *Rwanda: Poverty Reduction and Sustainable Growth*, Report No. 12465-RW, May 16, 1994, 12–13.

34. During this period, the government operated without a budget, and local-level officials no longer received salaries. See Gasana, *Rwanda*, 240, 250.

35. On mutual rearmament, see Gasana, *Rwanda*, 243–44.

36. These points are emphasized in many accounts of the genocide. For those who focus specifically on the history of ethnicity in Rwanda, see in particular Chrétien, *The Great Lakes of Africa* (as well as his various works in French); Philip Gourevitch, *We Wish to Inform You that Tomorrow We Will Be Killed with Our Families* (New York: Picador, 1998); Prunier, *The Rwanda Crisis*; Mamdani, *When Victims Become Killers*; and Aimable Twagilimana, *The Debris of Ham: Ethnicity, Regionalism, and the 1994 Rwandan Genocide* (Lanham, MD: University Press of America, 2003).

nickname for Habyarimana's inner circle. Others refer to a Hutu Power clique. But the baseline argument is that the genocide had specific, powerful architects—the hardliners who between 1990 and 1994 radicalized and prepared to do what was necessary to keep power. The argument is fundamental to the prosecution at the UN-created International Criminal Tribunal for Rwanda (ICTR), to every major human rights report and international commission on Rwanda, and to most scholarly works on the genocide.[37]

Third, scholars and human rights activists emphasize that the hardliners planned the genocide before it happened. The genocide is presented here as carefully, even "meticulously," planned before the presidential assassination and as an "efficient" "machine" that emanated from the capital after the assassination. The military commission that defined Tutsis as enemies, the civilian defense program, the militia training, the distribution of weapons, the "genocide fax," the racist propaganda, and the anti-Tutsi massacres are all viewed here as evidence of a pre-1994 genocide plan. Authors also claim that Rwanda's intensive, even "totalitarian," state administration was critical to an "efficient" implementation of the genocide plan, as were military chains of command, irregular militia forces, and radio propaganda.[38]

37. For human rights accounts, see Des Forges, *Leave None;* and African Rights, *Rwanda.* For an international commission account, see Organization of African Unity, "Rwanda: The Preventable Genocide: Report of International Panel of Eminent Personalities to Investigate the 1994 Genocide in Rwanda and the Surrounding Events," July 7, 2000. For documents from the ICTR, see the court's first decision, "The Prosecutor versus Jean-Paul Akayesu," Case No. ICTR-96–4-T, 23: "The Chamber's opinion is that the genocide was organized and planned not only by members of the RAF [Rwandan Armed Forces], but also by the political forces who were behind the Hutu Power." For scholarly works that emphasize that a small group of elites organized and planned the genocide to keep power, see, among others, Bruce Jones, *Peacemaking in Rwanda;* Filip Reyntjens, *Rwanda: Trois jours qui ont basculer l'histoire* (Paris: Cahiers Africains, 1995); Prunier, *The Rwanda Crisis;* and Helen Hintjens, "Explaining the 1994 Genocide in Rwanda," *Journal of Modern African Studies* 37, no. 2 (1999), 241–86.

38. This argument is fundamental to most works on the genocide. Prunier claims a genocide plan was likely established in 1992 (Prunier, *The Rwanda Crisis,* 169). Alison Des Forges claims that "Hutu Power leaders were determined to slaughter massive numbers of Tutsi and Hutu" by late March 1994 (Des Forges, *Leave None,* 5). Linda Melvern claims that plans for genocide began in 1990, *Conspiracy to Murder,* 19. In the court's first decision, the ICTR judges found that "in the opinion of the Chamber, this genocide appears to have been meticulously organized." ICTR, "The Prosecutor vs. Jean-Paul Akayesu," paragraph 235. See also ICTR, "The Prosecutor Versus Clément Kayishema and Obed Ruzindana," Case No. ICTR-95-I-T, paragraph 275. Johan Pottier refers to "a masterplan for the extermination of Habyarimana's political opponents and all Tutsi . . . a plan already in existence in 1993." Pottier, *Re-Imagining Rwanda: Conflict, Survival, and Disinformation in the Late Twentieth Century* (Cambridge, UK: Cambridge Uni-

The major analytical themes of the new consensus take us a long distance from the ancient tribal hatred model. Rather than seeing the violence as chaotic frenzy, as state failure, or as an explosion of atavistic animosities, scholars and human rights activists alike stress that the violence was modern, systematic, and intentional. Specific Hutu leaders planned the violence—they drew on modern, colonially manipulated ethnic categories and a modern ideology of ethnic nationalism; they used the state to execute their plans; and they deliberately attempted to eliminate a racially defined minority. What happened in Rwanda was not tribalism run amok; it was genocide.[39]

Unanswered Questions

That said, the new consensus leaves a number of questions unanswered and underexplored, and in some cases the new consensus goes too far. The questions that the new consensus leaves unanswered are not about whether genocide happened, and they are not about whether particular leaders are responsible. Rather, the questions that remain unanswered are more social scientific in nature. The questions are about how and why genocide occurred in Rwanda and about how to evaluate how and why genocide occurred. I identify four principal questions that the new consensus leaves unanswered—these are the questions that will dominate the rest of the book.

First, how and why did the violence start and spread? The new con-

---

versity Press, 2002), 31. A final example comes from journalist Jean Hatzfeld, who in three pages refers to a pre-1994 "precise plan of extermination," to the Rwandan state as "totalitarian," and to the genocidal process as "efficient." See Hatzfeld, *Machete Season: The Killers in Rwanda Speak*, trans. Linda Coverdale (New York: Farrar Straus and Giroux, 2005), 56–58. Many other examples could be cited here. For further references to the Rwandan state as "totalitarian," see Christian Scherrer, *Genocide and Crisis in Central Africa: Conflict Roots, Mass Violence, and Regional War* (Westport, CT: Praeger, 2002), 109; Melvern, *A People Betrayed*, 24; and Twagilimana, *The Debris of Ham*, 161. For further references to the way that the genocide was "meticulously" or "scrupulously" planned, see, in addition to the citations above, African Rights, *Rwanda*, xix and OAU, "Rwanda," Chapter 14, paragraph 2. The two Public Broadcasting Service *Frontline* specials, "The Triumph of Evil" and "The Ghosts of Rwanda," also use the expression "meticulously planned." In the former, the narrator uses the phrase; in the latter, American diplomat Joyce Leader does. For a reference to the "machine" metaphor, see Pottier, *Re-Imagining Rwanda*, 31. For reference to "efficient" killing, see Melvern, *Conspiracy to Murder*, jacket, and OAU, "Rwanda," Chapter 14, paragraph 3.

39. The "modernity" of the Rwandan genocide is emphasized in Robert Melson, "Modern Genocide in Rwanda: Ideology, Revolution, War, and Mass Murder in an African State," in *The Specter of Genocide: Mass Murder in Historical Perspective*, ed. Robert Gellately and Ben Kiernan (New York: Cambridge University Press, 2003), 325–38.

sensus focuses on the top, it focuses on the history of ethnicity and nationalism, and it focuses on the leadership most responsible for planning the genocide. But what happened in local areas throughout Rwanda? Most of Rwanda is in fact rural, yet we know little about how the violence spread from the capital or the major regional towns to the rural areas. Who were the people who instigated the killing? Who were the people who followed? How did the mobilization occur? When did the killing start in different areas? These questions are critical for understanding the empirical details of the genocide, and the empirical details are critical to understanding why genocide happened in Rwanda.

Second, how and why did so many ordinary Rwandan civilians, with no preexisting history of violence, take part in the killing? The question is especially pertinent in an African context because most African states have a weak capacity for civilian mobilization and shallow roots in the countryside.[40] The question is also relevant because a defining characteristic of the Rwandan genocide is large-scale civilian participation. Thus, how and why did hundreds of thousands of civilians take part in killing? To date, there has been little systematic evaluation of this question, even though explaining perpetrator behavior is a critical issue in many studies of mass violence and genocide. Rather, most analyses of the Rwandan genocide rely on limited information, anecdote, and speculation to make generalizations about perpetrators' behavior and motivations.

Third, what is the rationale for genocide? The new consensus holds that the hardliners pursued genocide to keep power. The argument is right as far as it goes. But why did the hardliners choose genocide over a number of other possible strategies? What drove them to choose violence against civilians? What, moreover, drove them to order the destruction of the Tutsi enemy, which in practice meant killing all Tutsis regardless of age or gender?

Fourth, what is the right model for explaining the origins of genocide? In other words, how did the policy of genocide emerge? The new consensus presents a series of calculated moves that the hardliners took with the intent of committing genocide. Is that model empirically accurate? Did the hardliners plan to commit genocide as far back

---

40. On weak state capacity in rural Africa, see, for example, Joel Migdal, *Strong Societies and Weak States: State-Society Relations and State Capabilities in the Third World* (Princeton: Princeton University Press, 1988); and Goran Hyden, *Beyond Ujamaa in Tanzania: Underdevelopment and an Uncaptured Peasantry* (Berkeley and Los Angeles: University of California Press, 1980).

as 1990? If not, when did they decide on a genocide plan? Did the hard-liners take decisions that over time escalated to genocide? If so, what drove the escalation? The question here is not whether the hardliners at some point ordered genocide—they did. The questions here are when and why they did so.

These four questions are clearly interrelated, but each is critical for understanding how and why genocide happened in Rwanda. It is not enough to say that leaders decided to exterminate Tutsis and then ex-termination happened. We need to know what drove the leaders to choose an extreme strategy, and we need to know why those leaders succeeded. It is not enough to trace Rwanda's history of ethnicity and the hardliners' racist propaganda. We need to investigate whether and how ethnicity and propaganda drove the killing. These dynamics are critical for explaining why genocide happened.

Hypotheses

The questions I have outlined are empirical and theoretical in na-ture. They are empirical in that little is known about the dynamics and specificities of the genocide at the micro or local level. They are theoretical in that we need hypotheses of genocide and participation in genocide to answer the questions. Much of the rest of the book is about generating and examining evidence to evaluate different theo-ries. Here I want to summarize some the main hypotheses I will test. Broadly, I examine four intersecting literatures: (1) theories that au-thors have put forward to explain the Rwandan genocide; (2) theories that authors have put forward to explain genocide, whether in a com-parative or a case study context; (3) theories that explain ethnic con-flict; and (4) theories that explain individual-level participation in violence. Taken together, these four literatures are quite vast. To com-pensate, I focus here on the main hypotheses that frame the rest of the book.[41]

One major claim about the spread of violence and about participa-tion in it concerns ethnicity. Even if the violence was not tribal, many authors suggest that ethnic identity and nationalism drove the killing and drive genocide in general. Some authors point to prejudice or to a culture of discrimination as a key mechanism. Others point to wide-

41. For a more in-depth theoretical discussion, see my doctoral thesis: Scott Straus, *The Order of Genocide: Race, Power, and War in Rwanda,* Ph.D. dissertation, Univer-sity of California at Berkeley, 2004, chs. 1, 5. For a good overview, see also Helen Fein, "Genocide: A Sociological Perspective," *Current Sociology* 38, no. 1 (1990).

spread belief in nationalism.[42] Here is one typical construction by a well-known author on the Rwandan genocide:

> [In] Rwanda political life would fall under the influence of a monstrous racial ideology that preached intolerance and hatred. . . . In the years between 1959 and 1994, the idea of genocide although never officially recognized, became a part of life.[43]

The idea of a "monstrous racial ideology" that saturated society is a recurring analytic theme in the literature on genocide, in particular in relationship to the Holocaust.[44]

There are a number of mechanisms that might lead from ethnicity to violence. One is dehumanization. Whether because of prejudice or ideological indoctrination, individuals may degrade people in a different ethnic category; such degradation in turn facilitates violence. Another mechanism is antipathy: individuals commit violence because they distrust or abhor members of another ethnic category. A third mechanism is ideological commitment: individuals commit violence because of their strong political beliefs and desires. A fourth mechanism concerns media effects, in particular how propaganda indirectly or directly conditions people to kill. Some claim that propaganda "instills" dehumanizing stereotypes of ethnic others; others claim that propaganda directly "incites" violence; still others claim that the propaganda "brainwashes" the perpetrators.[45]

42. The argument is very common in the literature on Rwanda. See Prunier, *The Rwanda Crisis*, 40, 246, 248; Chrétien et al., *Les médias*; Gourevitch, *We Wish To Inform You*, 94; Shaharyar Khan, *The Shallow Graves of Rwanda* (London and New York: I.B. Tauris, 2001), 66; Mamdani, *When Victims Become Killers*, 14; and Scherrer, *Genocide and Crisis*, 119–22—among others.

43. Melvern, *Conspiracy to Murder*, 7–8.

44. On prejudice or culture of hatred driving the Holocaust, see, for example, Daniel Jonah Goldhagen, *Hitler's Willing Executioners: Ordinary Germans and the Holocaust* (New York: Random House, 1996), 9; and Lucy Dawidowicz, *The War Against the Jews, 1933–1945* (New York: Holt, Rinehart, and Winston, 1975), 219. More generally, on deep divisions driving genocide, see Leo Kuper, *Genocide: Its Political Use in the Twentieth Century* (New Haven: Yale University Press, 1981), 57. On ethnic nationalism and genocide, see Michael Mann, *The Dark Side of Democracy: Explaining Ethnic Cleansing* (New York: Cambridge University Press, 2005).

45. On dehumanization in the Rwandan context, Colette Braekman claims that a "genocidal culture" existed in Rwanda (*Rwanda*, 161); see also Alain Destexhe, *Rwanda and Genocide in the Twentieth Century*, trans. Alison Marschner (New York: New York University Press, 1995), 28. On antipathy, see Donald Horowitz, *The Deadly Ethnic Riot* (Berkeley and Los Angeles: University of California Press, 2001), 541; on propaganda effects—especially salient in the Rwanda case—see, for example, Francois Misse and Yves Jaumain, "Death by Radio," *Index on Censorship* 4, no. 5 (1994), 72–74; and ICTR, "Ferdinand Nahimana et al."

Another cluster of arguments concerns the relationship between deprivation and violence. Some scholars argue that structural violence or difficult life conditions created hardship and stress among Rwandans, which in turn manifested as violence. The mechanism here is frustration leading to aggression leading to "scapegoating." Versions of the argument are common in the literature on Rwanda and on genocide more generally.[46] Authors claim that Rwanda is a poor country and that many Rwandans had few life chances. There were land shortages. Many young people faced a future with little prospect for unemployment So Hutus lashed out against Tutsis.

Yet another cluster of arguments centers on social pressure and legitimization. There are several versions of the argument. One version stresses "obedience" in a context of legitimate authority.[47] Another emphasizes peer pressure and group conformity.[48] A third version stresses a "culture" or "tradition" of obedience and authoritarianism.[49] The latter is most common in commentary on the Rwandan case— many observers point to a strong "culture of obedience." Hutus, it is often argued, habitually obey orders. The argument may seem sim-

---

46. On structural violence—a catchall term encompassing malnutrition, poverty, inequality, discrimination, exclusion, oppression, authoritarianism, and regionalism— and for an application to Rwanda, see Peter Uvin, *Aiding Violence: The Development Enterprise in Rwanda* (West Hartford, CT: Kumarian Press, 1998). On population growth and environmental stress, see James Gasana, "Remember Rwanda?" *World Watch* 15, no. 5 (2002), 26–35; on population growth and land scarcity, see Catherine André and Jean-Philippe Platteau, "Land Relations under Unbearable Stress: Rwanda Caught in a Malthusian Trap," *Journal of Economic Behavior and Organization* 34, No 1 (1998), 1– 47; on the effects of coffee prices and structural adjustment program, see Jean-Claude Willame, *Aux sources de l'hécatombe rwandaise* (Brussels: CEDAF, 1995), 109–32, 159. For more general accounts on the frustration-aggression mechanism driving violence, see Ted Robert Gurr, *Why Men Rebel* (Princeton: Princeton University Press, 1970), 13, 23–24, 36; and James Rule, *Theories of Civil Violence* (Berkeley and Los Angeles: University of California Press, 1988), 200–223. On difficult life conditions, see Ervin Staub, *The Roots of Evil: The Origins of Genocide and Other Group Violence* (Cambridge, UK: Cambridge University Press, 1989), 15–23. Finally, on how resource scarcity indirectly contributes to violence, see Thomas Homer-Dixon, *Environment, Scarcity, and Violence* (Princeton: Princeton University Press, 1999), esp. ch. 5.

47. Stanley Milgram, *Obedience to Authority: An Experimental View* (New York: Harper and Row, 1974), 1–2; and Herbert Kelman and V. Lee Hamilton, *Crimes of Obedience: Toward a Social Psychology of Authority and Responsibility* (New Haven: Yale University Press, 1989), 89–90.

48. Christopher Browning, *Ordinary Men: Reserve Police Battalion 101 and the Final Solution in Poland* (New York: HarperCollins, 1993), 184–85; and Stanley Milgram, *Obedience to Authority*, 113–15.

49. On the Holocaust and a culture of authoritarianism, see Elie Cohen, *Human Behavior in the Concentration Camp*, trans. M. H. Braaksma (New York: W.W. Norton, 1953), 278–79.

plistic, but it is frequently offered as an explanation for how the violence spread in Rwanda so quickly and why participation happened on such a large scale.[50] Arguments about social pressure and legitimization are analytically similar to theories that link crowd behavior to violence. In crowds, individuals lose a sense of individual responsibility and inflict harm they might not otherwise commit.

Yet another approach views violence as "deviant" behavior. The focus here is on biological or psychological characteristics that predispose individuals to violence.[51] Perpetrators might be sadists, for example. The argument is less common in the Rwandan context, and many scholars of genocide explicitly refute it.[52] Nonetheless, the argument is still plausible and deserves empirical examination. Another common argument stresses material incentives: individuals commit violence in order to steal, loot, or otherwise profit. Because Rwanda was so poor and because there was much looting during the genocide, many authors favor the theory.[53]

Yet another important argument pivots on fear. Here the central claim is that perpetrators commit violence because they seek to protect themselves against dangerous adversaries. In the field of political science, the most common version of the theory is that of a "security dilemma." The central idea is that in the context of anarchy or war, individuals will attack first to avoid being attacked. People commit violence, in short, because they are afraid of violence being committed against them.[54]

50. See Prunier, *The Rwanda Crisis*, 57, 245; International Criminal Tribunal for Rwanda, "The Prosecutor Versus Jean-Paul Akayesu, Case No. ICTR-96–4-T: Judgement," paragraph 151; Scherrer, *Genocide and Crisis in Central Africa*, 113; Khan, *The Shallow Graves*, 67; and Regine Andersen, "How Multilateral Development Assistance Triggered the Conflict in Rwanda," *Third World Quarterly* 21, no. 3 (2000), 441–56.

51. An excellent review, especially with reference to the Holocaust, can be found in James Waller, *Becoming Evil: How Ordinary People Commit Genocide and Mass Killing* (Oxford: Oxford University Press, 2002), 55–87.

52. For example, Hannah Arendt's *Eichmann in Jerusalem: A Report on the Banality of Evil*, rev. ed. (New York: Penguin Books, 1965); Browning, *Ordinary Men*; and Robert Jay Lifton, *The Nazi Doctors: Medical Killing and the Psychology of Genocide* (New York: HarperCollins, 1986), 5.

53. Waller, *Becoming Evil*, 69; Des Forges, *Leave None*, 10–11; Prunier, *The Rwanda Crisis*, 248; Gourevitch, *We Wish To Inform You*, 94; and André Sibomana, *Hope for Rwanda: Conversations with Laure Guilbert and Hervé Deguine*, trans. Carina Tertsakian (London: Pluto Press, 1999), 69–70.

54. There are different versions of this argument, but see especially Barry Posen, "The Security Dilemma and Ethnic Conflict," *Survival* 35, no. 1 (1993), 27–47; Jack Snyder and Robert Jervis, "Civil War and the Security Dilemma" and Rui de Figueiredo Jr. and Barry Weingast, "The Rationality of Fear: Political Opportunism and Ethnic Conflict," in *Civil Wars, Insecurity, and Intervention*, ed. Barbara Walter and Jack Snyder (New

There are a number of other relevant theories of genocide. Some authors focus on social upheaval and crisis, other authors focus on authoritarian regimes as a precondition for mass violence, others focus on modernity and modern bureaucracy, and still others focus on ideologies of utopia.[55] The literature on genocide and violence is, in fact, fairly vast—much too vast and varied to summarize here. Moreover, theories are not mutually exclusive. At the level of perpetrators, an individual might distrust or fear members of another group *and* feel deprived. Genocide is also a complex event in which different people can have different motivations and motivations can change over time. Ethnic antipathy might drive one perpetrator, while fear may drive another, even if both participate in the same genocide. Obedience may have led a person to kill the first time, but thereafter he might have wanted to steal goods or he might have become acculturated to killing. In short, motivation—the mechanism driving individuals—can be both heterogeneous within individuals as well as among them, even during a single event.

The main point, however, is that we do not know which variables and mechanisms drove the Rwandan genocide. Many of the above hypotheses are plausible. The analytical task is to find out whether and how much these mechanisms mattered, and that is the main purpose of the rest of the book. To do so, detailed evidence collected systematically is necessary. And therein lies the rub: with a few exceptions, most existing evidence is focused on the top, and most of the existing evidence was not collected with social scientific goals in mind.[56] Most of the rest of the book is an effort to correct that tilt.

York: Columbia University Press, 1999), 15–37 and 261–302; David Lake and Donald Rothchild, "Spreading Fear: The Genesis of Transnational Ethnic Conflict," in *The International Spread of Ethnic Conflict: Fear, Diffusion, and Escalation,* ed. David Lake and Donald Rothchild (Princeton: Princeton University Press, 1998), 3–32. On war and genocide, see Browning, *Ordinary Men,* 186; Robert Melson, *Revolution and Genocide: On the Origins of the Armenian Genocide and the Holocaust* (Chicago: University of Chicago Press, 1992), 273; Erik Markusen, "Genocide and Warfare," in *Genocide, War, and Human Survival,* ed. Charles Strozier and Michael Flynn (Lanham, MD: Rowman and Littlefield, 1996), especially 77–81; and Martin Shaw, *War and Genocide: Organized Killing in Modern Society* (Oxford: Polity 2003), among others.

55. On social upheaval and crisis, see Barbara Harff, "No Lessons Learned from the Holocaust? Assessing Risks of Genocide and Political Mass Murder since 1955," *American Political Science Review* 97, no. 1 (2003), 57–73; on authoritarian regimes, see Rudolph Rummel, *Death by Government* (New Brunswick: Transaction Books, 1994); on modernity, see Zygmunt Bauman, *Modernity and the Holocaust* (Ithaca: Cornell University Press, 1989); and on the importance of utopia, see Eric Weitz, *The Century of Genocide: Utopias of Race and Nation* (Princeton: Princeton University Press, 2003).

56. The notable exceptions are Des Forges, *Leave None,* which has two long sections on genocide in the prefectures of Butare and Gikongoro; Timothy Longman, "Genocide

---

The trajectory of thinking on the Rwandan genocide has followed a clear path. The initial commentary, which still pervades public discourse on Rwanda, pinned the label of "ancient tribal hatred" on the genocide. Rwanda's violence was seen as a frenzy of deep-seated enmity in the context of state failure. Rwanda's violence was thus seen as an extreme version of tribal violence that is typical for Africa.

However, in the first decade since the genocide, scholars, human rights activists, and international jurists labored to show why the tribal hatred model is deeply flawed. Rwanda does not have tribes. Rwanda has a very specific history of ethnicity, one that has to do with the colonial introduction of race thinking and the rise of majoritarian ethnic nationalism at independence. Moreover, particular Hutu leaders planned the genocide and then used the state to execute the extermination. The genocide was thus not a chaotic outcome of state collapse; it was specific, prepared, state-driven, and based on modern constructions of ethnicity and nationalism. The result is a new consensus in academic and human rights communities that stresses the planning, the elite responsibility, and the elite's modern instruments and elements.

However, there is much that remains. The new consensus has made considerable advances on the tribalism model, but our understanding of the genocide is still at a largely macro and sometimes superficial level. What is needed now is a more micro-level, social scientific investigation, one that identifies and evaluates the mechanisms and dynamics driving the genocide. Is the planning model accurate? How did the violence spread? What led people to kill? These are the questions that frame the rest of the book. The answers I offer will help answer the key question of how and why genocide happened in Rwanda in 1994—and answering that question has implications that extend well beyond the Rwandan case.

---

and Socio-Political Change: Massacres in Two Rwandan Villages," *Issue: A Journal of Opinion* 23, no. 2 (1995), 18–21; and Michele Wagner, "All the Bourgmestre's Men: Making Sense of Genocide in Rwanda," *Africa Today* 45, no. 1 (1998), 25–36. Despite the high quality of analysis and knowledge of Rwanda reflected in these sources, the level of detail is at times fairly general and the information sometimes anecdotal.

2 Genocide at the National and Regional Levels

On April 6, 1994, Rwanda's fate changed. At 8:20 that evening, the plane carrying Rwandan President Juvénal Habyarimana and his entourage was shot down over Kigali. Quickly after the assassination, Hutu hardliners took control of the Rwandan state. In short order, they physically eliminated their main rivals in the political opposition, drew the RPF into combat, attacked international peacekeepers, and sidelined dissenters in the army. From there, the hardliners unleashed an all-out war against the "Tutsi enemy," and Rwanda hurdled horribly and swiftly toward genocide. One hundred days later, Rwandans had murdered at least half a million other Rwandans, including an estimated 75 percent of the resident Tutsi population. It was the twentieth century's fastest genocide.

This chapter examines the genocide's details at the national and regional levels. In the first main section, I focus on the fateful days when the hardliners set Rwanda on a path of genocide. I argue that the decisions that led to genocide were inextricably linked to the events that happened in that period. In particular, the president's assassination and the resumption of war were central to the dynamic of escalation and the logic of killing that drove the genocide. In the second main section, I focus on the details of the violence itself, including the estimates of the number of civilians killed in the genocide. Then I focus on regional differences in the level and timing of violence. For the latter, I create a dataset of onset periods nationwide and map the results. I then zoom in on Kibuye Prefecture, one of Rwanda's eleven prefectures during the genocide, and present a detailed graph of the temporal distribution of killing. The results are striking: while there were important regional differences in when violence started, once killing started in an area the violence rapidly spiked. That finding has a number of important implications that I discuss.

In the final main section, I do some preliminary hypothesis-testing. The starting point for the analysis concerns the regional differences in timing, which I interpret as indicators of willingness to commit genocide. I then test different arguments that might explain why people in some areas were more willing to commit genocide than in others. I find that ethnic prejudice, deprivation, obedience, and exposure to radio broadcasts are *not* variables that can predict when violence starts in different regions. Political party support for the ruling party is the strongest predictor. The findings do not conclusively explain why people committed genocide, but the results provide insights that the next chapters develop.

The Eve of Genocide

To recap the last chapter in slightly different form: on the eve of the genocide, Rwanda had four major political forces operating at the national level: (1) *Hutu moderates:* the mainstream Hutu political opposition that had some support within the army; (2) *Hutu hardliners:* the representatives of the ruling MRND party, the ultranationalist Coalition for the Defense of the Republic (CDR), and their allies in the military and media; (3) *Tutsi rebels:* the Rwandan Patriotic Front (RPF); and (4) *International actors:* the roughly 2500 United Nations peacekeepers and the diplomatic corps.

By and large, the Hutu moderates and the international actors backed the Arusha Accords. By contrast, the Hutu hardliners and the Tutsi rebels covertly prepared for war (despite nominally committing to peace). The hardliners trained and armed militias; they strengthened loyal military units, including the Presidential Guard; they distributed weapons; they ramped up the racist propaganda against Tutsis; they prepared plans to assassinate high-level opposition politicians; and they trained militias to kill Tutsi civilians, especially in the capital. For its part, the RPF imported weapons into Kigali and elsewhere reinforced their positions. Both parties—especially the Hutu hardliners—blocked efforts to install a new broad-based government, which was a key requirement of the Arusha Accords.[1]

---

1. In addition to the material in the previous chapter, for evidence of the hardliners' distrust of the RPF, efforts to sabotage Arusha, and fear of loss of control, as well as the

The current consensus interprets the Hutu hardliners' behavior as evidence of a scrupulous plan to commit genocide. But closer inspection reveals slightly different dynamics. In particular, the hardliners were now operating under new constraints. Hutu moderates controlled key government posts, and segments of the military were openly siding with the opposition.[2] The RPF had a battalion in Kigali, and the hardliners faced new international scrutiny from the peacekeepers in Kigali and elsewhere in the country. Moreover, the hardliners were convinced that the RPF was abrogating its stated commitments and secretly readying for battle. Events in Burundi only heightened the hardliners' suspicion: Tutsis, some hardliners reasoned, would never share power. In short, the hardliners' power had eroded; they were deeply suspicious of their rivals and, critically, in that context they invested in alternative measures and institutions to keep power.

Take, for example, statements the hardliners made to international peacekeepers within a week of the genocide's onset. Déogratias Nsabimana, the Rwandan army chief, warned Belgian peacekeeper Luc Marchal that the RPF was preparing an offensive. Nsabimana was fateful and apocalyptic: he warned Marchal that the international community did not understand the conflict and that the government had to adopt the same tactics as its adversaries.[3] Marchal also reports an encounter with Théoneste Bagosora a few days before the president's assassination. Bagosora took the same line as Nsabimana. The RPF, Bagosora insisted, had no interest in peace and wanted only to take power militarily. Bagosora further claimed that Rwanda would have peace only if the rebels were eliminated.[4]

I do not interpret the hardliners' statements as evidence of meticulous planning for full-blown, countrywide extermination of Tutsis but rather as evidence of contingency planning and a frame of mind that could easily lend itself to genocide. The hardliners were preparing to

---

RPF's preparations for war, see Roméo Dallaire with Brent Beardsley, *Shake Hands with the Devil: The Failure of Humanity in Rwanda* (Toronto: Random House Canada, 2003), ch. 7, esp. 141–42, 155–57, 163–64.

2. James Gasana, the former minister of defense who has written an account of Rwanda, stresses the division within the Rwandan army: Gasana, *Rwanda: Du parti-état à l'état-garnison* (Paris: L'Harmattan, 2002), 256–57. A high-ranking Hutu military officer I interviewed also stressed this in repeated interviews in Kigali in July 2002.

3. Luc Marchal, *Rwanda: La descente aux enfers: Témoignage d'un peacekeeper Décembre 1993–Avril 1994* (Brussels: Éditions Labor, 2001), 210.

4. Marchal, *Rwanda,* 213. Similar statements can be found in Dallaire's autobiography and in Alison Des Forges, *Leave None to Tell the Story: Genocide in Rwanda* (New York: Human Rights Watch, 1999), 145, 146, 147, 149, 166, 168, and 170.

defend themselves and defeat the RPF once and for all, *if war resumed*. The hardliners were facing new constraints and found themselves with incomplete control over a state they once dominated. In that context—of compromised power and deep distrust of their armed rivals—the hardliners invested in institutions they could control (militias and loyal military units) and they pursued extreme tactics (assassination plans and virulent propaganda). The hardliners' measures reveal deeply distrustful contingency planning for war in an institutional environment where their power was compromised.

The Habyarimana Assassination

It was in that context that President Habyarimana was assassinated. On April 6, two ground-to-air missiles sailed out across Kigali's sky and struck Rwanda's presidential jet. All aboard died, including Habyarimana, Nsabimana, President Cyprien Ntaryamira of Burundi, and key Rwandan Hutu hardliners Elie Sagatwa, chief of presidential security, and Juvénal Renzaho, a chief political adviser of Habyarimana. In one fell swoop, the downing of the presidential plane knocked out several of the most important Hutu hardliners, in particular those in the military.[5]

Who killed Habyarimana is a critical question, but one that current evidence cannot definitively answer. There are two principal hypotheses: one blames the Hutu hardliners who subsequently took over and orchestrated the genocide, and the other blames the RPF, who subsequently launched an offensive and ultimately won the civil war.[6] There are problems with both theories, but the current balance of evidence suggests that the RPF was responsible.

The thinking behind the first theory is that the hardliners were angry about Habyarimana's concessions to the RPF in the Arusha Accords. Rather than share power, the hardliners would have decided to sacrifice the president and destroy the Tutsi threat once and for all.[7] The theory has a number of problems, but two stand out. First, the as-

5. Filip Reyntjens, *Rwanda: Trois jours qui ont basculer l'histoire* (Paris: Cahiers Africains, 1995), 44–45.

6. For reviews of different theories, see Des Forges, *Leave None*, 181–85; Reyntjens, *Rwanda*, 28–38; and Gérard Prunier, *The Rwanda Crisis: History of a Genocide* (New York: Columbia University Press, 1995), 213–26.

7. While authors accept that the question remains open, the extremist assassination theory is favored in many seminal works on the genocide, including Prunier, *The Rwanda Crisis*, 222–26 and African Rights, *Rwanda: Death, Despair, and Defiance*, rev. ed. (London: African Rights, 1995), 96–99.

sassination was a terrible blow to the hardliners. Not only did the assassination kill key players in the hardliners' camp—presumably those who would have planned the genocide had it been planned before April 6, 1994—but other key officials were also out of the country, including the defense minister and the chief of military intelligence. The timing for the hardliners, in short, was quite poor.[8] Second, since the genocide, neither the RPF nor the well-funded International Criminal Tribunal for Rwanda (ICTR) has produced concrete evidence to implicate the hardliners in the assassination. Generating such evidence is strongly in the interest of both parties.

The thinking behind the second theory is that the Tutsi rebels would have desired a clean military victory rather than a negotiated political settlement. Fed up with the hardliners' obstacles to implementing the Arusha Accords and unsure of their popular support, under this theory the RPF opted for a lightning strike and quick offensive.[9] There is evidence to support the theory. To date, the most comprehensive investigation of the assassination—a six-year French magistrate inquiry—concluded that the RPF was responsible for the assassination. (The magistrate investigated because the plane's two pilots, who also were killed, were French.)[10] Several RPF dissidents also blame the rebel leadership, in particular former rebel leader Paul Kagame, for planning and ordering the assassination.[11] The main problem with the theory is that the assassination triggered the genocide. If the theory is correct, then the RPF leadership must have miscalculated their ability to win the war quickly, the impact of the president's assassination, or the depravity of their opponents—or some combination of the three.[12]

---

8. Linda Melvern, *Conspiracy to Murder: The Rwandan Genocide* (London: Verso, 2004), 136–37; Reyntjens, *Rwanda*, 51.

9. The RPF lost elections in the eight communes under its control in late 1993 and had by 1993 lost support among the majority of the domestic political opposition, at least according to some close observers of Rwandan politics: Reyntjens, *Rwanda*, 41; Gasana, *Rwanda*, 223; and Stephen Smith, "André Guichaoua: 'L'assassinat du président Habyarimana a été programmé dès 1993,'" *Le Monde*, May 6, 2004.

10. The investigation was led by Jean-Louis Bruguière; see Stephen Smith, "L'enquête sur l'attentat qui fit basculer le Rwanda dans le génocide," *Le Monde*, March 9, 2004. For further discussions of the thesis that the RPF ordered the assassination, see Reyntjens, *Rwanda*, 38–46; and Prunier, *The Rwanda Crisis*, 215–22.

11. Charles Onana with Déo Mushayidi, *Les secrets du génocide rwandais: enquête sur les mystères d'un président* (Paris: Duboiris, 2002); and Adbul Ruzibiza, *Rwanda: L'histoire secrète* (Paris: Éditions du Panama, 2005).

12. A meeting between Dallaire and Kagame in May suggests that the rebel leader was willing to win at all costs. Asked about concerns that the massacres of Tutsis, Kagame

The Hardliners Take Power

Whoever killed Habyarimana, the hardliners moved quickly to take control of the Rwandan state. The night of April 6, Bagosora called and chaired a meeting of the top military officers.[13] At the meeting, he argued that the military should take power—quickly. However, the majority of other assembled officers rejected Bagosora's proposal. They argued that a civilian government should rule, and after all Prime Minister Agathe Uwilingiyimana was still alive. Uwilingiyimana was an MDR politician, a Hutu but an opponent of the MRND. Bagosora in turn angrily rejected her authority, claiming that the prime minister did not command the confidence of the population. The assembled officers also voted down another of Bagosora's recommendations, namely the appointment of Colonel Augustin Bizimungu, a hardliner, as new army chief of staff. Instead, the officers appointed Marcel Gatsinzi, a moderate from the Butare region. The officers also agreed to pursue the Arusha process and work with the UN peacekeepers.[14] In short, the moderates won the first round after the assassination.

After the meeting, Bagosora accompanied Dallaire to see Roger Booh-Booh, the UN Secretary General's Special Representative in Rwanda. Booh-Booh heard Bagosora out but stipulated that the prime minister was still the head of government and should be consulted. Booh-Booh announced a meeting the next morning, to which he invited Bagosora, who agreed to attend. Dallaire further spoke with the prime minister, who agreed to address the nation at daybreak. To protect her during the night, Dallaire dispatched ten peacekeepers from Belgium and five from Ghana. The move would prove a fateful one.[15]

Sometime that evening, however, Bagosora and his allies turned the tables and very quickly gained the upper hand. Their first order of business was to eliminate the domestic opposition. In a series of actions, which Dallaire and others describe as well-organized, Presidential Guard and other elite soldiers fanned out across the city. They surrounded the radio station, followed by the prime minister's residence. The soldiers took the Belgian peacekeepers guarding the prime minister hostage. The prime minister subsequently fled, but the soldiers

---

responded, according to Dallaire, that "If the [Tutsi] refugees have to be killed for the cause, they will be considered as having been part of the sacrifice." Dallaire, *Shake Hands*, 358.

13. Des Forges, *Leave None*, 185; Reyntjens, *Rwanda*, 52–54; and Dallaire, *Shake Hands*, 222–23.

14. The account in this paragraph is based primarily on Dallaire, *Shake Hands*, 222–25; Marchal, *Rwanda*, 218–19; and Des Forges, *Leave None*, 185–86.

15. Dallaire, *Shake Hands*, 226–27; Marchal, *Rwanda*, 221–23.

hunted her down and assassinated her, along with her husband. The Rwandan soldiers captured the Belgians who had been guarding the prime minister, took them to a military camp, and savagely murdered them. The operation did not stop there. Elite soldiers systematically found and assassinated key opposition politicians and their families—many of whom were on the "death lists" described in the previous chapter. In short, within hours of the assassination and after losing the immediate initiative to the moderates and the international community, the hardliners struck back. They did so violently and by using the parallel institutions they had cultivated during the months prior to the assassination.

Late the morning of April 7—still within twenty-four hours of the president's assassination—Bagosora broadcast a communiqué claiming that the army was in the process of "restoring order." The broadcast called for calm. In effect, Bagosora signaled that the army was in charge and, more particularly, that the hardliners in the army were in charge.[16]

Bagosora completed the hardliner takeover on April 8. That morning, he met with MRND chairman Joseph Nzirorera to form a new government. The ministers they named nominally came from a range of political parties, but in reality they either represented hardliner factions within their respective parties or were malleable. They named Théodore Sindikubwabo, an elderly southern pediatrician from the MRND, to be the next president, and they named Jean Kambanda, an MDR politician and economist, to be the new prime minister.[17] Kambanda apparently did not want the post, but he reluctantly agreed to accept his new appointment.[18] Several years later, Kambanda told international investigators that he and anyone else who opposed the hardliners or opposed killing civilians would have been killed if they openly dissented.[19]

For its part, the RPF prepared to attack on April 7. Early that afternoon, Kagame warned Dallaire that if the killings in Kigali did not stop, the RPF would strike. Dallaire relayed the message to Bagosora, who summarily dismissed it.[20] And, indeed, after receiving fire during the late afternoon, RPF soldiers stationed at the parliament broke

16. This paragraph and the preceding one are based on Dallaire, *Shake Hands*, 226, 230–35; Marchal, *Rwanda*, 217–37; Des Forges, *Leave None*, 185–91; and Gasana, *Rwanda*, 252.

17. Des Forges, *Leave None*, 196; Reynjtens, *Rwanda*, 86–88.

18. Des Forges, *Leave None*, 197; author interviews, Kigali, June 2002.

19. Melvern, *Conspiracy*, 190.

20. Dallaire, *Shake Hands*, 253–54, 267; Marchal, *Rwanda*, 226, 238; and Des Forges, *Leave None*, 189.

out of the building and advanced on the Presidential Guard camp. In response, government soldiers, militias, and civilians set up hundreds of roadblocks throughout Kigali.[21]

On April 8, the RPF launched a full offensive, advancing swiftly from its northern positions. Meanwhile, violence was exploding across Kigali. Dallaire describes scenes of "chaos." Civilians fled the violence in large numbers. Militias loyal to the hardliners and government soldiers manned roadblocks. They rampaged on the streets, and they started killing civilians on April 7 and 8. The scene was so violent that the same day the hardliners announced the new government, the newly appointed officials had to spend the night in a hotel. The next day—April 9—the new government was sworn in—at the hotel where they had taken shelter. Three days later, on April 12, the new government fled southwards because the RPF were threatening to take Kigali.[22] The government, in short, was on the defensive.

There were two other major developments in this critical period. First, the international actors with a strong presence in Rwanda decided to abandon Rwanda and neuter the UN peacekeeping force. Less than a year after U.S. army soldiers died in Somalia, the Clinton administration had no appetite for another humanitarian mission in Africa. The relevant UN agencies were similarly risk averse, and all the more so after the murder of the Belgian peacekeepers, which triggered the Belgians to withdrawal their soldiers from the UN operation. The French started evacuating nationals and some Hutu allies (including the president's wife) April 9. The Americans and Belgians followed suit a day later. Shortly thereafter, despite Dallaire's strong objections, the UN Security Council voted to reduce the peacekeepers to a token force.[23] In effect, the international community signaled that the war and the unfolding violence were Rwanda's problems. The international community would not intervene to halt the killing.

The second major development came when the Hutu hardliners sidelined the moderates within the military. Having watched Bagosora and the other hardliners outmaneuver them on April 7 and the days thereafter, moderate officers made a last appeal for peace on April 12. That day, several officers broadcast a statement over the radio calling

---

21. Dallaire, *Shake Hands*, 245–62.

22. Dallaire, *Shake Hands*, 277; Linda Melvern, *Conspiracy*, 175.

23. On the international response, see especially Michael Barnett, *Eyewitness to a Genocide: The United Nations and Rwanda* (Ithaca: Cornell University Press, 2002); as well as Linda Melvern, *A People Betrayed: The Role of the West in Rwanda's Genocide* (London: Zed Books, 2000); and Dallaire, *Shake Hands*, 289–99.

for an end to the unfolding tragedy. The broadcast had little effect. In fact, at least one of the officers went into hiding after the broadcast because he learned that the communiqué had prompted an order to assassinate him.[24] In the end, the moderates were no match for the hardliners. The latter commanded the most elite military units, including the Presidential Guard and the Paracommando and Reconnaissance battalions, and the RPF advance and ensuing war weakened the moderates' claims.[25]

What does all of this show? Habyarimana's assassination created an initial gap in authority. In that context, Hutu moderates and hardliners initially competed to control the resulting headless state. The moderates initially won (the night of April 6), but the hardliners quickly regained the upper hand. To do so, they ignited their parallel institutions, wiped out the domestic political opposition, sidelined moderate military officers, prompted the international community to withdraw, and drew the RPF into full combat. It was in this context that the hardliners set Rwanda down a path of genocide. The hardliners narrowed Rwanda's political arena to two major players: the Hutus (as represented by the hardliners) and the Tutsis (as represented by the RPF). The hardliners in turn declared war on the latter. The result was swift and devastating, as we shall see in a moment. What I hope is clear is a dynamic of escalation that cannot be divorced from context and events. The hardliners pursued radical and violent measures from a position of eroded power and in response to the actions of their opponents, including the Hutu opposition and the international community, but in particular and especially the RPF rebels.

The Genocide

When exactly the genocide started is difficult to say. By "genocide" I mean a systematic and coordinated attempt to physically eliminate the entire Tutsi population of Rwanda. That is ultimately what happened. The Hutu hardliners fomented mass violence against the Tutsi population in order to combat the RPF. But when the hardliners first gave the orders to do so—assuming that they did in fact issue an explicit private order to attack Tutsi civilians—is unclear, as it may always remain.

What is clear is that by April 7 violence against Tutsi civilians had

24. Dallaire, *Shake Hands,* 293; and Des Forges, *Leave None,* 204–5.
25. Des Forges, *Leave None,* 194–95; Marchal, *Rwanda,* 239.

begun in several areas around the country, especially where hardliners had strong support. By April 9, there was evidence of systematic massacres against Tutsi civilians, at least in Kigali.[26] By April 12—the same day the interim government fled Kigali to Gitarama—the hardliners openly called on the population to attack Tutsi civilians. In a broadcast aired on state radio and signed by the Ministry of Defense, the army's top brass instructed soldiers, gendarmes, and "all Rwandans" to "unite against the enemy, the only enemy and this is the enemy that we have always known. . . . It's the enemy who wants to reinstate the former feudal monarchy."[27] Such was the command and logic that led to widespread attacks against Tutsi civilians around the country. Hutus had to put aside their differences to fight their common "only enemy," which here vaguely refers to those wanted to reinstate monarchy. Such language became a license to attack Tutsis, to destroy the "Tutsi enemy"—as we shall see.

By April 14, violence against Tutsis had started in most parts of the country. The main holdout areas were Butare and Gitarama Prefectures, where there was considerable resistance from Hutu moderates. The hardliners ultimately removed the prefect (the leading administrative authority) in Butare, deployed the president and prime minister to both prefectures, and threatened any Hutus who refused to join the fight against Tutsis. By April 21, widespread and systematic violence against Tutsi civilians had become the norm in almost every area of the country that had not yet fallen to the rebels.

For the next two and a half months, the conflict's broad outlines did not change. In areas under the hardliners' control, genocide was the order of the day. However, as the hardliners devoted energy and resources to killing Tutsi civilians, the RPF rebels steadily advanced. By late April, the RPF rebels controlled most of north central and eastern Rwanda. By the end of May, they controlled most of central Rwanda (though not Kigali, which did not fall until July 4). By mid-July the rout was complete: three months after Habyarimana's assassination and the resumption of war, the rump genocidal regime fled into what was then Zaire, taking with them the remnants of the army, the militia, the civilian administration, and more than one million Hutu civilians. Close to another million fled eastward into Tanzania.

---

26. See descriptions in Dallaire, *Shake Hands,* 279–81; and David Hawk, *Genocide in Rwanda: Documentation of Two Massacres during April 1994,* U.S. Committee for Refugees, November 1994.
27. International Criminal Tribunal for Rwanda, "The Prosecutor vs. Jean-Paul Akayesu," Case No. ICTR–96–4–T, paragraph 203; Des Forges, *Leave None,* 202–3, 263.

We may never know precisely how many civilians died in the genocide. The standard international estimate in journalist and United Nations reports is 800,000 killed.[28] However, according to the last government census taken before the genocide (in 1991), Rwanda had only 600,000 Tutsis living in the country.[29] Given Rwanda's population growth, there may have been as many as 660,000 Tutsis in Rwanda at the time of the genocide.[30] It is possible that government officials or Tutsis themselves disguised the true number of Tutsis, but there is no concrete evidence of widespread fabrication, and the 1991 census data correspond to data in the last census conducted in the colonial period.[31] The 800,000 figure is thus probably too high. The best aggregate estimate of the number killed during the genocide comes from historian and human rights activist Alison Des Forges, who has written the most comprehensive book documenting genocide at the national level. Des Forges triangulates data from three sources and estimates that at least 500,000 Tutsi civilians were killed in the genocide. That sum amounts to roughly three-quarters of Rwanda's pre-genocide Tutsi population.[32]

Tutsis were not the only civilians killed in this period. The hardliners also targeted and sometimes killed other Hutus. How many is difficult to say, given the poor data on the subject. Des Forges estimates 10,000 Hutus killed in the genocide.[33] The number is consistent with my research in Rwanda. I found that in rural communities those committed to the genocide punished and beat Hutus who refused to participate in the violence. Some Hutus were killed as examples for repeatedly resisting the killing and for personal vendettas, but not as a rule. The RPF also killed MRND political leaders and Hutu

28. United Nations, *Report of the Independent Inquiry into the Actions of the United Nations during the 1994 Genocide in Rwanda,* December 15, 1999, and Organization of African Unity, *Rwanda: The Preventable Genocide. The Report of the International Panel of Eminent Personalities to Investigate the 1994 Genocide Rwanda and the Surrounding Events,* 2000, chapter 14, paragraph 2. For a higher estimate of 934,218 killed, see République Rwandaise, "Dénombrement des victimes du génocide: Analyse des resultats, draft" (Kigali, Rwanda: Ministère de l'administration locale et des affaires sociales, 2001), 7. This last document is discussed later in the chapter.

29. République du Rwanda, *Recensement général de la population et de l'habitat au 15 août 1991: Analyse des résultats définitifs,* Kigali, Rwanda, April 1994, 124.

30. République du Rwanda, *Recensement général,* 12–13. The reported annual growth rate is 3.1 percent.

31. Des Forges, *Leave None,* 15.

32. Des Forges, *Leave None,* 15–16.

33. Personal communication with the author.

civilians as they advanced; again, the number is not known.[34] Des
Forges cites two estimates ranging from 25,000 to 60,000.[35]

Details of how the genocide happened in rural areas is the focus of the
later chapters, but, briefly put, Hutus formed both small and large
groups to attack Tutsis. Some groups included military-trained militias;
most did not. Some groups included soldiers; some included government authorities; others had representation from neither. Hutus went
house to house searching for Tutsis. Hutus formed roadblocks at commercial centers and road crossings. They combed marshes, fields, and
hills to find Tutsis. And they attacked central congregation points, such
as churches, schools, and government buildings, where Tutsis had fled
for safety. Most large-scale massacres took place at these congregation
points, and the massacres often entailed hundreds, sometimes thousands, of attackers and generally included both soldiers and civilians.

Killing was the modal form of violence, but both looting and sexual
violence were also widespread. The extent of this sexual violence is
unclear and may never be fully revealed. A commonly cited figure is
250,000 rapes committed during the genocide. The number is derived
from the total number of "rape babies" reported after the genocide.[36]
However, according to the 1991 census, in Rwanda there were only
163,738 Tutsi women over the age of fourteen years old.[37] Some Tutsi
girls under the age of fifteen were surely raped, and some women were
undoubtedly raped multiple times. However, as we shall see in a moment, the killers quickly murdered most women, and they killed
women at the same time as men. Thus, the figure of 250,000 rapes is
probably too high, but a more accurate estimate is not currently possible. What can be said with certainty is that sexual violence was common and was an important dimension of the genocide.[38]

34. On RPF targeting of MRND politicians, see Gasana, *Rwanda,* 254. For local-level
estimates of Hutu civilians killing by the RPF, see Philip Verwimp, "Testing the Double-Genocide Thesis for Central and Southern Rwanda," *Journal of Conflict Resolution*
47, no. 4 (2003), 423–42.

35. The latter figure includes estimates of Hutus killed through August 1995.

36. The logic is as follows: there were about 2000 to 5000 pregnancies caused by rape.
The standard estimate is 100 rapes per pregnancy, hence the estimate of 250,000 rapes.
See Human Rights Watch, *Shattered Lives: Sexual Violence during the Rwandan Geno-
cide and Its Aftermath* (New York: Human Rights Watch, 1996), 15–16.

37. République du Rwanda, *Recensement général,* 84. I took the total number of
Rwandan women older than fourteen and multiplied that number by the percentage of
Tutsis in the country, according to the census (8.4 percent).

38. For further information on sexual violence during the genocide, see ICTR, "Jean-
Paul Akayesu," and Human Rights Watch, *Shattered Lives.*

Regional Variation

Many analyses of the Rwandan genocide stop with what I have just described. The specific dynamics of violence and mobilization remain a black box—something that the rest of this book aims to remedy. I begin that process in this chapter by disaggregating the genocide to examine regional patterns of violence. Disaggregation matters especially for hypothesis-testing. If analysts treat "the genocide" as an undifferentiated event, it is difficult to judge what drove the violence. But focusing on variation can lead to inferences about the factors that drove the violence. In the remainder of this chapter, I examine differences across regions in terms of level and timing of violence. The central questions are: was the violence against Tutsis more intense in some areas than in others and did the violence start at different times? If so, then the analytical question becomes why—why was the violence greater or faster in some areas than in others? Answers to those questions will offer us clues into the mechanisms driving the violence.

For level of genocidal violence, the operational question is how many Tutsis died in an area as a percentage of the preexisting Tutsi population. It is clear that more Tutsis died in some areas than in others. But it is also true that before the genocide more Tutsis lived in certain areas than in others. Thus, if level (or intensity) is being measured, the question is how many Tutsis in a region died as a percentage of how many lived there before the killing began.

Unfortunately, the data to answer the question are not very good. The only document that shows regional differences in the number killed countrywide is a "genocide census" that Rwanda's post-genocide, RPF-led government conducted in 2000. However, there are serious problems with the document, including the fact that the total number of Tutsis listed as dead is about 150 percent of the total number that the 1991 census listed as living in Rwanda. Given that, I compare ratios: I compare the percentage of Tutsis living in a region (as a function of the total Tutsi population) to the percentage of the Tutsis killed in a region (as a function of the total number of Tutsis killed during the genocide). Table 2.1 reports the results.

Broadly speaking, table 2.1 shows that the level of killing was similar countrywide. With some exceptions, the percentage of Tutsis killed in a prefecture as a function of all Tutsis killed is similar to the percentage of Tutsis living in a prefecture as a function of all Tutsis in

39. Administrative redistricting in 2000 created the prefecture of Umutara from

Rwanda. This is true for areas that the RPF captured quickly (such as Byumba) and ones it captured late (such as Butare and Gisenyi).

The notable exceptions are Cyangugu, Kibuye, Kigali-City, and Ruhengeri Prefectures. But problems in the data limit what inferences may be drawn. First, there were administrative changes between when the population census was recorded and when the genocide census was.[39] Second, the general census lists where Tutsis lived, while the genocide census lists where Tutsis were killed, which may skew results. Moreover, other data do not support the findings. For example, a study of three prefectures found less anti-Tutsi violence in Gitarama than in Kibuye.[40] In short, the findings in table 2.1 matter but should be treated with caution.

What about timing? Did the violence start at different times in different regions? Anecdotally, most studies of the genocide indicate that there were regional differences in when violence started. To answer the question more systematically, I created a dataset of onset dates at the commune level using six principal sources (see Appendix table 2.1).[41] I then mapped the results (see figure 2.1).

The results clearly show that there were regional differences in when genocide started. In some areas, Hutus rapidly complied with the call to attack the Tutsi enemy and began eliminating Tutsis only

---

Byumba and Kibungo, elsewhere expanded Kibungo, significantly expanded the boundaries of Kigali-City, and reduced the size of Kigali-Rural. See Republic of Rwanda, *Law No. 47/2000 of 19/12/2000 Amending the Law of April 15, 1963 concerning the Administration of the Republic of Rwanda as Modified and Completed to Date,* Ministry of Local Government and Local Affairs, Kigali, April 2001.

40. The study is based on a household survey and is, to my knowledge, the only other systematic effort that compares subnational levels of genocidal violence. Based on information from twenty-seven Tutsi-headed households and 151 Tutsi individuals, the survey found comparatively less (anti-Tutsi) genocidal violence in Gitarama than in the two other studied prefectures (Gikongoro and Kibuye). See Verwimp, "Testing the Double-Genocide Thesis," 423–42, esp. 433. Though carefully selected, the small sample size limits the nationwide implications of the study. Another critical source of comparison is a painstaking list of every genocide victim in the prefecture of Kibuye. That survey, which was conducted by the survivors' organization Ibuka and which I discuss in more detail below, recorded 59,050 Tutsi victims. If we assume that the annual population growth for Tutsis resembled the national rate of 3.1 percent, then we can estimate the total Tutsi population in Kibuye to be 75,947 persons at the time of the genocide. That would mean that approximately 78 percent of all Tutsis were killed in Kibuye. That number is fairly close to the national estimate of 75 percent of all Tutsis killed during the genocide, as per calculations by Alison Des Forges.

41. I consider "onset" when genocidal violence started. In some locations, the initial violence consisted of isolated, sporadic, sometime surreptitious attacks against specific individuals. This type of violence gave way—sometimes quickly, sometimes not—to public, generalized attacks against Tutsis. I consider the latter to be "genocidal violence." The map was created with the assistance of Heather Francisco.

Table 2.1 Regional variation in the level of genocidal violence*ᵃ*

Prefecture where Tutsis lived in 1991 and prefecture where Tutsis were killed in 1994	Pre-genocide percentage of Tutsis as a function of total Tutsi population in Rwanda	Percentage of Tutsi deaths as a function of total Tutsis killed in 1994
Butare	21.7%	22.3%
Byumba	1.9	1.6
Cyangugu	9.6	5.9
Gikongoro	9.9	10.4
Gisenyi	3.5	3.7
Gitarama	13.0	12.2
Kibungo	8.3	9.9
Kibuye	11.6	7.8
Kigali-Rural	13.2	14.6
Kigali-City	6.6	10.5
Ruhengeri	0.6	1.1
Total	100	100

Sources: République du Rwanda, *Recensement général de la population et de l'habitat au 15 aout 1991: Analyse des résultats definitifs,* April 1994, 124; and République du Rwanda, *Dénombrement des victimes du génocide: Analyse des résultats,* Ministère de l'Administration Locale et des Affaires Sociales, March 2001, 7.

*ᵃ*The following assumptions and calculations were made for this table: (1) the percentage of Tutsis in a prefecture is based on the number of Tutsis in a prefecture taken as a percentage of the total number of Tutsis in Rwanda. (2) After the genocide, the new government created the prefecture of Umutara from Byumba and Kibungo. To compensate, I have taken the genocide victim population for Umutara and evenly distributed it to Byumba and Kibungo Prefectures. (3) Because the "genocide census" includes several different categories of victims, my estimation is based on 93.7% of prefecture totals because that is percentage that the census lists as having been killed because they were "identified as Tutsi." See République du Rwanda, *Dénombrement des victimes,* 3, 18.

days after Habyarimana's assassination. In other areas, Hutus did not kill for a significant period of time, even though (for reasons discussed in the next chapter) their opposition was ultimately overcome. The difference in onset was short—a week, sometimes two—but in most cases the delays represent real and significant resistance to killing.

Timing and Intensity: The Case of Kibuye

The genocide's patterns of violence are strikingly evident in data that a survivor's organization collected for the western prefecture of Kibuye. The organization, Ibuka, recorded the name of every genocide victim in a "*dictionnaire nominatif*" (a dictionary of names). The document is simple in construction, but it is one of the most remarkable items to emerge from the genocide: a massive book of the dead that runs more than a thousand pages long.

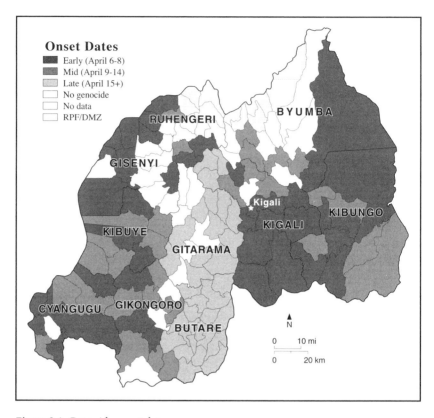

Figure 2.1 Genocide onset dates

In total, the *dictionnaire nominatif* records 59,050 names, or about 78 percent of the resident Tutsi population in Kibuye before the genocide.[42] For 43 percent of the entries, the book lists the exact dates when people died. The dates in turn offer a detailed picture of when the killing happened in one of Rwanda's eleven prefectures. In fact, although the Ibuka dictionary has some limitations (mainly that the dates are based on a surviving family member's recollection), the data in it are the most detailed available for reconstructing regional temporal patterns of violence. The findings are extraordinary. To depict them, I present four diagrams.

The first graph (figure 2.2) shows the pattern of violence for all Tut-

42. The percentage is based on numbers in the 1991 census and assuming a 3.1 percent population growth rate. See note 40.

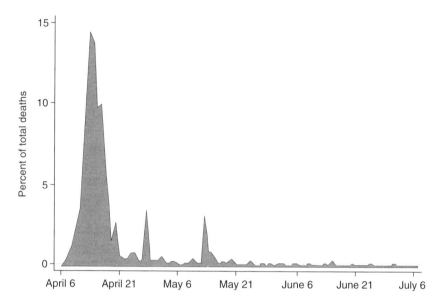

Figure 2.2 Percentage of total genocide deaths in Kibuye Prefecture by day

sis killed. Prefecture-wide, the violence was relatively slow to start, at least compared to some other prefectures. By April 10, only 2.5 percent of all observed deaths had happened within the prefecture. But that number doubles on that date and then rapidly takes off. By April 19, some 77.7 percent of the total observed deaths occurred. In other words, some 75 percent of the genocidal killing that happened in Kibuye happened in nine days—from the start of April 10 to the end of April 18.

The *dictionnaire nominatif* reveals other critical details. In particular, the book helps determine whether the violence began as genocide or whether the violence evolved into genocide. I measure that question by comparing dates of death for females and children to the dates of death for all killed. I do so under the assumption that most females and children were clearly not combatants and thus that killing them is direct evidence of genocide. The results (figures 2.3 and 2.4) show dramatically that the violence started as genocide, at least in Kibuye. The temporal pattern for females and children tracks almost identically with the temporal pattern for all Tutsis killed. Another cut on the evidence reveals the same. Figure 2.5 depicts the percentage of female deaths as a function of total deaths. For the first sixty days of

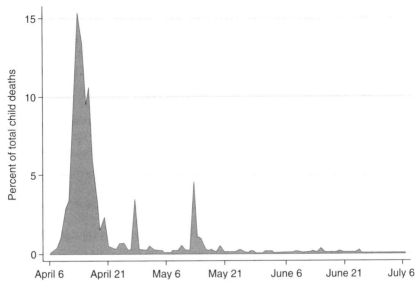

Figure 2.3 Percentage of total deaths of children in Kibuye Prefecture by day

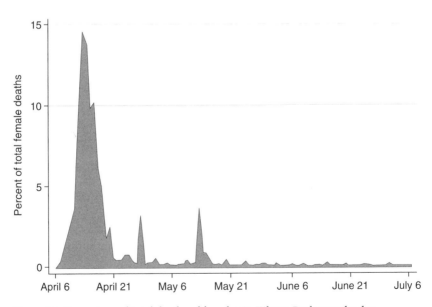

Figure 2.4 Percentage of total deaths of females in Kibuye Prefecture by day

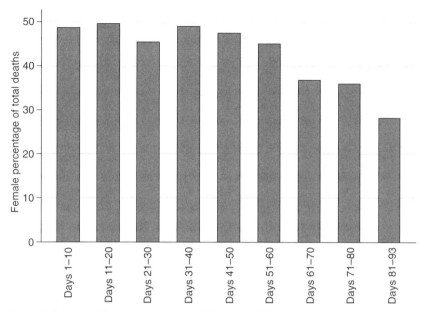

Figure 2.5 Ratio of female deaths to total deaths in Kibuye Prefecture

the genocide, about 50 percent of the deaths were consistently those of females.

The graphs also help resolve an apparent paradox. The findings that I presented in the previous section suggest that while there were important differences in when violence started across regions, those differences tended to even out, in terms of level of violence, during the course of the genocide. In other words, timing varied, but level of violence did not. The detailed data from Kibuye help answer why. Once violence reached a critical mass, it was extraordinarily intense. Therefore, despite important differences in when violence began in a particular area, the killing rapidly spiked shortly after it began.

The swiftness and intensity of violence are principal characteristics of the Rwandan genocide and require explanation. Why did the violence take off? The spike also has important theoretical and practical implications. Theoretically, the evidence strongly suggests the importance of situational factors. Something changed to cause the violence to surge. Practically, the findings show that, all things being equal, any international intervention would have needed to take place very early in the overall genocide. In Kibuye at least, less than two weeks after the genocide started, more than three-quarters of the victims already had been killed.

Regional Factors Determining Onset of Genocidal Violence

I want to turn now to what might explain regional differences in timing. The question has theoretical import. If genocide started earliest in areas where poverty was greatest, where unemployment was highest, or where land was in shortest supply, that would support theories that link deprivation to violence. Similarly, if genocide started earliest in areas with the fewest number of Tutsis, that finding would suggest that prejudice mattered (under the theory that interethnic interaction reduces prejudice). There are, in fact, many plausible theoretical avenues here.

In this section, I look for meaningful relationships between onset and a range of explanatory variables. The prefecture is the unit of analysis. (Above I measure onset at the commune level, but most data for relevant explanatory variables are measured at the prefecture level, hence I use the prefecture as the common unit of analysis.) To proceed, first I classify prefectures as having early, middle, or late onset (see Appendix table 2.2).[43] Then I run a series of simple bivariate regression analyses whereby the dependent variable is onset at the prefecture level and the independent variables are different plausible explanatory variables. I run eighteen analyses in total (see Appendix table 2.3 for regression results).

The findings are interesting for the relationships that emerged—and failed to emerge. I start with the latter. Education, profession, parcel size, population density, age distribution, ethnic diversity, proximity to Kigali, and refugee presence all prove *not* to have statistically significant relationships with onset. Violence does not radiate directly from the capital Kigali. In fact, Gitarama's regional center is among the closest to Kigali, but the violence took quite long, comparatively, to materialize in that prefecture. The areas with the most Tutsis are not those where violence started earliest or latest. Before the genocide,

---

43. The criteria for the classification are the following: (1) early onset occurs in those prefectures where 75 percent or more of the communes (on which I have data) initiated genocidal violence during the first interval (April 6–8); (2) middle onset occurs in those prefectures where about half of the communes initiated genocidal violence during the first interval and about half during the second and third intervals (the second interval refers to April 9–11, the third to April 12–14); and (3) late onset occurs in those prefectures where 75 percent or more of the communes initiated genocidal violence during the fourth through the seventh intervals (April 15 and beyond).

many Tutsis lived in Kigali-City, Kigali-Rural, Gitarama, and Butare Prefectures. Violence started quickly in the first two prefectures and late in the latter two.[44] Similarly, regional education levels appear to have no consistent relationship with onset. The same is true for areas with large numbers of refugees and displaced persons. Butare is where many Burundian refugees were in 1994, but again genocide took comparatively longer to start in that region. The finding runs contrary to the claim that Burundian refugees instigated the killing in Rwanda.

The findings on deprivation are particularly interesting. A region's relative wealth and unemployment level are statistically significant with onset variation. But the relationship runs contrary to expectation. Though the correlation is not strong, the findings indicate that poorer areas with higher unemployment were *not* those where violence started earliest. The findings suggest the opposite.[45]

As for other statistically significant variables, the strongest relationship is between onset and support for the ruling MRND party. In areas where Habyarimana's party had the strongest support, violence materialized quickly; in areas where the opposition had the strongest support, there was the most resistance to the violence. The finding could have different meanings. It could be that individuals supported the ruling party and killing for the same reasons. It could mean that those who were most upset by the president's death were the first to be violent. Or it could mean that violence started most quickly in regions where the hardliners who took control in Kigali had the most connections and support. At a minimum, however, the findings suggest that in some way political commitments and alliances drove early participation.

The other two statistically significant variables concern proximity to the war and degree of population growth. With regard to war, on balance violence against Tutsi civilians happened earlier in prefectures that were closer to RPF positions. In and of itself, the finding suggests

44. Kigali-Rural is varied. In the Bugesera region and areas east of Kigali-City, violence started very quickly. However, in areas of the prefecture northwest of Kigali-City, violence started later.

45. A different World Bank report suggests a similar pattern. According to the World Bank, the greatest concentration of poverty occurred in the south and southwest, which were late and middle onset areas respectively, while the wealthiest area was the northwest, which was an early onset region. The World Bank calculates the poverty severity as 5 percent in the south central region (late onset), 3 percent in the north central (middle and early onset), 2 percent in the northwest (early onset), southwest (middle onset), and east (middle and early onset), and 1 percent in urban Kigali (early onset). See World Bank, *Rwanda: Poverty Reduction and Sustainable Growth*, Report No. 12465-RW, 1994.

that war and fear related to war played some role in triggering the violence. The finding on population growth is harder to interpret in light of the other findings that population size and density in a region are not good predictors of when violence starts. But in and of itself the finding suggests that where adults had more children violence started earlier. More children could be an indicator of stress on families and individuals, but the other results that indicate that deprivation does not drive onset do not support the interpretation.

These findings are suggestive theoretically but hardly conclusive. Both the method of analysis and the data are blunt, and the sample size is small. Most independent variable data come from government sources, which in some cases are questionable. (For example, the census records the unemployment range as being between 0.13 to 5.5 percent per prefecture. However, less than 8 percent of the economically active population received a salary.) I created ordinal scales on the independent variables from the census data, but in some cases the incremental differences between different categories were relatively small. Finally, data sources for some important variables, such as political party support, are weak. (My estimation is based on secondary sources and my research in Rwanda.) In short, the analysis is useful, but the results should not be treated as proof of one theory or another. Triangulation is necessary.

―――――――――

This chapter develops two sets of arguments. The first concerns genocide at the top or, more specifically, the context and conditions under which Hutu hardliners pursued a policy of extermination. I reconstructed the periods just before and just after the genocide began. There is much that we do not yet conclusively know about this period, including the hardliners' exact decisions and the identity of President Habyarimana's assassins. But the hardliners' fateful choices were made in the context of new constraints on their power and ultimately a defensive war: the hardliners radicalized as their power eroded and as they faced armed combat.

It is difficult to say for certain whether the genocide was planned beforehand. There is no question that after Habyarimana's assassination, the hardliners chose genocide. Their actions were deliberate and organized, and they used the power of the state to murder massively. But what led them to take that decision? An instrumentalist or intentionalist model of the genocide would suggest that the decision came earlier, probably around the time Habyarimana signed the

Arusha Accords. By this model, the genocide would have been "meticulously prepared" before Habyarimana's assassination. But that model misses the dynamics of escalation that occurred as well as the factors that were driving the escalation. On balance, the evidence suggests a far more contingent set of decisions and dynamics.

In particular, it was the hardliners' fractured power that initially drove their radicalization. The hardliners had stiff resistance in the army and the political arena (the Hutu moderates), even while they faced an armed enemy (the Tutsi rebels). The hardliners claimed they had to take extreme measures to safeguard their power and defend the country. The president's assassination, the ensuing leadership crisis, and the quick resumption of war exacerbated the radicalization. The hardliners found themselves on the defensive, facing advancing rebels and opposition internally from politicians and the international community. It was in that context that they authorized mass violence against Tutsi civilians. If true, then these factors—fractured control, the assassination, and a defensive war—would be essential to the causal structure of the genocide. Immediate context mattered.

The chapter also focuses on regional patterns of violence in order to understand how and why the violence spread so quickly. To explain the genocide, we need to understand not only what led the hardliners to make their decisions but also why they were successful. The main findings are that while violence started at different times in different regions, the level of violence appears to even out over the course of the genocide. Data from one prefecture further showed that the violence was extraordinarily intense. Once a threshold was reached, the killing spiked. The next chapter explores why. The regional differences in timing are important. They indicate that the Hutu response to the hardliners was not monolithic: in many places, Hutus resisted the violence. That finding runs contrary to theories of genocide that stress ethnic identity, a culture of hatred, or even radio incitement. Identity and culture cannot explain why in some regions violence started earlier and why in some places violence started later. The same holds for radio incitement: the radio reached places where violence started earlier as well as places where the violence started later. Nor for that matter is a "culture of obedience" sufficient: in some regions Hutus obeyed; in others they did not. Something other than these factors played a role in igniting violence.

The chapter explores some other possible factors. Again, some common assumptions seem not to hold. Deprivation, for example, does not seem to explain why a region is prone to starting violence earlier than another. Neither does ethnic diversity, education levels, land shortage, or proximity to the capital. The most statistically significant variable is degree of support for the ruling party, followed by proximity to RPF positions. The political party finding is hard to interpret but suggests that regional support for the hardliners or possibly anger at the president's death may have played a role. The finding about RPF proximity is another indicator that war is an important part of why genocide happened. These are not conclusive findings, but they suggest that ethnic identity, prejudice, radio incitement, deprivation, and other factors that are commonly seen to drive participation do not seem to explain why violence starts. Rather, something else related to party support and war matter. Areas start as quiescent and then they explode into genocidal violence. The question is why—a topic I take up in the next chapter at a more fine-grained level of analysis.

3 Local Dynamics

The last chapter showed the awesome horror of Rwanda's genocide. In a few days, a community transformed from quiescence to mass killing; the result was that in three months at least half a million civilians died countrywide. But the regional patterns and killing rates do not really illustrate what happened in local areas where the violence took place. Who were the key actors? What did they do? How did the violence start? Why did the violence take off at a certain point? What, in short, were the dynamics that drove the genocide at the local level?

This chapter addresses those questions through a micro-comparative study. The chapter compares dynamics in five communes, including Giti, the one commune under government control where genocide did not take place. The specifics of mobilization differed in each of the other four communes, and each was located in a different prefecture. Yet, despite the variation, the comparison reveals important similarities. In particular, I find that the president's assassination and the resumption of war ruptured the preexisting order, creating a feeling of intense crisis and uncertainty in local communities. There followed a play for power *among Hutus,* what I call a "space of opportunity." Some wanted peace or to preserve the status quo; others hot-headedly called for war against Tutsis. But over time—sometimes very rapidly, other times less so—and for different reasons, Hutus vowing war on the Tutsis won the upper hand. A tipping point was reached; once that happened, mass mobilization of Hutu men swiftly followed, with devastating consequences for Tutsis.

The micro-comparative study leads me to diagram and re-conceptualize the dynamics of violence. Chaos is not the right model; neither is a carefully constructed, hierarchical "machine" of killing. Rather, a more contingent process happened: the call to kill Tutsis emanating from the top became a de facto basis for authority. Killing became akin to policy. Local elites claimed power and legitimacy because they had allied with the hardliners. Genocide was the new order of the day, one that overwhelmed Hutu opposition, demanded mass compliance, and ultimately took on a life of its own. The hardliners' call to destroy the Tutsi enemy set these dynamics in motion. The hardliners had the balance of power among Hutus in the country at the time. They dominated the central state, key army units, militias, and radio broadcasts. They succeeded partly because of their raw power, partly because of the general climate of heightened anxiety and fear in the country following the assassination and resumption of war, and partly because of Rwanda's institutions and geography.

Setting the Stage

Before turning to the five communes, I want to discuss briefly my case selection process as well as the major social groups at the local level in Rwanda. During the course of my research, I identified four principal ways in which genocidal violence started at the commune level: (1) mobilization from above by civilian authorities; (2) an intra-commune challenge to existing authorities by subordinates, other elites, or angry young men; (3) military mobilization of civilian authorities and local elites; and (4) an invasion from outside the commune either to remove officials who had refused to start the killing or to pressure recalcitrant officials to change their position. Each pattern of mobilization resulted in mass mobilization and genocide, but how each arrived at that outcome differed.

The variation in mobilization guided my case selection process. I picked a commune from each of the four categories: Gafunzo in Cyangugu Prefecture, chosen as an example of administratively led genocide; Kayove in Gisenyi Prefecture, chosen as an example of an internal challenge to existing officials; Kanzenze in Kigali-Rural Prefecture, chosen as an example of military-led mobilization; and Musambira in Gitarama Prefecture, chosen as an example of determined early resistance followed by an external incursion. And, as mentioned above, I also selected Giti to study as a "negative case"—where geno-

Figure 3.1 Field research sites

cide did not happen. Figure 3.1 depicts the location of the five communes on a map.

Rwanda is overwhelmingly rural, and the five communes I studied are no exception. Rwandan communes, of which there were 145 in 1994, average 182 square kilometers in size and more than 50,000 inhabitants. The largest social category in rural areas is that of farmers and shepherds: nationally, before the genocide, the primary economic activities of a little more than 90 percent of the adult population were farming, animal husbandry, and hunting, according to the census.[1] In general, these Rwandans have little education and little social power.

1. République du Rwanda, *Recensement général de la population et de l'habitat au 15 août 1991: Analyse des résultats définitifs,* Kigali, Rwanda, April 1994, 108.

Rwandans often call them the *rubanda rugufi*, literally "the low people," whose ranks also include itinerant laborers, domestic workers, petty business owners, and hawkers who sell merchandise in markets and commercial centers.

The next most important social stratum in Rwanda is the rural elite: those with substantial influence, status, and power at the local level. They generally have some education beyond primary school and earn a substantially higher salary than the average Rwandan (for example, the equivalent of $100 a month or more). Rwandans sometimes refer to the members of this social stratum as *les intellectuals.* They are political party leaders, clergymen, teachers, doctors, nurses, civic association directors, employees of international aid organizations, and important businessmen at commercial centers. There is some overlap between these categories: businessmen, for example, can also be political party leaders. Nationally, this stratum constituted about 5 percent of the adult population, according to the census.[2]

Another key stratum at the local level consists of administrative officials, including the burgomaster (mayor), assistant burgomasters (two to three per commune), a communal accountant, a communal secretary, *conseillers* (sector heads), and members of the *cellule* committee. In addition, every commune employed a school inspector, a school director, an agricultural inspector, a police brigadier, and about eight communal policemen. The burgomaster was the most powerful local official; he had the most authority in the commune and controlled the security apparatus. However, in the communal outskirts, *conseillers* often wielded the most authority. On average, each commune had eleven sectors, and each sector had about four *cellules*, each controlled by a five-person committee and led by a *responsable.* (See p. 204 for a diagram of the Rwandan state administration.)

Other categories of social actors existed, though not uniformly across the country. Some areas had parastatal companies—tea processing factories, cement factories, oil processing plants—which employed teams of local workers. In 1994, some areas had internally displaced persons who had fled from territory that the RPF controlled; in some areas of southern Rwanda, Burundian refugees also had taken refuge. In addition, among the civilian population were some paramilitary political party youths as well as retired soldiers and "reservists." All political parties had youth wings, though the MRND appears to be the only party that systematically gave military training

2. République du Rwanda, *Recensement général*, 108–9.

to members of its youth wing (called the *interahamwe*, as discussed in chapter 1). In short, there are a number of different local actors to consider, but keeping these basic distinctions in mind will help make sense of the dynamics described in detail below.

Gafunzo

Gafunzo is a rural commune with a seemingly average level of development. In 1994, the commune had one major and several small commercial centers, a major parish (Shangi), and electricity and phone lines.[3] Politically, the commune was divided between the ruling MRND party and the opposition MDR party. The commune did not have military-trained party militia, though both the MRND and MDR had active youth wings. According to the former burgomaster, Tutsis were 12 percent of the population, and intermarriages were common. Yet an estimated 6,000–6,800 Tutsis were killed in Gafunzo during the genocide, according to officials.

Violence in Gafunzo started immediately after Habyarimana's assassination, but the first targets were political leaders from opposition parties. On the night of April 7 and the morning of April 8, the MDR and PL heads in the commune, a Hutu and a Tutsi respectively, were attacked and killed. The early signal to Hutus and Tutsis alike, according to various interviewees, was that the violence would be between parties. "We heard there was fighting between the MDR and the MRND," summarized one Hutu man not implicated in the killings. The MDR commune president described his decision to go into hiding as a local leader of the opposition:

> We thought we were dead. . . . The president was killed. The Prime Minister was killed. [National MDR leader Faustin] Twagiramungu was being hunted. As head of MDR, you had no choice. All you could do was hide your skin.

In short, inhabitants of the commune knew of violence at the national and local levels, and in general they were conscious of a confused and

---

3. Interviewed for this case study were five sentenced perpetrators, chosen randomly; the former burgomaster; a former *conseiller*; two former soldiers (both sentenced in prison; one refused to speak); the current mayor (in 2000 the new, post-genocide government relabeled "burgomasters" to be mayors); a current *conseiller*; the commune head of IBUKA (a survivor's organization); a former *conseiller* and survivor; the former MDR commune president; three Hutu men who did not participate in the genocide; and two members of the clergy. These interviews took place in Cyangugu central prison, in the commune (now called Impara and called a district), and in Kamembe over the course of eleven nonconsecutive days in May and June 2002.

unsettled situation. But the early violence was not clearly anti-Tutsi. Indeed, survivors and perpetrators alike report that in several sectors, Hutu *conseillers* organized patrols to fight possible intruders. As in many other areas throughout Rwanda during this period, the patrols were composed of both Hutu and Tutsi men.

But the climate changed rapidly. By April 9, key members of the rural elite as well as a posse of armed reservists and former soldiers had taken control and were leading widespread violence against Tutsis. By April 10, they had initiated a genocidal dynamic throughout the commune. Interviewed in prison, the former burgomaster, Charles Karorero, maintained that, since his authority was already weakened in multipartyism and since he was ill in early April, he had no control over what happened. He said that he called a security meeting for all *conseillers* and other rural elite on April 8, but only two *conseillers* came. Karorero also said that he deployed communal police and gendarmes to a church where Tutsis congregated, but both forces ultimately were overpowered. (These claims were corroborated.) On balance, though, the burgomaster appears not to have made much effort either to prevent or to promote the violence, at least publicly. As such, his role is best described as passive—a response that allowed pro-violence forces to take control.

Judging from interviews with perpetrators, survivors, and Hutu nonparticipants, two groups formed. The first was composed of the MRND commune president, the CDR commune president (a businessman), a school director, a school inspector, and other businessmen. Some had familial ties to the burgomaster. The second group consisted of former soldiers and army reservists, in particular one nicknamed "Pima." Though it is difficult to prove, the two groups appear to have worked together. One perpetrator described an April meeting in which some of the elite who had assumed control instructed the armed men how to proceed:

> They welcomed us. They gave us something to drink. They told us there were killings, but only men had been killed. They said it was now necessary that women also be killed because foreign radio had reported killings in Rwanda. [The concern was that] these women would denounce those who had killed people and those who had demanded others kill. . . . These leaders stayed in the house. They did not want to be noticed. They did the politics. Three soldiers and I, we arrived at the "city" [a commercial center]. We sensitized others there, [saying that] the authorities had just said [Tutsis] had to be killed. We became many.

The respondent is here describing the dynamics of mobilization. Hardliners among the rural elite—MRND and CDR political party leaders, businessmen, and school officials—issued orders (in this case, to kill women) to retired soldiers and army reservists. The armed men in turn went to a common meeting place in the commune—a commercial center—and relayed the order to an assembled crowd. They did so in the name of "the authorities": the official order became to kill Tutsis, even though in this case the burgomaster and other local officials had not been present.

The violence spread quickly in the commune from April 10 onwards. As the violence spread, Tutsis fled to government offices, to the Shangi parish, and to neighbors' homes. But the attacks followed them there. According to several witnesses, Pima led the first large-scale attack on April 11 at a government office. Then on April 14, he led an even larger-scale attack on Shangi, which Tutsis, police, and gendarmes posted there resisted with some success. However, the final blow in the commune came from the outside. Further south in the prefecture, Yusuf Munyankazi—an MRND stalwart and militia leader who headed an agriculture association prior to the genocide—led attacks in several communes, according to numerous witnesses. Later he would travel as far as Kibuye Prefecture to attack Tutsis there too. But on April 27, Yusuf—as he is known—arrived in Gafunzo with several busloads of armed militias. According to several accounts, Yusuf's team easily overwhelmed the resistance and decimated the Tutsi population at the parish. Witnesses and survivors describe a scene of unbelievable horror, of death all day and night.

The mobilization outline seems to be the following. Although from a distance the pattern seemed to be administrative-led genocide, closer analysis shows that the top officials' primary response was passivity. Some *conseillers* organized early resistance while others did not, but none emerged in my research as an active promoter of violence. The burgomaster was publicly absent for all of April. With the early attacks on the opposition, the leaders of those groups were absent too. Thus, the early days of violence appear to be characterized by an initial gap in social authority, confusion, and fear—a short rupture. That gap in turn opened what I call a "space of opportunity," captured in this case by a pro-MRND rural elite working with a nucleus of military-trained individuals. All this points to a pattern also seen elsewhere: a nucleus of rural elite working with aggressive killers, or thugs, who in turn mobilized others to join the killing.

Kayove

About fifty miles north of Gafunzo is the hilly lakeside commune of Kayove, in Gisenyi Prefecture.[4] Rich in coffee and strongly supportive of President Habyarimana, Kayove had a smaller concentration of Tutsis than Gafunzo, estimated at around 10 percent with a high concentration in several sectors around Lake Kivu. Prior to the war, both Hutus and Tutsis recall, relations were good, with much intermarriage. However, there was an episode of anti-Tutsi violence in the commune in 1990, just after the first RPF attack in late October of that year. Hutus from northern sectors with fewer Tutsis attacked sectors with more Tutsis, claiming that the RPF had collaborators there; Tutsis also were attacked around Gishwati forest. A former burgomaster, Anselme Nzabonimpa, is widely credited with stopping this violence; he circulated throughout the commune, sent for and received gendarme reinforcements, and eventually arrested looters and attackers, including a communal agent. However, in 1992, after opposition political parties were made legal, Nzabonimpa resigned, because, as he told me, there was too much disobedience in the commune. His replacement was a political appointee from Kigali, an ally of President Habyarimana. The MRND went largely unchallenged in the multiparty era, though the CDR and the MDR had marginal support. By all accounts, there was no interparty violence prior to the genocide.

The reconstruction of early genocidal dynamics in Kayove is distinguished by several remarkable sources. First, there are letters from former *conseillers* written to the burgomaster during the genocide. Second, the MRND party leadership in Kayove is not implicated in the genocide—a very rare occurrence in Rwanda—so some can be interviewed. And third, one of the most active genocide leaders is open and articulate about what he did and why, and I interviewed him over the course of three days. Overall, the pattern of mobilization in Kayove appears to be that of a rural elite working with party and other aggressive youth, initiating genocide against Tutsis, and intimidating

---

4. Those interviewed for this case study include ten confessed and sentenced perpetrators chosen randomly as well as six other prisoners who had been charged but not convicted of genocide. The latter include a former *conseiller* and a former vice president of the *interahamwe* in the commune. Also interviewed were the current mayor (a returnee), the current head of IBUKA for the commune and current district administrator (a survivor), a businessman (a survivor), a current *conseiller* (a survivor), the former MRND president, the former commune accountant and current head of *Gacaca*, the commune's burgomaster from 1982 to 1993, a *conseiller* during the genocide not accused of genocide, a former teacher, and several members of the clergy. The interviews were conducted in April and June 2002.

anyone who tried to stop them. The burgomaster's role is disputed. Some claim he orchestrated everything that happened from behind the scenes, but closer examination suggests he took a more tacit position of acceptance.

By all accounts, the violence started on April 7 in numerous sectors and spread to all but one by April 8. In the holdout sector, Hutus and Tutsis, with the *conseiller*'s encouragement, mounted a joint defense against attacks from other sectors. They succeeded until April 10, when the burgomaster came and, according to two witnesses, claimed he could do nothing to halt the violence. The current *conseiller*, a survivor, said:

> The burgomaster came and talked to the *conseiller* who came and told us, "Things are difficult. Everyone must arrange for himself." We heard from a businessman who hid our family that the burgomaster had said [to the *conseiller*], "Things are difficult. We must leave people be. These are things done throughout the country." . . . Then things changed immediately, and the attack began and the young bandits and people of bad ways saw it was a law to kill the Tutsis.

In a different sector, the burgomaster claimed the same. According to the former MRND secretary and current commune *Gacaca* president:

> At 10 a.m. on the 7th I saw a band of these *interahamwe* and the *impuzambigumbi* [CDR youth]. They had killed three people at the school. . . . I went to see the burgomaster about the situation. I met him near the school. He had a vehicle. There were two gendarmes and two communal police with him. I told him the situation. He said, "What can we do? I can do nothing." And the fighting continued. . . . The *interahamwe* passed everywhere. If they found you, no matter whom they found, they took you by force. They were crazy in the head.[5]

In another example, a Hutu former school director said that he witnessed an attack on a health center, where a crowd of attackers took away the guns of the two gendarmes who were guarding the center:

> I lived next to a health center. At 6 a.m., I was there. There were many people at the center, around 100. . . . They had local weapons, clubs, sticks, machetes. . . . They took the gendarmes' guns and told the gendarmes to face the wall [indicating that the gendarmes had to stand

---

5. "*Gacaca*" is a form of traditional justice that in 2002 was remodeled to try genocide suspects. Most *Gacaca* officials are considered not to have participated in the genocide. The interviewee was Kayove's *Gacaca* president in 2002.

down]. Then they looked for the woman [a Tutsi who had given birth the night before and was hidden in the clinic]. They did not find her. They tried to destroy the door. It was chaos. The burgomaster arrived there. He tried to calm the population and to get the population to return the weapons to the gendarmes. Then the burgomaster left with the gendarmes.

By these accounts and others, the burgomaster's main public course of action was to claim powerlessness. In so doing, the burgomaster tacitly accepted the attacks. However, judging from perpetrator testimony and from the *conseiller* letters, the authority of officials was, in fact, violently challenged during this period. Let's start with a key perpetrator, a member of the rural elite who came from a well-connected family and who had worked for Rwanda's national ballet troupe:

It was Wednesday during the night [of April 6]. A veterinarian, a neighbor, came to tell me that he had just heard on the radio that Habyarimana had been shot. In my mind, I understood right away that the Tutsis were responsible. I was angry, and I said to myself, "It is true. The Tutsis are mean." And I said everything people say about them is true. I went to the cabaret [a local bar]. I found that the peasants had set up roadblocks. It was then they said, "No Tutsi can remain in our sector." That is what they decided at this meeting at this roadblock. It was like a meeting; there were a lot of people. Those they found this day they did not kill. It was the 7th. The 8th, we heard a woman had been killed; we heard that in the other sectors people were being killed. So we too attacked those who were our neighbors.

Further describing his attitude, he said:

We said . . . we are going to kill them before being killed by them. I immediately thought of Ndadaye [the former Burundian president killed in October 1993] and of those from Byumba [internally displaced by war fighting]. I no longer had a conscience to be able to love someone. I thought that even all those people in other parties, like the MDR and PL—that I had to kill them. I did not remember that I was educated by Tutsis, or that I had once lived with priests. I did not even think about the fact that my older brothers had Tutsi wives or that my mother-in-law was Tutsi.

Over the next seven days, the perpetrator said he led a group that ranged in size from three hundred to five hundred people. He said they killed all but one of the seventeen Tutsis in the sector and one Hutu. Describing himself as "a terrorist," he said that only five men did the actual killing, including a former soldier and a former prisoner who had been released:

> It was said my team was very strong because I came from a strong family where there were Tutsis and that I no longer supported them. No one could stop me . . . even the burgomaster could not arrive before me in this period. *Why not?* Because he knew that one of my older brothers was a secretary of an embassy; another was a sub-prefect; another was a priest; and another was a lieutenant.

Asked about those who did not participate, he cited an example:

> Our *conseiller* refused to help us, saying that he could not tolerate people being killed. So we went to look to kill him. We could not find him. His wife gave us 100,000 FRW [roughly $715, an enormous sum in rural Rwanda]. The *conseiller* had fled to the burgomaster. When the burgomaster brought him with the gendarmes, we threw rocks at the vehicle. The burgomaster gave 100,000 FRW so that we would allow the *conseiller* to return to his house, but if we had not [eventually] fled [to Zaire] we would have killed him.

When interviewed, the *conseiller* in question corroborated this account, describing how he repeatedly fled and hid during the course of the genocide.

The dynamic here is that the rural elite and peasants took control; they initiated violence against Tutsis; they overpowered local officials; they threatened to kill anyone who resisted. The same pattern is evident in other sectors. Several *conseillers* wrote to the burgomaster during the genocide, pleading for help. In one sector, the *conseiller* described how on April 7 an army sergeant, a reservist, and two agents of the state tourism agency, ORTPN, one of whom was armed, led an attack against Tutsis. The attack killed the man of the household, but the survivors fled to the *conseiller*'s home. On April 8, the *conseiller* wrote:

> I gave them money, but they would not leave me alone. They searched the whole house and found there [name withheld] and certain members of his family. They took them by force and beat them with gun butts. Mr. Burgomaster, I am asking you to help us quickly because if this continues, no one will remain. I am weakened, I am afraid.

A letter of April 19 from a different *conseiller* is even more dramatic. The *conseiller* describes how his older brother, who was among those leading the violence in the sector, told him that he was next to die:

Mr. Burgomaster,

I am writing you this letter with great sadness. Those who are called *interahamwe* (they are called that because we did not choose them) have informed me that I must be killed tomorrow morning. [Name withheld] (my older brother) gave me the message; he is part of them. I asked him why I must be killed. He responded that I will be informed tomorrow morning before dying. . . . It is sad that someone is targeted because of his goodwill.

Another *conseiller* wrote on April 18 to say that he could not make a meeting:

I want you to know that there is not security for me and in the sector. When it is day, we don't know if night will come; when it is night, we don't know if day will come. There is looting. I ask you to help me render justice.

In an interview, another former *conseiller*—and former MRND commune president—described a similar situation. He told me that Tutsis fled to his house for protection, but the attackers followed them there. The *conseiller* and the survivors in turn fled, and the house was looted. As in other sectors, the leader of the attack was a member of the rural elite: a former court employee who had worked in Kigali. "He said I was *Inkotanyi* [a synonym for the RPF]," the former ruling party leader said. "It was grave."

In retrospect, the pattern of mobilization in Kayove was not substantially different from Gafunzo. In both, President Habyarimana's death and the onset of violence in Kigali and the commune environs unsettled existing power relationships and created a space of opportunity. A rural elite very quickly emerged to claim that the time had come to kill Tutsis. The burgomaster tacitly accepted the new course of action, but the new rural elite intimidated and overpowered any who resisted the killing—including local officials. The dynamic again shows how power was in play during this period, and how promoting violence was a means by which to establish power in an unstable environment.

Kanzenze

Outwardly, the genocidal dynamic in Kanzenze looks quite different from those in the other communes examined because of the military's role there, but on closer inspection, as will be shown, the similarities are greater than the differences.[6] Kanzenze is an hour's drive southeast of Kigali. Prior to the genocide, the region received successive waves of settlers, both Tutsis escaping violence in the 1950s and 1960s and Hutus from the northwest and elsewhere looking for land. Numerous sources report a nearly equal Hutu/Tutsi ratio in the commune before the genocide. Politically, the MRND controlled the leading administrative posts in the commune, but the PL and the MDR had substantial support among the rural elite and among the *rubanda rugufi*. As in Kayove, there was violence against Tutsis before the genocide, in March 1992. But the key factor that distinguishes this commune from others is the presence of a large military camp, called Gako.

Both perpetrators and survivors agree that the first killing occurred on the night of April 8 when soldiers from Gako killed a Tutsi businessman and threatened other rural Tutsi elites. Before then and especially in the two days following, the climate in the commune was tense. The insecurity and violence prompted some Tutsi civilians to flee to two major hilltops in the commune, Kayumba and Rebeho. Both survivors and perpetrators report skirmishes between these groups and Hutus in the vicinity. The change came on April 10 and 11, and all accounts assign a decisive role to the Gako soldiers. The existing evidence suggests that the local military camp commander initiated the attacks, whether independently, after being ordered to do from Kigali, or in response to requests from local officials—or some combination thereof.

The discussion below benefits from the testimony of two very aggressive killers in the commune, interviewed separately. The first is an army reservist and CDR party activist; the second is an *interahamwe* member. Both admit to, and are widely credited with, being among the foremost attackers in the commune. According to the reservist, the order to kill Tutsi civilians came from officers in the camp on April 10:

> The lieutenant ordered revenge. We had to kill the enemy. The Tutsis had killed the president. We had to kill the Tutsis.

6. Those interviewed for this case study include the former assistant burgomaster, the former *Interahamwe* president in the commune, a reservist, two other perpetrators in prison, the current mayor, two other current commune authorities, the IBUKA head in the commune (also is a communal authority), a current *conseiller* (also a survivor), four Tutsi survivors, and a nonparticipating Hutu. These interviews were conducted in January and July 2002.

In the interview, the reservist emphasized that the entire ethnic group—all its members—were defined as the enemy. (I will return later to the rationale present in this perpetrator's short but telling account.) The reservist further elaborated that the military strategy was to contact civilian officials, who in turn would mobilize the Hutu population. Soldiers considered the local population "intelligence," he said, meaning they used civilians to find out where Tutsis were located. Numerous perpetrators from the communes surrounding the camp report a similar process, in which soldiers arrived and either summoned local authorities to mobilize the population or did so themselves.

The *interahamwe* perpetrator gave a slightly different but not inconsistent account. He said he was summoned to a meeting at the commune offices on April 10. In the meeting, he said, a top military official from Kigali—General Kabiligi—took the floor and said that, in response to the resumption of hostilities and the president's assassination, the Tutsis had been declared the enemy. According to the *interahamwe* member, the general ordered the commune authorities to participate in the annihilation of the enemy. A sub-prefect was there, as was the burgomaster. Both, according to the perpetrator, reiterated the message. The logic, he said, was:

> The enemy attacked the country. They were *Inkotanyi.* They said we
> had to defend ourselves. If not, they could kill us.

Everyone assembled at the meeting understood this to mean that Tutsis had to be killed, the *interahamwe* perpetrator said. After the meeting concluded, the burgomaster ordered a local businessman to hand out machetes to the local youths; the perpetrator himself got one, he said. Violence started the next day.

On April 11, according to perpetrators, bystanders, and survivors, busloads of soldiers descended on Kanzenze. Working in conjunction with *interahamwe* and other Hutu *rubanda rugufi* men, the soldiers led an attack on Kayumba, the first of a series of large-scale attacks in the commune. Tutsis surviving this attack and others fled to churches, the commune offices, and a cultural center. Attacks on these gathering points and another place continued through April 16, all with significant military involvement. Each attack resulted in a major massacre, similar to the one attributed to Yusuf in Gafunzo described above.

Prior to the genocide, the burgomaster, Bernard Gatanazi, was considered by most to be a moderate. But several perpetrators and survivors report Gatanazi's direct, active encouragement of the violence. One survivor recalled a change in the burgomaster's behavior after he returned from a meeting in Kigali on April 7: "Before, he was a friend," he said. "But Thursday, after his return, he was very angry. He wouldn't talk to you." But Gatanazi was not alone. Perpetrators and survivors alike claim that the CDR commune president (a business-man), the MDR president (a businessman), and the MRND president (the commune's agricultural officer) all encouraged the violence. The lone Hutu elite political party member who opposed the genocide, it appears, was the PSD leader. A Hutu, he was killed along with his Tutsi wife, according to two survivors.

In retrospect, the onset dynamics in Kanzenze are not a major departure from the other communes analyzed so far. In the first three days, fear and confusion prevailed. Tutsis fled and some Hutus attacked. However, the course of violence was not yet set. The tipping point came on April 10 with the military's aggressive entry into the civilian arena. The military's entry into the arena appears to have had several effects. For the burgomaster, whose participation was directly demanded, a passive response was no longer possible. If he had opposed, he would have lost power and probably his life. If he accepted, he would have retained his position. He accepted. For the other rural elite, the military backing of civilian authorities left little opportunity for political maneuver or a local power struggle. In short, the military set the dynamics within the commune, as it did in the neighboring Ngenda and Gashora Communes, as well as in other locations throughout the country. Where soldiers entered into the civilian arena and promoted violence against the "Tutsi enemy," that entry swiftly determined the balance in favor of genocide.

Musambira

Outwardly, again, the pattern of genocidal violence in Musambira Commune looks different, and the violence started later in the commune, as it did throughout south central Rwanda.[7] But closer inspection shows that while the shift to widespread genocidal violence took longer to materialize—for reasons that will be explored below—the dynamics of violence were similar to what occurred elsewhere.

7. Those interviewed for this case study include four perpetrators selected randomly, the former burgomaster, the former subprefect (both sentenced prisoners), a detainee accused of being an active participant, the current mayor, two current *conseillers,* the current Ibuka head in the commune, and the commune's elected *Gacaca* president.

Musambira is in Gitarama Prefecture, southwest of Kigali, and was strongly supportive of the opposition MDR party before the genocide. Although precise details about the preexisting ethnic population are not available, the commune had a sizeable Tutsi population and much intermarriage—on a scale comparable to Giti (see below). Not apparently particularly wealthy, Musambira had a commercial center on a par with the main centers in Kayove and Gafunzo, though larger than Giti's and marginally smaller than Kanzenze's. About a year prior to the genocide, a new burgomaster was elected: Justin Nyandwi, a young former teacher from the moderate wing of the MDR party.

By all accounts—from perpetrators, survivors, Hutu bystanders, and current authorities—Nyandwi mobilized people to prevent violence from spreading to the commune in the first days after President Habyarimana's death. Nyandwi himself said:

> People knew there were killings in Kigali. Together with our prefect, we took the decision to thwart the killings, to repulse them, and each commune organized to do this. . . . In my commune, I ordered the communal police to be ready on the borders of the commune.

In the first week, the strategy worked for Musambira. Even so, Nyandwi described a harrowing experience when he traveled to Kigali:

> On the 10th, a friend came to my place. He told me his brothers were in danger. I thought I should do something to save them. I went to Kigali, but I was arrested at a roadblock. . . . They told me a lot of things: that I was against the *interahamwe,* that I had a conflict with the president of MRND, and so on. They said they had decided to kill me and my three policemen.

The burgomaster and his companions were brought to a pit where perpetrators had discarded various corpses. Nyandwi described the horrific scene; he told me he expected to die at that point. But, he said, a police commander there intervened; the commander recommended calling Gitarama to verify if Nyandwi really was the burgomaster of Musambira (Nyandwi had been accused, among other things, of being an RPF infiltrator). The call was made, and the commander released the Musambira team the following day.

On his way back home, Nyandwi stopped to see the burgomaster in neighboring Runda Commune. The burgomaster there was a friend, and Nyandwi wanted to inform him of what had happened in Kigali. However, Nyandwi said his colleague's authority had been compromised. In the early days, the Runda burgomaster had imprisoned people who had started killing. But, Nyandwi said, a militia leader had come from Kigali and forcibly released the detainees. An even more devastating event, he said, occurred the following week:

> I continued to struggle. . . . The week of the 11th, there were *interahamwe* incursions. There was also a very serious incident for me. The population killed an *interahamwe* and that was very expensive for me. On RTLM, it was said that I was killing *interahamwe* and helping Tutsis. That was repeated many times. It was the 14th. The population [in the commune] began to be afraid, calling a burgomaster an enemy! . . . It was grave for me. The population helped me, but the police began to get scared. They asked themselves, "What will we do?" I tried to calm them. We continued all the same, up until the 20th.[8]

In fact, the balance of power had begun to shift slightly earlier. Three main changes happened. First, on April 18, a meeting was held with the other burgomasters in Gitarama, with the prefect and the prime minister, in which the latter threatened to replace burgomasters who reported insecurity—a clear signal not to resist violence.[9] In Mugina, a neighboring commune, the burgomaster who had opposed the violence was killed that day or the following one.[10] Second, soldiers arrived in Musambira on April 19, killed Tutsis, and ordered peasants to continue killing. And third, the dynamic in neighboring Taba Commune changed.

Regarding the soldiers' arrival, three interviewed witnesses said soldiers stopped on the main road and threatened to kill Hutus who did not take part in killing Tutsis. One perpetrator said:

> I was on the road. A soldier came. He said, "Others have killed the Tutsis and you, you are like that [doing nothing]! If you don't kill them, I will begin on one side without leaving a house—I will kill everyone." . . . The war had not yet started in Musambira. . . . I was with delinquents. They profited by taking cows and looting.

8. Interviews with others in the commune have corroborated key elements of this story: that Nyandwi led resistance against killing, that there were incursions, that an attacker (here called an *interahamwe*) was killed, and that Nyandwi was denounced on RTLM. Given the private nature of what happened to Nyandwi in Kigali, I have not been able to corroborate this aspect of the story. However, nothing I have heard calls it into question.

9. See International Criminal Tribunal for Rwanda, "The Prosecutor versus Jean-Paul Akayesu," Case No. ICTR–96-4-T," 32.

10. ICTR, "Jean-Paul Akayesu," 32; author interview with Nyandwi.

As for Taba, the burgomaster there, Jean-Paul Akayesu, apparently changed his position on April 19 (see below). On that date, according to several sources, Akayesu entered Musambira looking for someone who supposedly was plotting to kill him. The incursion generated insecurity in Musambira, and Tutsis also began fleeing from Taba to Musambira. Nyandwi tried to calm the situation on April 20, but when he returned, his wife told him that men dressed in military uniform were looking for him. Having been threatened already and with his control already tenuous, Nyandwi concluded that the soldiers had come to kill him. He decided to flee, first to the prefect's house and from there to others' homes.[11]

Immediately after Nyandwi fled, by all accounts, a Musambira native on the MRND national committee, Abdulraham Iyakaremye, took control of the commune. "Wherever he went, whatever he wanted was done," said the current *Gacaca* president, a Hutu. Prior to the genocide, Abdulraham was a director of an agricultural association. After taking control, Abdulraham established a "security crisis committee" that had representatives in every sector. According to several accounts, the representatives were ordered to mobilize the population for nightly patrols, which became attacks on Tutsis. At first, only men were killed; the killing of women was ordered later.

Several Hutus—perpetrators and nonperpetrators—said the pressure to participate was intense. "It was difficult to escape" participation, said the *Gacaca* president. One day, a Hutu group went to his house in search of adult men to join them. "The chance we had is that we were children. We were students. They did not require someone from our house to go." What the respondent is describing here is a dynamic we will see later. In many locations during this period, groups of men went house to house, requiring at least one adult member of the household to participate in the attacks against Tutsis. The pattern is consistent with preexisting institutions of labor mobilization in Rwanda (the history of which I discuss in chapter 8). In his case, there were no adult men—all the males in the house were children of school age—and hence no one from the household took part in the violence, according to the man I interviewed. The pressure on Hutus to participate was intense in other ways too. Perpetrators, survivors, and current authorities all report that Hutus who hid Tutsis were also killed.

---

11. Current authorities, survivors, and perpetrators corroborated this story.

Even those who tried to calm others were threatened: "They would call you an accomplice, and if you were called an accomplice you were killed like the others," said the *Gacaca* president.

In retrospect, the main difference in Musambira was that the anti-violence forces remained active longer than in the other communes I examined above. The question is, why? The answer seems to lie in the politics of the area. By and large, the peasants, the rural elite, the administrative officials, and the prefectural authorities were initially all solidly in the opposition. On April 7 in Kigali, the first attacks came against MDR politicians from the south, and those who killed were loyal to the MRND Hutu hardliners. Thus, the call to violence did not resonate in Musambira—at first. Nyandwi did not face a strong local challenger (Abdulraham appears not to have been a resident of the commune prior to April 20); the burgomaster did not face initial military pressure or an initial attack from a neighboring commune. Nyandwi was thus able to remain in effective control and maintain a plurality of force against violence. However, his authority was challenged at the national level—the prime minister threatened those who resisted the violence, soldiers later invaded the commune, and violence began in neighboring Taba and Runda Communes. The final blow was the arrival of soldiers, who sought out the burgomaster. With these changes, the balance of power tipped: the burgomaster gave up, and the genocide began.

The dynamics in neighboring Taba Commune make for an instructive comparison.[12] The burgomaster from Taba, Jean-Paul Akayesu, was the first convicted criminal at the International Criminal Tribunal for Rwanda (ICTR), so there is a well-documented public record of what happened in Taba. Although one commentator claims Akayesu typifies the genocide-supportive "middle management" in a "land of followers" with a "culture of obedience," Akayesu's case resembles Musambira's, with only one key difference.[13] Like Musambira, Taba was a MDR stronghold, and until April 18, by all accounts, Akayesu tried to prevent violence.[14] As in other places, Tutsis conducted night

12. Although I interviewed several perpetrators from Taba, the key source of information for the following discussion comes from the ICTR decision that found Akayesu, Taba's burgomaster, guilty of genocide.

13. Bill Berkeley, *The Graves Are Not Yet Full: Race, Tribe, and Power in the Heart of Africa* (New York: Basic Books, 2001), 254.

14. On Akayesu's attempts to prevent violence, see ICTR, "Jean-Paul Akayesu," 31–32, 37; on MDR's strength, 35.

patrols with Hutus until April 18, and the burgomaster and his allies made a concerted effort to ward off incursions and prevent an outbreak of violence.[15] But on April 18, according to numerous witnesses and in the opinion of the ICTR chamber, a "marked change" occurred.[16] According to the ICTR's findings, Akayesu switched to cooperating with the militia and adopted a pro-genocide position. In the words of the chamber, Akayesu "called on the population to unite and elimi-nate the sole enemy: accomplices of the *Inkotanyi.*"[17] Widespread vi-olence started immediately.

What prompted the switch? Akayesu claims variously that he was "overwhelmed," that he lost control, and that he was coerced.[18] But closer inspection suggests that as the balance shifted toward violence, at a certain point Akayesu chose to adapt, to switch his own position. Up until April 18, as in Musambira, Taba faced incursions and Tutsi influxes. These probably weakened his authority, but Akayesu had the support of prefectural authorities and seemingly did not face a strong rural elite challenge. But on April 18, two external conditions changed. First, the prime minister threatened noncompliant burgo-masters, as already mentioned. Second, violence became widespread on April 18 in a neighboring commune, Runda.[19] Moreover, pro-vio-lence forces arrived from Kigali. On April 19—after resisting vio-lence—Akayesu appeared before a crowd beside an *interahamwe* waving a document given to him that he said showed that the RPF and local accomplices were plotting to kill Hutus and seize power.[20] In short, the pattern is similar to elsewhere: once the balance of power shifted toward the violence position, the burgomaster faced a new choice: switch, remain passive, or flee. Musambira's burgomaster fled; Mugina's was killed. Akayesu switched.

This pattern is similar to what occurred in other areas that at first resisted the violence. The dynamics are well documented in opposi-tion-dominated Butare Prefecture.[21] There, most burgomasters and the prefect actively resisted the genocide for nearly two weeks. But na-tional authorities intervened, replacing the prefect and removing an anti-violence gendarme commander. In a local public meeting, the

---

15. On trying to stop incursions, ICTR, "Jean-Paul Akayesu," 31.

16. ICTR, "Jean-Paul Akayesu," 31.

17. ICTR, "Jean-Paul Akayesu," 52.

18. ICTR, "Jean-Paul Akayesu," 32, 51.

19. ICTR, "Jean-Paul Akayesu," 36.

20. ICTR, "Jean-Paul Akayesu," 43, 51.

21. The account below is based on Alison Des Forges, *Leave None to Tell the Story: Genocide in Rwanda* (New York: Human Rights Watch, 1999), 432–594.

prime minister then warned that the government "would no longer tolerate those who sympathized with the enemy."[22] The president in turn threatened those who refused to "work."[23] These interventions shifted the balance of power. Some burgomasters switched too, others passively accepted, and at least one fled but was killed. Having been resisted for two weeks, violence started immediately and spread rapidly.

In communes where violence started earlier but where there was initial hesitance or resistance—such as Nyakizu in Butare and Musebeya in Gikongoro—the pattern was similar. In Nyakizu, the burgomaster faced strong pressure from the rural elite to start violence; the commune was already host to Burundian refugees and, being on the prefecture border, faced incursions, pressure, and Tutsi influxes from neighboring Gikongoro Prefecture.[24] In Musebeya, the burgomaster actively resisted but faced internal rural elite pressure, external pressure from a former colonel and the MRND president, and attacks from other communes. He resisted until he finally went into hiding in his home.[25]

Giti

Giti is an exception—genocide did not occur in Giti—but there is no a priori reason why this was the case.[26] The commune is just north of the capital and in Byumba Prefecture, where President Habyarimana and the MRND had strong political support. The burgomaster and all *conseillers* were in the MRND, and the party was dominant in the commune. Prior to the genocide, the burgomaster had distributed firearms as part of the civil defense program, and nightly patrols had been instituted. The commune was host to Rwandans displaced by the war, though many had returned to their homes just prior to the genocide. All radio stations could be heard in the commune. Socioeco-

22. Des Forges, *Leave None*, 458.
23. Des Forges, *Leave None*, 460.
24. Nyakizu is discussed in detail in Des Forges, *Leave None*, 353–431, esp. 372–76. The internal pressure in this account came from a MDR-*Pawa* local leader and from other apparently pro-violence rural elite.
25. For an account of what happened in Musebeya, see Des Forges, *Leave None*, 316–45.
26. Interviewed for this case study were the burgomaster during the genocide (Hutu), the burgomaster immediately after the genocide (Tutsi), the current mayor of Rwamiko (Tutsi; the commune of Giti no longer existed in 2002 as it was fused with another and renamed), a former subprefect who is from Giti (Tutsi), the current police inspector (Tutsi), two survivors, two current *conseillers*, one former *conseiller*, a current school director (Hutu), and one perpetrator chosen randomly (from Rutare).

nomically, the commune had normal levels of education and population growth rates, according to former officials. The economy was
peasant-based, without factories or any large-scale commercial centers. If anything, the commune was marginally poorer than most and
entirely rural; in 1994, it had neither electricity nor phone lines.

Giti did have an above average number of Tutsis—25 to 30 percent
of the population, according to the former burgomaster—and much
intermarriage. Many inhabitants spoke of a culture of tolerance in the
commune's subregion of Buganza. Indeed, although the MRND was
dominant, political party contests prior to the genocide were, by all
accounts, not violent, and the burgomaster, Edouard Sebushumba,
was considered a moderate. There were no armed *interahamwe* militias in the commune. Many rural elites lived in Kigali, some of which
were associated with the moderate wing of the MDR.[27] However,
moderate politicians, a lack of armed irregulars, and a high Tutsi concentration were not anomalous; those conditions existed throughout
Butare and Gitarama Prefectures, as we have seen.

But there was no genocide in Giti. On April 6, the day of President
Habyarimana's assassination, the burgomaster said he knew there
could be trouble in his commune. "Fear took hold of me," Sebushumba told me in an interview. "I said that the consequences would
be bad. A president who died! One expected something terrible." Almost immediately, he saw houses burning in a neighboring commune, but he decided he would try to prevent violence from breaking
out in Giti. "One cannot fight for one's country by killing people," he
said.

It is also true that the burgomaster did not face a strong internal
challenge to his authority. He said that he and the *conseillers* "spoke
the same language" and that a rival from the rural elite did not make
an early bid for control. Still, "a tension in the population" existed,
and some wanted to foment violence, he said. On April 8, youths
slaughtered cattle that belonged to Tutsis—often an early act of violence. But Sebushumba arrested them and multiplied nightly patrols
to prevent further breakouts. He told me, "If you do not put people in
prison and they take cows, the next day they would kill."

The burgomaster also faced an external attack from the neighboring
commune of Murambi, where a former burgomaster, a national-level
MRND politician named Jean-Baptiste Gatete, was in control. The

27. The minister of information, one of the first victims on April 7 in Kigali, was from
Giti.

conseiller of the attacked sector mobilized the local population to resist the invaders. Even so, Sebushumba felt that he was close to losing control. "It was nearly finished," he said. "If things had continued, I could have lost control."

The critical change that stopped the violence from taking hold was the arrival of RPF rebel troops. Although the troops did not set foot in the communal administrative headquarters for another week, they arrived in neighboring Rutare Commune the night of April 9, and knowledge of their presence was widespread in Giti on April 10.[28] Just knowing the RPF troops had arrived and had stopped the violence in Rutare was enough to calm the situation and block a dynamic of violence from taking hold in Giti, according to several survivors and former officials. Summarizing the situation, one Tutsi survivor told me, "If the *Inkotanyi* had not arrived, there would have been massacres."

Although the outcome in Giti was anomalous, its early dynamics were not. They resemble the dynamics in other communes where local officials hesitated or resisted the violence immediately after President Habyarimana was killed, such as in Musambira and Taba. The critical difference that stopped a genocidal dynamic from taking hold in Giti was the arrival of the RPF, which calmed the situation. Elsewhere where the RPF did not arrive, the balance tipped to those promoting violence and claiming authority on that basis; mass mobilization and violence swiftly followed, as we have seen.

Dynamics of Violence

I am now in a position to reconstruct the local dynamics that led to genocidal violence starting in communities throughout Rwanda. At the most general level, two different but often simultaneous dynamics drove the killing. On the one hand, the presidential assassination, the resumption of war, the assassination of political leaders, and the spreading violence deeply destabilized Rwanda. The period was one of acute uncertainty, heightened anxiety, fear, and confusion. The pre–April 1994 events only deepened the sense of confusion; in other words, the crisis was particularly acute because of the civil war, the multiparty politics, and the regional violence that preceded it. That was the first dynamic: acute uncertainty and insecurity. On the other

28. My account is based on interviews with witnesses. See also the International Criminal Tribunal for Rwanda (ICTR), "The Prosecutor v. Laurent Semanza," Case No. ICTR-97–20-T, Judgment and Sentence, May 2003, paragraph 114, which discusses Giti and Rutare.

hand, hardliners who had taken control of the national state issued a directive to destroy the Tutsi enemy. That call became a basis for authority: locals around the country could claim allegiance to the hardliners, which meant killing Tutsis, and leverage power on that basis. Killing Tutsis, in short, became a source of legitimacy and power in the context of acute crisis. Genocide became the new order of things or, as some of the participants put it, "the law."

The micro-comparative study illustrates how the dynamics unfolded at the local level. In most locations, the national events of April 6 and 7 unsettled rural authority. Many people knew the situation was very serious, but they did not know what was happening. The uncertainty played out differently in different places. In Giti, for example, there was looting; in Kanzenze, there were limited skirmishes; in Gafunzo, local opposition political leaders were assassinated. Elsewhere in the country, people slept in fields, fearing attacks; sometimes both Tutsis and Hutus fled for safety to central congregation points, such as churches or schools. But the course of genocide was not yet set. Insecurity and uncertainty prevailed, but in many areas Hutus and Tutsis had not yet divided, and often they jointly patrolled their communities, trying to prevent any trouble or violence.

At this stage, a "space of opportunity" opened at the local level. The crisis created a new field of contestation at the local level because the preexisting political order had been ruptured. The president was dead; the prime minister was assassinated; war was on the horizon. Power, in short, was indeterminate. In this climate, influential actors were able to take charge at the local level. In Gafunzo, political party leaders, reservists, and armed youths took the initiative; in Kayove, a well-educated man from a powerful family stepped forward; in Kanzenze, the burgomaster eventually took control; in other places, a *conseiller* led the call to attack Tutsis; in still other places, aggressive young men did. But what we are seeing here is a contest among Hutus—an *intra*-Hutu struggle for dominance and authority at the local level in a period of acute crisis.

Eventually, the Hutus promoting violence won: the balance of power shifted to those claiming that the time had come to attack Tutsis. In most communities, there appeared a clear point when this happened—a tipping point—when pro-violence forces in a particular community consolidated control. From that point forward, those forces mobilized other Hutu men to participate in the attacks. A new "us or them" dichotomy took shape, quickly marginalizing opposition, and the killings spread like wildfire across the communities.

Genocide became the new law of the land, one to which Hutu men had to demonstrate their loyalty and compliance.

The key question is *why* this happened. Why did the hardliner position of genocide trump everything else? There are a number of reasons. Most importantly, the hardliners had the most power countrywide among Hutus. The hardliners controlled the national state; radio broadcasts reinforced the message, as did roving militia bands and hardliner military officers stationed throughout the country. Why genocide succeeded cannot be divorced from the hardliners' position of power and their order to destroy the Tutsi enemy.

It is also true that the president's assassination, the resumption of war, the killing of the most senior Hutu opposition leaders, and the international community's inaction undermined the peacemakers and moderates in rural communities throughout Rwanda. Having almost no opportunities for external backing and support—in the middle of a wartime emergency that only radicalized and emboldened the hardliners—the moderate space for action steadily shrank and ultimately disappeared. Think back to the man from Kayove who described himself as a "terrorist." The president's death pushed him over the edge. From that point forward, he was angry and blamed the Tutsis—all Tutsis—and forgot all the ways in which he had close ties to Tutsis. Recall too the apparently moderate *conseillers* who cowered during this period and pleaded for help in the face of overwhelming violence. The space for moderation had shriveled up. The assassination, the war, and the ensuing violence emboldened aggression and marginalized peacefulness.

There is another factor that comes through clearly in interviews with perpetrators (and is discussed in subsequent chapters): the violence had momentum. That is, once a point was reached when those promoting violence consolidated control and once men started killing, they themselves became increasingly violent and demanded conformity from their peers. Men traveled throughout their communities telling other men, in effect, "Since we have killed, so must you," and "Since killing has started in neighboring regions, it must start here too." This is evident in many interviews. Recall the Kayove man who said that when on April 8 people in his area learned that in a neighboring area a woman had been killed, they too decided to attack. A dichotomous, us-or-them logic based on alliance to the genocidal program followed. All Hutu men were pressured to participate, while all Tutsis were targeted for murder.

This analysis offers some insight into the regional patterns of violence seen in the previous chapter. In particular, it is now clearer why violence started earlier in some areas and later in others, why violence tended to start at similar times in different regions, and why the violence was so intense once it started. I examine these issues in turn.

Judging from the micro-comparative analysis, there was an initial balance of power in different communes throughout the country. In some areas, the balance favored the hardliners who asserted control after Habyarimana's death. These were areas, typically, where either the MRND had very strong mass and local elite support—such as Kayove—or some type of hardline player, such as locally stationed military officers, could decisively shape events. Kanzenze is an example of the latter. In these areas, the consolidation of power by pro-violence forces was very swift. The local authorities, in particular the burgomaster, were either part of the coalition launching the violence, or they remained passive. In the latter case, key members within the rural elite would move in to assume control.

However, in other areas, the initial balance was not favorable to the hardliners; the initial balance opposed violence. These tended to be areas of strong opposition support (Musambira) or areas with moderate political leaders (Giti). Given the area's politics, the calls to violence by the MRND hardliners who controlled the central government found little resonance. The burgomasters' main response was to maintain order by preventing a breakout of violence or by remaining passive. However, the balance shifted over time. The change came from a military or militia incursion, an invasion from a neighboring commune, or direct pressure from prefectural or national authorities. But the change also was sometimes subtler: houses burned on a neighboring hill; Tutsis and Hutus fled into a community, fearing violence in their home commune; a rival began consolidating power. At this stage, the play for power came to a head, and violence looked inevitable. Burgomasters in turn faced a second choice: switch to a pro-violence position, remain passive, or flee. Once the pro-violence position consolidated, the same dynamic took over as in places where violence started earlier: mass mobilization of Hutus and mass violence against Tutsis. The main difference in Giti was that at the point when the balance of power looked to be shifting, RPF soldiers arrived.

It is useful to diagram these dynamics. To review, the stages are the following: (1) the assassination, the war, and the killings destabilized local authority; (2) a space of opportunity opened at the local level; (3) national hardliners meanwhile launched violence and made that violence a new basis for authority; (4) a struggle for local dominance en-

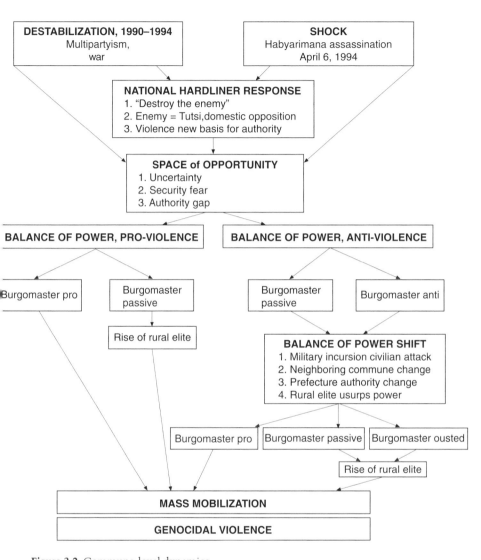

Figure 3.2 Commune-level dynamics

sued; (5) in some areas, local hardliners advocating killing quickly won control; in other areas, the process was slower; and (6) in all locations (save Giti, where the RPF arrived before the moderates lost) once the balance tipped toward those willing to promote violence, mass mobilization and mass killing quickly followed. Figure 3.2 depicts these processes.

My discussion has made use of the concept of "balance of power." The central ideas here are that a plurality of force existed at the local level and that this plurality could be tipped one way or the other in a context of destabilization, assassination, and war, as occurred in April 1994. That plurality of force depended on two main dimensions, one internal to the commune and one external. The first consisted of administrative officials, armed elements within the commune, the rural elite, and ordinary villagers (the *rubanda rugufi*). The second consisted of national officials, prefecture officials, the military, and activity in neighboring communes. To tip the balance—to consolidate a pro- or anti-violence position—some combination of intra- and extra-communal elements were needed.[29]

In Kayove, the dynamic was primarily internal to the commune: the rural elite and the *rubanda rugufi* directly initiated violence, sidelining the *conseillers* and the burgomaster. In Gafunzo, pressure came from the rural elite, irregular internal armed forces, and distant reinforcement from extra-communal armed elements such as Yusuf. In Kanzenze, the primary tip came from forces external to the commune—the military—but commune officials and the rural elite also contributed to consolidating a pro-violence position. In Musambira, with prefectural backing, the burgomaster maintained an anti-violence position for two weeks. The tip came from a military incursion, national pressure, and a change in a neighboring commune. In Giti, the burgomaster lacked a strong challenge from within the commune, and he was able to maintain an anti-violence position. But as conditions changed in neighboring Rutare, the balance began to tip—only to be interrupted by the arrival of the RPF.

Implications

There are a number of important implications from the micro-comparative study. First, recall the two principal models for how genocide spread: that of an efficient, administratively led "machine of killing" stemming from "meticulous planning" or that of all-against-all, state failure, and "chaos." Neither model is completely right. Rather, the violence spread as a cascade of tipping points, and each tipping point

29. In addition to the communes detailed in this chapter, a similar pattern is evident in Mukingo and Nkuli Communes, in Ruhengeri Prefecture, which were discussed at some length in an international court case. See International Criminal Tribunal for Rwanda, "The Prosecutor v. Juvénal Kajelijeli," Case No. ICTR-98-44A-T, December 1, 2003, 98–100, 107–8.

was the outcome of local, intra-ethnic contests for dominance. The context for the cascading tipping points was acute crisis following the presidential assassination, war, and killing of leading opposition figures. At the same time, hardliners took control in the capital, and they declared war on the Tutsi enemy. In so doing, the hardliners equated killing Tutsis with policy and made violence a source of power, legitimacy, and authority countrywide. Once that position won enough local adherents, violence was swift, the space for opposition and moderation was eliminated, and genocide became the order of the day.

Whether or not the violence was scrupulously planned, the national hardliners who took control after Habyarimana's death played a central role in setting Rwanda on a path to genocide. If the hardliners had not authorized violence against Tutsi civilians, moderates in various areas would likely have won the upper hand even if local challengers had emerged to advocate killing as revenge for Habyarimana's death. Order would have meant the absence of killing, not the promotion of it. So too do we see here the importance of international inaction: in the absence of an alternative to the hardliners, the moderates throughout the country lost; they had no basis for standing down those who advocated killing. In short, that the immediate context of war and assassination matters does not eliminate the hardliners' responsibility. To the contrary, it shows how critical their actions were and ultimately how critical the international abandonment of Rwanda was.

There are other implications. The major explanations of participation in genocide turn on ethnic prejudice, hatred, identity commitments, radio incitement, obedience, and deprivation. The micro-comparative study does not disprove any of these theories. However, the micro-comparative study does show that the explanations are insufficient and can be misleading. What we have seen in this chapter is how killing Tutsis at a certain point became a form of policy, to which local Hutus had to demonstrate their loyalty. That in turn triggered an unfolding set of choices for individuals. Many faced a choice between being punished by other Hutus or committing violence against Tutsis. Many chose the latter, but the dynamics driving that choice were less about hatred, dehumanizing indoctrination, obedience, and deprivation and more about insecurity, relationships to power, and, in some cases, intra-ethnic coercion.

The micro-comparative study also shows that the category of "perpetrators" should be disaggregated. We know from previous chapters that the main national actors include the regime's inner circle, military commanders, central committee political party leaders, government ministers, members of parliament, and those running both radio and print media. Actors at this level are responsible for launching the violence after Habyarimana's death and for equating killing with state policy. There also were regional actors who moved between communes but remained in one or two prefectures. They include prefects, sub-prefects, army and gendarme camp commanders, and *interahamwe* militia.

The micro-comparative study provides details about perpetrators at the commune level. At the top were influential rural elites who organized, legitimized, and directed the killing within their communes. The composition of rural elites varied across locations, but they were primarily administrative officials and well-educated Rwandans with high social status in their locations. Next were a relatively small group of aggressive and often young men—political party youths, unemployed youths, "delinquents," army reservists, former soldiers, and policemen. These aggressive men killed and, working with the rural elite, mobilized as many adult Hutu males as possible to join the attacks. They were the elites' principal enforcers. Finally, there was a large group of mostly male civilians, who ultimately made up the largest portion of attackers—the rural elite and aggressive young men recruited them to join the killing. In short, the micro-comparative study helps us see the dynamics among perpetrators—which the next three chapters discuss in more depth.

4 The *Génocidaires*

Why individuals kill is a critical question for any observer of mass violence.[1] The question is especially relevant for the Rwandan case because civilian participation in the genocide was so high and so critical to the outcome. The question hovered behind the previous two chapters, but the analysis remained at an aggregate level: I examined regional and local dynamics of violence, which led only to indirect inferences about the factors driving individuals to kill. I face the question more directly in this chapter and the following two. I do so by examining the characteristics and motivations of perpetrators using my core research in Rwanda—extensive interviews with perpetrators.

Any search for a single motivation that causes individuals to commit genocide is surely a futile exercise. Motivation and participation were clearly heterogeneous in the Rwandan genocide, and Rwanda is not exceptional in that regard. Some Rwandans killed for multiple reasons. Others joined in the attacks for one reason, but then continued for other reasons; their motivations changed over time. Still other men

1. The question is salient in studies of the Holocaust, violence, and genocide. For three statements on this, see Dick de Mildt, *In the Name of the People: Perpetrators of Genocide in the Reflection of their Post-War Prosecution in West Germany: The 'Euthanasia' and 'Aktion Reinhard' Trial Cases* (The Hague: Martinus Nijhoff, 1996), 15; Roger Petersen, *Understanding Ethnic Violence: Fear, Hatred, and Resentment in Twentieth-Century Eastern Europe* (Cambridge, UK: Cambridge University Press, 2002), 2; and James Waller, *Becoming Evil: How Ordinary People Commit Genocide and Mass Killing* (Oxford: Oxford University Press, 2002), 9.

enthusiastically attacked Tutsis day in and day out, and they took the lives of many. Other men brandished weapons, searched houses for Tutsis, and maybe helped capture a Tutsi, but never actually killed. In short, motivation and participation varied during the genocide. There is no one reason why all perpetrators took part in the violence.

That said, certain patterns emerge from my research, and, on balance, the findings run contrary to many common expectations about which individuals committed genocide and why they did so. In particular, I do not find that preexisting ethnic animosity, widespread prejudice, deeply held ideological beliefs, blind obedience, deprivation, or even greed motivated the majority of Rwandan perpetrators. Nor do I find that most perpetrators were unattached young men, poorly educated, or militia members. There are exceptions, to be sure. Ethnic hatred drove some, as did ideological commitment, as did obedience, as did the desire to loot or seize land. Militias did play an important role in some areas. But in the aggregate my findings do not support these claims.

Rather, the overwhelming majority of perpetrators in rural areas were ordinary men. They were fathers, husbands, and farmers who had average levels of education and who had no prior history of violence. The evidence presented in this chapter shows that the demographic profile of perpetrators is very similar to the demographic profile of adult Hutu men at the time of the genocide. For the most part, Rwanda's genocide perpetrators—"*génocidaires*"—were regular citizens.

Their reasons for committing genocide are also, in the aggregate, quite banal. Many men chose to join groups of attackers because they feared punishment from other Hutus if they refused to take part in the violence. Other men were scared of the advancing Tutsi rebels and, after their leaders encouraged them to do so, attacked Tutsi civilians as a way to counter the rebels. Still other men opportunistically exploited the confusion of the moment to grab power or to steal from their neighbors. Rwanda's perpetrators may not be the Nazi careerists that scholars of the Holocaust have consistently found, but the Rwandan perpetrators' reasons for taking part in genocide resemble their Nazi counterparts in important ways. In particular, the Rwandans' motivations were considerably more ordinary and routine than the extraordinary crimes they helped commit.

All this is consistent with the findings from the previous chapter. The basic pattern that I find for rural areas is as follows. After Habyarimana's assassination and the resumption of war, a small core of local actors seized the initiative, consolidated control, and then mobilized adult Hutu men to destroy the "Tutsi enemy." The actual war that was happening in the country was critical to the dynamics of mobilization as well as to the logic of killing. Common perceptions about state power and authority also mattered for the mass mobilization, as did expectations derived from preexisting institutions of labor mobilization. But the overall picture is not one that points strongly to a "culture of hatred" toward Tutsis, to a deep dehumanization of Tutsis, or unemployment and rage among angry young men. Rather, the main dynamics driving participation in the violence are pressure from other Hutus, security fears, and opportunity—and those mechanisms were salient in a context of national state orders to attack Tutsis, war, dense local institutions, and close-knit settlements.

The findings are surprising—at least they were to me—and I will take the next three chapters to present evidence to support and illustrate them. The discussion may occasionally be dry, but the point is to present and interpret evidence about individual-level participation in a careful and methodical fashion.

My starting point, again, is the gap in information about perpetrators. We know little about the basic facts of the perpetrator population in terms of who perpetrators were, how they compare to the rest of the Rwandan population, and how many perpetrators there were. This chapter focuses on these issues and, more specifically, three main concerns. First, I focus on methodology. Interviewing *génocidaires* raises obvious concerns about validity and credibility, and I want readers to understand my procedures, why I decided on them, and their limitations. Second, I focus on perpetrator characteristics such as age, education level, occupation, and other dimensions. I also test hypotheses about whether differences in various characteristics can explain differences in levels of participation. Were, for example, younger men more violent than older men during the genocide? Third, I focus on the attacks themselves. I discuss who led the attacks against Tutsis, as well as how large the attacks were. I use my findings here to estimate how many perpetrators there were in the genocide. Overall, the chapter helps clarify the dynamics of genocide at the local level and thereby provides an empirical base from which I try to interpret what drove the violence.

Methodology

I start with a brief discussion of methodology. The issue matters because a central problem for those who want to explore why individuals commit genocide is empirical, not theoretical. There is a large range of hypotheses that purport to explain individual participation in genocide (as I discussed at the end of chapter 1). However, with the exception of the literature on the Holocaust, where the evidentiary record is deep, there is little detailed and systematically collected micro-level evidence for most cases of genocide and mass violence. That lacuna is especially acute in the Rwandan case despite the volume of material published on the genocide.[2]

The need for more and better evidence is obvious, but the question of how to find and gather that evidence is less clear. Mass violence in a country directly affects almost everyone, and it traumatizes many. This is particularly true in Rwanda, where the rate of participation was high, where the killing took place in public locations across the country and where, after the genocide, more than two million citizens (nearly a third of the remaining population) fled the country as refugees. Moreover, mass violence often is subject to criminal proceedings and of enormous political importance to the authorities in power (again, especially so in Rwanda). For these reasons, empirical research on mass violence after the fact is a major methodological challenge, and no informant or method should be treated as unbiased or objective.

I chose to focus on perpetrators because I wanted to answer questions about the reasons that individuals commit genocide and the dynamics of mobilization. The method followed the research question. To be sure, the approach does not exclude other sources of data; triangulation is essential, as I have made clear. I also do not treat perpetrator testimony as unbiased. Rather, I consider the testimony to be self-interested narratives that need to be critically and skeptically examined.

In Rwanda, the justice system is the obvious point of entry to collect information about perpetrators. After the genocide, the RPF-led government chose maximal prosecution, meaning that the government charged everyone who participated in the genocide in some fashion. Rwandans who killed or participated in killing faced prosecution, as did those who looted during the genocide. By 2000, the government had arrested nearly 110,000 individuals on genocide charges, of whom about 6,000 had been sentenced by 2002 (the year I conducted my prin-

---

2. Many scholars recognize this gap in the evidence. For example, Neil Kressel writes: "No studies have addressed the question of why individual Hutus, from the militias and the general public, joined in the slaughter." Kressel, *Mass Hate: The Global Rise of Genocide and Terror* (New York: Plenum Press, 1996), 112.

cipal research).[3] One research strategy could be to analyze court documents from these cases. However, the only publicly available documents in 2002 were judgments, and I found the information therein too general for either reconstructing the dynamics of violence or hypothesis-testing. That being the case, I decided that the best method for generating theoretically relevant information about perpetrators was to interview them.

Given the large number of detainees and the methodological problems inherent in interviewing perpetrators, the matter of sampling is crucial. I had four main selection criteria. First, I chose to interview detainees who had been sentenced. Sentenced detainees have fewer incentives to lie than detainees awaiting trial. Moreover, guilty verdicts provide a modicum of verification, however imperfect, and that trials already had taken place meant that the material in them already had been publicly discussed (an important consideration for the university institutional review board charged with protecting "human subjects" whose approval I needed). Second, I interviewed detainees who had pled guilty.[4] In 2000, I conducted a pilot study and found that interviewees who had not confessed were not helpful for the questions I asked. My objective in the interviews was to understand the dynamics of genocide, so talking to a respondent who denied doing or seeing anything related to the genocide would not make for particularly rewarding research. Third, I sampled randomly where possible. Here the issue was to avoid biases that would be introduced by others choosing respondents for me. In previous experience in Rwanda, I had seen how prison officials or prisoners had chosen specific perpetrators for re-

3. For the former, see Office of the Prosecutor, "Abantu Bafungiye mu Magereza Kasho na Burigade," Ministry of Justice, Kigali, Rwanda, August 2002. These statistics were the latest available when I conducted field research in Rwanda in 2002. For the latter, see Office of the Prosecutor, "Décisions judiciares rendues par années (Déc. 1996–Juin 2002)," Ministry of Justice, August 2002. By June 2002, 7211 detainees had been judged, of whom 1,386 had been acquitted.

4. Rwanda's law for prosecuting genocide crimes included a provision for reduced sentences if suspected perpetrators confessed and pled guilty to their crimes. See Official Gazette of the Republic of Rwanda, "Organic Law on the Organization of Prosecutions for Offences Constituting the Crime of Genocide or Crimes against Humanity Committed since 1 October 1990," Kigali, Rwanda, September 1, 1996, 16–18. The confession process has four stages. First, detainees must indicate they want to plead guilty. Second, they must write out their confession. Third, the public prosecutor must read and accept their confession. Fourth, the confession is publicly handled in a court proceeding and either accepted or rejected by a three-judge panel. According to data provided to me by the Prosecutor General's office, in 2002, 25 percent of the prisoner population had confessed, which refers to detainees who were at any one of these four stages.

searchers or journalists to interview. I wanted to sidestep that problem. Fourth, I sampled nationally, meaning that I sampled in every prison where there was a population of perpetrators who had been sentenced and had confessed. Sampling nationally was important given the regional variation in Rwandan politics and in when the killing campaign started.

In total, I interviewed 210 detainees in fifteen central prisons during a six month period, and the survey represents the largest study of perpetrators of which I am aware. My procedure was the following. At each prison, I made an advance request to prison officials for a list of sentenced confessors in a particular prison. On an agreed date, I returned to the prison, obtained the list, and then used computer-generated random numbers to select individuals from the list. In some prisons, the number of sentenced confessors was too small to use random numbers. One prison had only six sentenced confessors, and I interviewed all of them. In four other prisons, I simply interviewed every other prisoner on the list. For the remainder, I used random numbers.[5] (The differences in the size of the sentenced confessor population per prison led me to weight my findings—more on this below.)

I also limited my sampling to men. To be clear, women did play important roles during the genocide. In particular, where women were in leadership positions at the national and local levels, they often were instrumental in organizing, promoting, and authorizing genocidal killing. Women participated in other ways during the genocide. Sometimes women looted, in particular after Tutsis were killed. Sometimes women told bands of killers where Tutsis were hiding. Sometimes women encouraged their husbands or sons to attack Tutsis.[6] However, based on all my preliminary research I concluded that men formed the overwhelming majority of perpetrators. Prisoner statistics reflect this: in 2001 and 2002, women constituted only about 3 percent of the prisoner population.[7] Of those, very few had both confessed to commit-

5. Nyanza prison (Butare province) is where I interviewed all six prisoners. The ratios of those interviewed to the population in my sampling frame are the following: Gitarama (1 of 2); Rilima (1 of 11); Gikongoro (1 of 2); Butare (1 of 2); Kigali Central (1 of 4); Kibungo (1 of 7); Nsinda (1 of 29); Byumba I (1 of 6); Byumba II (1 of 6); Ruhengeri (1 of 3); Gisenyi (1 of 6); Kibuye (1 of 3); Cyangugu (1 of 6); and Kimironko (1 of 2). To account for this variation in sampling, I weight all statistical analyses in the pages to come according to the sampling proportion per prison.

6. I base this statement on my research. For a thorough discussion of women's participation in the genocide and on the primary ways they participated, see Nicole Hogg, "I Never Poured Blood": Women Accused of Genocide in Rwanda, M.A. thesis, Faculty of Law, McGill University, Toronto, Canada, November 2001, 76.

7. Hogg, "I Never Poured Blood," 58.

ting genocide and been sentenced. Since my sampling criteria were to interview sentenced confessors and since the overwhelming majority of perpetrators were men, I limited my survey to men. My findings thus pertain to male perpetrators.

To conduct the interviews, I designed a semi-structured questionnaire to test various hypotheses. The questionnaire included both closed and open-ended questions. The order of the questions and the way in which I asked them proved important to the respondents' degree of openness. I found it essential to begin the interviews with unthreatening questions, and I found that indirect, open-ended questions often elicited the most rewarding responses. I also found it important that I conduct the interviews myself so that I could evaluate, or at least try to evaluate, the respondent's veracity in each case. I also found it essential to ask follow-up questions to clarify responses I did not understand. The interviews were conducted in private rooms out of earshot of other prisoners, with only my research assistant, the respondent, and me present.

My research assistant was critical. Though French and Swahili are spoken in Rwanda, and I speak some of both, some 98 percent of the respondents in my sample wanted to speak in their mother tongue, Kinyarwanda, which meant I needed an assistant. After much thought, I decided that the best assistant would be a Rwandan who had lived in the country before and during the genocide and whom respondents would not associate with the ruling regime. The former mattered because the assistant could judge each respondent's credibility and, after the interviews, explicate his responses to me, if need be. The latter mattered because I wanted to create an atmosphere in which respondents would feel comfortable and not as if they were under criminal interrogation.

To meet these concerns, I chose an assistant whom respondents would identify as Hutu. In fact, my assistant was of mixed parentage, and he and various members of his family had been attacked, threatened, and robbed during the genocide.[8] He also had prior experience as a human rights investigator and had worked in Rwanda's prison system. In short, by his experience and identity—and also by his intelligence and manner—my assistant put respondents at ease, gave me insight into their testimony, and overall provided a first-stage verification on the interview material.

---

8. His mother is Tutsi, but because Rwandan ethnicity is patrilineal, he was considered Hutu.

Credibility is, indeed, a major concern when interviewing perpetrators. Some responses (such as perpetrator characteristics, which I analyze below) are less problematic. But it is clear that prisoners may lie, misremember, or reconstruct events in order to mitigate their responsibility or justify their conduct. My research design reduced these risks because I interviewed sentenced perpetrators who had pled guilty and because I sampled in different prisons (thereby preventing prisoners' ability to coordinate deception). But important credibility questions remain, particularly concerning the ways in which respondents may reconstruct pre-genocide Rwanda and the genocide itself.

While in Rwanda, I took several other measures to corroborate perpetrator testimony. First, I sought out specific survivors whom perpetrators had mentioned in order to verify the latter's accounts. Second, I identified Hutu men who survivors and local authorities agreed had not participated in the genocide. I then asked them to describe their experiences during the genocide, again with an eye on corroboration. Third, where possible, I checked the survey results against existing secondary sources. Many documents and studies of the genocide contain anecdotes and informed opinion, which I used to crosscheck my findings. These are not foolproof measures, but they add a layer of verification to perpetrator testimony.

The representative-ness of the sample is another important concern. My conclusion is that the sample well represents the confessor population, which, when I was conducting the research, was about 25 percent of the overall prisoner population.[9] Nothing suggests that the confessors the government prosecuted first were different from other confessors. However, whether my sample is representative of (a) the entire prison population or (b) the entire perpetrator population is unclear. The safe assumption is that the sample underrepresents the worst killers, who were more likely to have fled Rwanda for good, to have been subject to revenge killings by Tutsis, or to have chosen not to confess because of the scale of their crimes. This probable bias against hardcore killers should be kept in mind as I work through the results below.

Finally, I define a genocide "perpetrator" (*génocidaire*) as any person who participated in an attack against a civilian in order to kill or to inflict serious injury on that civilian. Perpetrators thus would be those who directly killed or assaulted civilians and those who participated in groups that killed or assaulted civilians. During the genocide, there were other kinds of participation. Many Rwandans joined state-mandated civilian night patrols. Sometimes the members of these pa-

9. See note 4.

trols killed civilians, and if they did they would be perpetrators under my definition. However, if they did not, they would not be. There also was a significant amount of looting during the genocide. If killing accompanied the looting, then looters would be perpetrators under my definition. However, if Rwandans looted property but did not join attacks in which civilians were killed, they would not be perpetrators. The central idea behind this definition is that a perpetrator is someone who materially participated in the murder or attempted murder of a noncombatant.

Perpetrator Characteristics

With that background in mind, let me now turn to the findings. I start with the basic demographic profile of the perpetrators: age, level of education, paternity rate, and so forth. Where possible, I compare my findings to national census figures before the genocide in order to determine how and whether perpetrators differed from the rest of the population.[10]

Age

How old were Rwanda's *génocidaires*? Many observers claim that young men and "unemployed city youth" were the genocide's main perpetrators.[11] If true, that might support a frustration-aggression argument: young people faced a future of meager employment prospects and a land shortage and thus, the argument goes, were prone to violence. To find out how old perpetrators were, I asked respondents to name the year in which they were born, and then I subtracted that number from the year when the genocide occurred (1994).[12] The results are reported in table 4.1, along with comparable census data.[13]

10. An alternative approach would be to create a "control group" of nonperpetrator Hutu men. However, when I conducted research in 2002, I could not be confident that non-imprisoned Hutu men were not perpetrators. Furthermore, in 2002 interviewing non-charged men about the genocide would have raised ethical concerns about whether I would put respondents at unnecessary risk and therefore would be unacceptable to my home university's institutional review board. In short, I chose not to collect data systematically on non-incarcerated Hutu men and instead I compare my results to national census data, where possible.

11. Alison Des Forges, *Leave None to Tell the Story: Genocide in Rwanda* (New York: Human Rights Watch, 1999), 11; for a reference to "unemployed city youth" playing an important role, see Waller, *Becoming Evil*, 69.

12. For example, if a respondent was born in 1965, I recorded his age during the genocide to be twenty-nine. The reason I asked for year of birth is that some respondents did not know the month or day when they were born.

13. The relevant census data are found in République du Rwanda, *Recensement*

Table 4.1 Age of perpetrators $(N = 210)$

Age range	Weighted sample	Rwanda adult male population (15+)	Rwanda male population
0–14	0%	~	48.2%
15–19	3.9	19.4%	10.0
20–24	12.0	15.7	8.1
25–29	11.6	14.4	7.4
30–34	28.6	13.3	6.9
35–39	18.5	9.9	5.1
40–44	11.6	6.5	3.3
45–49	6.8	4.3	2.2
50–54	1.0	4.0	2.0
55–59	2.4	3.4	1.7
60+	3.6	9.0	4.6
Median age	34	30	15

The results clearly show that my sample of perpetrators is not predominantly youthful. To the contrary, the perpetrators were primarily adult men: 89 percent were 20 to 49 years old and the greatest concentrations were men 30 to 39 years old. The median age was 34.[14] Even more striking is the comparison to the census data. My sample's age profile is similar to and, if anything, marginally *older* than the profile of the adult male population. The sample is considerably older than the general population, partly reflecting Rwanda's high birth rate.[15] I will return to these findings in a moment.

Paternity

The results for paternity rates are similar. Most perpetrators in my sample—some 77 percent—were fathers: they were not unattached youths (see table 4.2).

There are no precise comparative data on paternity rates in the census. However, extrapolating from data on maternity rates and my sample's medians for paternity and age, I conclude that the sample's

---

général de la population et de l'habitat au 15 août 1991: Analyse des résultats définitifs, Kigali, Rwanda, April 1994, 65, 84.

14. In a forthcoming study that includes interviews with perpetrators in two Rwandan prefectures, Lee Ann Fujii found a similar age structure. She has a sample of fourteen individuals, and the mean age was thirty-two years old. Lee Ann Fujii, *Killing Neighbors: The Social Dimensions of Genocide in Rwanda*, Ph.D. dissertation, George Washington University, Washington, D.C., forthcoming.

15. Rwanda's high birth rate means that the population frequencies will be biased toward younger populations.

Table 4.2 Paternity rates of perpetrators (N = 209)

Number of children	Weighted sample
0	22.9%
1	7.9
2	5.6
3	14.4
4	17.1
5	5.2
6	6.1
7	8.8
8+	12.2
Median	3

paternity rates are similar to those of Rwanda's adult male population.[16] Again, the perpetrators look like average adult Rwandan men.

Occupation

I also asked each respondent to identify his occupation. Two tables display the results. The first (table 4.3) displays the labels that perpetrators themselves volunteered when asked to name their occupations.

After several dozen interviews, I learned that many who identified themselves as farmers had other ways of earning money, which led me to ask an additional question about whether they earned money in other ways besides farming.[17] Of those to whom I put this question (N=128), a significant portion—55.5 percent—answered yes. Those activities included fishing, bricklaying, practicing apiculture, shepherding, riding a bicycle taxi, selling beer, being a domestic worker, being a farm laborer, being a carpenter, being a night watchman, and peddling wares in a market.

The second table (table 4.4) reorganizes the occupations listed in table 4.3 to correspond to the five occupation categories listed in the census.[18]

16. The steps in the logic are as follows: (1) the census reports "female fecundity" for women aged 15–49 years old to be 6.9 births; (2) of those births, 42.8 percent were born to women under thirty, which means that by their thirtieth birthday the average Rwandan woman had given birth to 2.95 children; and (3) men generally are older than women when they parent; and (4) in my sample I found that the median age was thirty-four and the median number of children was three. Hence I conclude that the sample's paternity rate was similar to national averages. For the census data, see République du Rwanda, *Recensement général*, 235, 247.

17. I thank Philip Verwimp for encouraging me to ask this question to respondents.

18. For the census data, see République du Rwanda, *Recensement général*, 108–9.

Table 4.3 Occupations of perpetrators ($N = 210$)

Occupation	Unweighted frequency
Farmer	77.6%
Driver	2.4
Builder/carpenter	1.5
Tailor	0.5
Mechanic	1.0
Business	1.0
Former businessman	0.5
Factory worker	1.0
Moneychanger	0.5
Cellule committee member	4.3
Cellule responsable	2.4
Conseiller	0.5
Political party leader	0.5
Associate director of schools	0.5
Teacher	0.5
Government agricultural agent	1.5
Medical assistant	0.5
Veterinary aide	0.5
Brigadier (head of commune police)	0.5
Reservist	0.5
Forest guard	0.5
Children	1.0
"None"	1.0

The census categories are ambiguous and overlap (especially since farmers sometimes had other ways of earning money), but I have done my best to reclassify my data accurately.[19]

Given some of the ambiguities in the census data and how the census categories correspond to the way that respondents identified their professions, it seems unwise to make too much of the reported differences. The conclusion to reach is that overall the sample's occupation profile is broadly similar to the national population. The main differ-

19. For first category, I include respondents who self-identified as "farmers," even if they were *cellule* committee members or *responsables.* For the second category, I include full-time salaried state officials, such as technical agents, *conseillers,* forest guards, and communal police. I also include teachers and factory workers in this category. For the third category, I include drivers, builders, carpenters, tailors, moneychangers, and mechanics. However, it should be noted that some "cultivators" also were carpenters, builders, mechanics, and tailors on the side. That being the case, when comparing the sample's occupation profile to the national one, the first and third census categories probably should be added together. For the fourth category, I include businessmen and ex-businessmen. For the fifth, I include those who said they had no profession, children, reservists, and political party leaders.

Table 4.4 Perpetrator and national occupation profiles

Occupation	Weighted sample	Census frequency
Agriculture, fishing, hunting, animal raising	86.1%	91%
Technical professions, administration, and specialized workers	6.7	2.0
Service sector	3.4	2.3
Commercial sector	1.1	1.0
Other	2.2	3.6

ence is an overrepresentation of professionals, administrative cadre, and specialized workers in the sample, which could reflect a large presence of those whom, in the last chapter, I labeled the "rural elite." But the major finding here is that, with the exception of an overrepresentation of local elites, the perpetrators strongly resemble the adult male Hutu population of Rwanda at the time of the genocide.

Education and Literacy

The findings on education and literacy show the same. Some 60.8 percent of the sample was literate (N=196, weighted) compared to 61.7 percent of all Hutu males older than six years old.[20] Table 4.5 compares the total years of education for my sample to males older than six.

Overall, the perpetrators appear to be slightly better educated than the average Rwandan man, but the differences are slight and may reflect a skew in the census.[21] Again, this evidence indicates that Rwandan perpetrators were representative of the adult male Hutu population at the time of the genocide and certainly were not undereducated.

Taken together, the findings in this section have important implications. Some theories posit that genocide perpetrators are different in some fashion. They might be sadistic, socially deviant, or otherwise predisposed to violence. Or perpetrators might be ignorant or deprived in some fashion. My findings run squarely against these arguments. Rwanda's perpetrators as represented in my random sample of sen-

20. République du Rwanda, *Recensement général*, 137.
21. The percentages in the census include all men from seven to seventy years old. However, almost by definition, boys under ten will receive less than four years of education. The census results thus slightly overrepresent lower education levels. République du Rwanda, *Recensement général*, 138.

Table 4.5 Perpetrator and national education levels (N = 204)

Years of education	Weighted sample	Rwandan males
0	32.2%	33.8%
1–3	13.5	22.9
4–8 (primary school)	48.6	36.1
9+ (post–primary school and up)	5.8	5.6

tenced confessors were quite ordinary. They were average adult Hutu men—in terms of age, education, paternity, and occupation. The average-ness of Rwandan perpetrators could mean many things. It could mean that there was a widespread culture of hatred against Tutsis. By this argument, since the average Hutu hated Tutsis, then the average perpetrator would look like the average Hutu man.[22] Based on my findings that I present below and in chapters to come, I conclude otherwise: namely, that the logic of mobilization of Hutu men corresponded to preexisting institutions and that many ordinary Hutu men took part in genocide because of banal situational reasons such as pressure from other Hutus, fear, and opportunity.[23]

Stated Political Party Affiliation

In addition to questions about demographic data, I also asked respondents about their social affiliations and networks. Here I wanted to find out both whether perpetrators came from particular political parties and whether preexisting social networks were the primary conduits for mobilization. There are no comparative national data for these findings, but the results are interesting in their own right. I start with political party affiliation (see table 4.6).

There is clearly a risk here that respondents might lie in answering this question. The expected bias would be to deny MRND and CDR party membership because those parties are especially implicated in the genocide. However, among those who said they belonged to a party, the MRND was the party most frequently cited. Moreover, the party affiliations generally corresponded to regional party strengths.

22. Such would be an extension of the argument in Daniel Goldhagen, *Hitler's Willing Executioners: Ordinary Germans and the Holocaust* (New York: Random House, 1996).
23. And thus my arguments conform more closely to those found in Christopher Browning, *Ordinary Men: Reserve Police Battalion 101 and the Final Solution in Poland* (New York: HarperCollins, 1992).

Table 4.6 Perpetrator political party affiliation
($N = 209$)

Political party	Weighted sample
MRND	37.5%
MDR	20.4
PSD	5.1
CDR	2.5
2+ Parties	2.0
None	32.4

Most respondents from northern and northwest Rwanda said that they were in the MRND and the CDR, while most from southwest and south central Rwanda said that they were in the MDR or the PSD. In short, the responses appear credible, and they suggest that party affiliation alone did not determine who became a perpetrator. Perpetrators belonged to every major party in the country.

Civic and State Involvement

During the interviews, I also asked a series of questions relating to civic and state involvement. I asked if respondents had a family member in the state administration or in the army—under the theory that civilian connections to officialdom might explain how and why Hutu men became *génocidaires*. The same principle holds for civic and commercial associations: since many Rwandans belong to collectives for borrowing money, for agriculture, for fishing, and for other activities, I wanted to see if those networks could explain how men came to take part in the violence. A third question concerned whether a respondent participated in a mandatory community service program for adults called *umuganda*. The program's activities included building schools, repairing roads, constructing bridges, digging anti-erosion ditches, and other community projects. The fourth question concerned whether a respondent participated in the nightly patrols called *amarondo*. These patrols were initiated in response to the 1990–94 civil war as part of a civil defense program, though the policy was implemented unevenly countrywide (see table 4.7 for results).

The strongest positive finding here concerns the *umuganda* community labor program: some 88 percent of respondents took part in the program. Without appropriate comparable data, I cannot say whether participation in the program predisposed men to commit genocide or

Table 4.7 Civic and state involvement of perpetrators (weighted results)

	Did you have a family member in the state?[a] (N = 203)	Were you in an association? (N = 174)	Did you do umuganda? (N = 203)	Did you do night patrols (amarando)? (N = 187)
Yes	25.8%	36.7%	87.5%	35.1%
No	74.2%	63.3%	12.5%	64.9%

[a]"State" here includes family members who were in government administration (not including teachers), the police, or the army.

whether the program itself was widespread. But at a minimum the finding demonstrates that a large number of genocide perpetrators had already complied with state orders to participate in unpaid labor *before the genocide.* Moreover, their compliance was apparently unrelated to the factors that many believe cause genocide participation, such as ethnic hatred or prejudice. I will return to this finding in chapter 8.

Nothing stands out among the other findings. Some respondents had family members in the government but most did not. Family affiliation with the government thus could explain how some men came to participate, but such affiliation appears not to have been the primary vehicle for mobilization. The same is true for associational membership. As for being part of the civil defense operation before the genocide, again this alone does not explain why most men took part in the genocide, but as with *umuganda,* here the findings indicate that the state had mobilized a significant proportion of perpetrators *before* the genocide to perform unpaid labor.

Disaggregating Participation and Statistical Analyses

Not all perpetrators were alike in their degree of participation. Some killed many Tutsis; others led the killing in their areas; others killed one person; still others joined attacks against Tutsis but did not kill. One way to measure different participation rates might be sentence length, but in reality this is not a valid measure. Based on my observations, Rwandan sentencing procedures were erratic. They varied year to year, region to region, and case to case, and they did not appear to correlate to the crime committed.

A better measure is the number of people a perpetrator killed or whether he was an avowed leader of the violence. This measure also has problems, chiefly credibility: there is no systematic way to verify whether the number of victims a perpetrator admits to killing reflects the actual number he killed.[24] Nonetheless, there is variation in my sample on how many people perpetrators admit to killing directly (as opposed to participating in an attack where one or more people were killed), and this variation can serve to measure degree of participation.

Can the results reported in table 4.8 be trusted? It is impossible to know for certain. Judging from my observations and those of my assistant, most respondents appeared not to be deliberately lying when answering this question. On the other hand, the respondents clearly had an interest either during the interviews or during their court cases in claiming they killed less than they actually had. That said, the results in table 4.8 have two important implications. First, the results indicate that the survey is biased toward lower-level killers, as argued above. Second, although the absolute numbers may not be perfectly valid, there is reason to believe that the relative degree of participation might be. In other words, if the numbers in table 4.8 do not accurately reflect the total number of victims these perpetrators killed by their own hand, they probably reflect real differences in the degree of violence respondents committed.

Measuring degree of participation matters for evaluating whether differences in participation correlate to differences in the characteristics discussed above. To look for these relationships, I use two different statistical procedures. The first is regression analysis, which I use for the variables whose differences can be measured by ordinal categories (such as age and education level). The second is cross-tabulation, which I use principally for those variables whose differences cannot be measured by ordinal categories (such as occupation and party affiliation).

Various regression analyses attribute statistical significance to age and paternity rates when degree of participation is regressed on those variables (see Appendix table 4.1 for various bivariate regression results). The correlation between education level and participation also looks strong enough to be worthy of further analysis, even if it does not have statistical significance. By contrast, literacy, associational

24. Court judgments do not help. The judgments that I read specify the number of deaths for which each defendant is held responsible. But most judgments do not distinguish between defendants who killed and those who participated in an attack. Therefore, the judgments cannot be used to check perpetrator statements about the number of deaths that each respondent specifically committed.

Table 4.8 Degree of genocidal participation

Weighted sample	N = 205
0 directly killed	71.5%
1 directly killed	20.4
2–4 directly killed	5.5
5+ directly killed	1.3
Self-identified leader of violence	1.3

membership, participation in the *umuganda* community labor program, and participation in the night patrols do not appear to be related strongly with degree of participation.

To examine these patterns further, I ran a multivariate regression analysis with the three variables—age, paternity, and education—that the bivariate analyses showed to be strongly related to degree of participation (see Appendix table 4.2 for results). The multivariate results indicate that age continues to have a statistically significant relationship with degree of participation when the other two variables are held constant. However, the paternity result changes: when controlled for age and education, paternity loses its statistical significance. By contrast, when the other two variables are held constant, education becomes statistically significant, but it has a negative relationship with degree of participation.

Why does all this matter? The regression analyses indicate that the younger perpetrators, those with fewer or no children, and those with lower levels of education tended to be the most violent during the genocide. The findings thus support some common wisdom about the genocide: namely, that Rwanda's killers were unattached youths and poorly educated. In other words, my primary finding in this chapter is that most perpetrators were ordinary men who broadly reflected the society in which they lived. However, the statistical analysis reveals that among perpetrators the most violent appear to have been younger, less well educated, and with fewer children, often no children.

Cross-tabulation analysis yields another nuance.[25] Of the self-identified leaders of the violence at the local level, all but one were between the ages of 33 and 37. All had finished their primary school education but had no further education, and all had between three and five children. In short, while overall the most violent individuals

25. I report the results from the cross-tab analysis but do not reproduce the tables.

in the sample tended to be younger with a low level of education (and had the fewest children), the local-level leaders of the violence tended to be well-integrated adult men with above average levels of education.

Occupation also matters. The self-described leaders were all administration officials, non-state rural elites, or farmers who had other ways to earn income (one was a tailor, the other a brickmaker). However, of those who killed two or more people, nearly 90 percent had preexisting firearms training (as in the case of an army reservist or a forest guard) or were farmers. These patterns suggest that the leaders of the violence tended to have some preexisting social status, while the most violent persons tended to be trained in firearm use or were young farmers.[26]

These statistical results have important implications. They confirm a general pattern seen in the previous chapter. In particular, there was a core group of perpetrators at the local level. These included local elites who tended to take charge during the genocide, whether they held government posts or not. Working with them were the "thugs": a small group of younger men or those who had firearms. The thugs were political party youths, angry young men, reservists, and, in one case, a forest guard. They were local specialists in violence or those who used their youth and strength to their advantage, and they did the lion's share of killing. The stereotype of the unattached youthful militia may not characterize the perpetrator population as a whole but rather those who were most violent at the local level. Otherwise, ordinary Hutu men formed the mass of perpetrators. They had few distinguishing features; they were average, regular men, and their participation in genocide, I will argue, is due to situational and institutional factors relating to war, Rwanda's state, and the crisis of the moment.

Characteristics of Attacks

In addition to information about individuals' characteristics and their affiliations, I also asked respondents to describe attacks against Tutsis in some detail. Table 4.9 reports what respondents volunteered when asked who led the attacks in which they participated.

26. The differences were marginal for farmers who had some other means of earning money and for those who did not (N=126).

Table 4.9 Leaders of attacks $(N = 184)$

Who led the killings in your area?	Weighted frequency[a]
Civilian authorities (Commune, sector, and/or cellule officials)	47.3%
Army soldiers and/or gendarmes	35.7
Non-state rural elite (e.g. businessmen, teachers, ex-officials, doctors, engineers, university students)	12.0
"Peasants who made themselves strong" or "peasants"	12.0
Interahamwe or other armed militia	11.4
Local political party leaders	9.7
National leaders (parliamentarians, ministers)	5.4
Respondent does not know who led killings	4.3
Reservists, demobilized soldiers, commune police	3.8
"Youths"	2.7
"Delinquents"	1.6
No leaders	1.0

[a]Many respondents identified more than one category of leader, such as a civilian authority working with a soldier or a teacher working with a militiaman. Recall, for example, how in the last chapter we saw that soldiers and civilian authorities worked closely in Kanzenze. The percentages reported in column 2 thus represent the incidence that any leadership category is mentioned. For example, if a respondent said that the burgomaster, soldiers, and a political party leader led the killing in his area, I would count each category once.

The evidence is consistent with the patterns seen elsewhere: the leaders of attacks tended to have preexisting social status—they were local authorities or local elites—or else they were officials in the army or the gendarmerie. Respondents also said that militias, youths, delinquents, and "peasants who made themselves strong" also led the killings. Taken together, the findings reported in table 4.9 provide further evidence that civilian elites and military personnel tended to direct the violence in rural areas, while aggressive young men—the "thugs"—acted as enforcers for the elites and the military. The evidence also shows how during the genocide, non-state authorities could opportunistically seize the initiative and lead the violence in their areas. All of these findings are consistent with the arguments made in the last chapter.

I asked a series of other questions to probe these issues further (see table 4.10).

Again, the findings show that civilian authorities and military personnel played a large role in the violence. Armed militias also played an important role, but their presence was less pervasive than is often claimed: they were present only in about a quarter of attacks. Moreover, according to the respondents, armed militias were in the attacks

Table 4.10 Perpetrator group compositions (weighted results)

	Were there members of the administration present in your attack? (N = 160)	Were there members of the military present in your attack?[a] (N = 166)	Were there armed militia members present in your attack? (N = 140)	Were there Burundians present in your attack? (N = 153)
No	26.6%	55.7%	73.4%	90.8%
Yes	73.4%	44.3%	26.6%	9.2%

[a]The "military" here includes members of the army, the Presidential Guard, and the gendarmerie as well as reservists.

without civilian authorities or soldiers in only 3 percent of the cases.[27] The perpetrators also indicate that Burundians were not strongly present in most attacks, a finding that runs contrary to the claim that Burundi refugees were key instigators of the violence. In short, the findings from these tables indicate that state authorities in the form of civilian administrators and military personnel played a large role in the killings. Authority and authorization were critical to the dynamics of mobilization.

I also asked respondents about the magnitude of the attacks in which they participated. The results are instructive in their own right, but I also use them to estimate the total size of the perpetrator population. The latter question has been subject to a great deal of speculation, and current estimates are widely discrepant: they range from tens of thousands of perpetrators to several million.[28] The high-end estimate—three million perpetrators—would mean that the entire adult

27. Valid N=133.

28. Senior government officials have estimated three million perpetrators in various interviews I conducted. See also Philip Gourevitch, *We Wish To Inform You that Tomorrow We Will Be Killed with Our Families* (New York: Farrar Straus and Giroux, 1998), 244. Mahmood Mamdani estimates "hundreds of thousands" of perpetrators. Mahmood Mamdani, *When Victims Become Killers: Colonialism, Nativism, and Genocide in Rwanda* (Princeton: Princeton University Press, 2001), 7. Christian Scherrer claims that 40–66 percent of male Hutu farmers, 60–80 percent of the higher professions, and "almost 100 percent" of the civil servants participated. No substantiation is offered for the latter. If properly calculated, those numbers would total more than a million perpetrators. Christian Scherrer, *Genocide and Crisis in Central Africa: Conflict Roots, Mass Violence, and Regional War* (Westport, CT: Praeger, 2002), 126. Alison Des Forges cites "tens of thousands" in *Leave None*, 260; Bruce Jones hypothesizes that 25,000 or fewer killers may have killed as many as a million over the course of a hundred days; see Bruce Jones, *Peacemaking in Rwanda: The Dynamics of Failure* (Boulder, CO: Lynne Rienner, 2001), 41.

Table 4.11 Perpetrator group sizes during the genocide

Group size (# of persons)	Weighted frequency	Group size per cellule (# of persons per cellule)	Weighted frequency
1–10	23.7%	1–10	44.1%
11–30	28.6	11–20	25.4
31–50	17.5	21–30	15.2
51–100	11.1	31–40	7.2
101–200	3.8	41–50	7.0
200+	15.3	50+	1.1
Weighted average	116 persons	Weighted average	22 persons

Hutu population at the time of the genocide participated in it.[29] My findings can yield an imperfect but better estimate.

To create an estimate, I calculate the average number of perpetrators per *cellule* (the smallest administrative unit nationwide) based on respondents' statements about the size and makeup of their groups.[30] I then estimate the number of *cellules* where genocide occurred, under the assumption that mobilization dynamics were similar countrywide once violence started in a particular community. I start here with table 4.11, which reports both average group sizes as well as average group sizes per *cellule.*

The numbers in the table have a number of important implications. First, violence during the genocide happened almost exclusively in groups. Of all the respondents I interviewed, only one said he launched on an attack on his own. The genocide was a group-perpetrated activity. Second, perpetrator groups varied in size, but many were quite large. Nearly 20 percent of all reported attacks had one hundred or more perpetrators, and some attacks exceeded a thousand persons.

29. According to the 1991 census, Rwanda had 2,813,232 citizens between 18 and 54. If 8.4 percent were Tutsi, the Hutu population was 2,576,920. Because of population growth between 1991 and 1994, the actual number was higher, and some perpetrators were younger than 18 and older than 54. Still, the estimate of three million accounts for the entire Hutu population. For the census figures, see République du Rwanda, *Recensement général*, 124.

30. I asked respondents the makeup of the attacks in which they participated. I assume an average of 4 *cellules* per sector, and 44 *cellules* per commune. Thus, if a respondent said there were 50 attackers from two cellules, I calculate a 25 person per *cellule* attack. If there were 100 attacks from all over the sector, the per-cellule average would be the same. For my administrative calculations, I used République du Rwanda, "Annexe à l'arrête présidentiel no. 251/03," Kigali, Rwanda, November 10, 1975.

As for the size of the perpetrator population, I estimate 5,852 *cellules* where genocide occurred, a number that I multiply by the estimate of the average number of perpetrators per cellule.[31] The product of these numbers is 128,744 persons, which is a base estimate for the number of perpetrators (22 persons × 5852 *cellules*). I also make a series of additional modifications. The most important is that respondents' estimates of group size were for single attacks, not for the genocide's duration. Often the same nucleus of perpetrators participated day in and day out, but group composition also changed over time. I know of no way to calculate this number systematically, but based on my research, my best estimate is an average of thirty to thirty-five perpetrators per *cellule* over the course of the genocide.[32]

If we assume a baseline standard of thirty perpetrators per *cellule,* the total number of perpetrators would be about 175,000, whereas if we assume thirty-five perpetrators per *cellule,* then the total number of perpetrators would be about 210,000. The main advantages of this estimate are that it is based on (1) a national sample, (2) direct perpetrator information, and (3) an explicit methodology. Indeed, if any assumption made here is wrong or if new research yields different findings, the estimate can be revised. The main weaknesses with the estimate are that it is based on (1) perpetrator observations about group size and makeup and it is not clear how accurate those observations are, (2) an assumption of broadly similar dynamics of mobilization across regions *once genocidal violence started at the local level,* and (3) informed guesswork about perpetrators in those areas not well represented in my sample.

If the figure of 175,000 to 210,000 perpetrators holds up as more ev-

31. The estimate is that genocide occurred in 133 communes nationwide and that there were on average 44 cellules per commune. In addition to Giti, those communes where genocide did not occur, because the RPF controlled them or because there in the demilitarized zone, include Kiyombe, Muvumba, Kivuye, Cyumba, Mukarange [Byumba Prefecture], Kigombe, Kinigi, Butaro, Nkumba, Cyeru, and Kidaho [Ruhengeri Prefecture].

32. I make two other modifications. First, of the estimated 40,000 soldiers and *interahamwe* in the country at the time of the genocide, I estimate that some 10,000 played a direct role in the genocide. Second, several communes had few resident Tutsis prior to the genocide, and there the relative number of attackers would likely be lower. Even if the above calculations are based on a national average, the bias is against those pockets of the country where genocide did not exist because no Tutsis lived there, or because the RPF seized the communes extremely quickly. I estimate an additional eleven communes where this occurred. They are: Tare, Rushashi, Musasa [Kigali-Rural], Nyakinama, Nyamugali, Nyamutera, Ruhondo [Ruhengeri], Gaseke [Gisenyi], Tumba, Kinyami, and Rutare [Byumba]. For these communes, I use a base estimate of 15 to 20 perpetrators per *cellule.*

idence becomes available, the estimate has two important implications. First, the numbers run counter to allegations that the current authorities are governing a "criminal population."[33] The Rwandan census defines "active adults" as eighteen to fifty-four years old. As such, my estimate of the number of perpetrators equals 7 to 8 percent of the active adult Hutu population and 14 to 17 percent of the active adult male Hutu population at the time of the genocide.[34] It was not all Hutus who participated in the genocide, nor all Hutu men. It was only a minority who did.

Second, even if not all Hutu men participated in the genocide, a very significant number did. Rarely do governments succeed in mobilizing 14 to 17 percent of an adult male population to participate in state-sanctioned behavior. This is especially true for African governments, which tend to have weak roots in the countryside and generally have weak mobilizational capacity. Some scholars argue that in most genocides direct participation in the murdering of civilians is limited to a very small minority of the population.[35] If true, then the magnitude of civilian participation in the Rwandan genocide would be anomalous when compared to other cases of genocide. In short, the large-scale civilian participation (1) characterizes the Rwandan genocide, (2) runs contrary to expectations about the power of African states, and (3) is anomalous compared to other genocides. Civilian participation also was critical to the rapid character of the Rwandan genocide: with so many men taking part, Tutsis and other targeted individuals had little room for escape. All this points to the importance of civilian participation in the genocide and the need to explain it—a question I discuss more explicitly in the next chapter.

This chapter is an introduction to my research on Rwanda's genocide perpetrators. I discuss the methodology I used to select 210 sentenced and self-confessed genocide criminals to interview. The chapter also discusses my main findings about the identity of Rwanda's perpetra-

33. As has been claimed in many interviews conducted with RPF officials and as cited in Mamdani, *When Victims Become Killers*, 7.

34. Rwanda had 2,813,232 citizens between 18 and 54 in 1991. If 8.4 percent were Tutsi, the Hutu population was 2,576,920, of which 48.7 percent were active men. Thus, the total number of active adult Hutu men was approximately 1,255,960. (The actual figure may be slightly greater because of population growth between 1991 and 1994.) For the census figures, see République du Rwanda, *Recensement général*, 74, 124.

35. On this point, see Benjamin Valentino, *Final Solutions: Mass Killing and Genocide in the Twentieth Century* (Ithaca: Cornell University Press, 2004), esp. ch. 2.

tors at the local level, as well as the principal characteristics of the attacks in which they participated. The main findings are that the perpetrator population strongly resembles the adult Hutu male population at the time of the genocide. Rwanda's perpetrators were ordinary in all but the crimes they committed. There were, however, different levels of violence. Some men killed more than others; some men led and authorized the violence at the local level. On the whole, those who killed the most were young, less well-educated men, militias, political party youth, and the like; they were the "thugs" I identified in chapter 3. Those who led the attacks were Rwandans with preexisting status—the rural elite—and in almost every attack some member of the state was present. The collective dimension of the violence is another critical attribute of the violence. Men committed Rwanda's genocide almost entirely in groups, often of a fairly large size. Men killed in groups and usually under the direction of those with rural authority.

These findings all clarify what happened at the local level during the genocide, but what do they mean? The ordinariness of Rwanda's killers, the group dynamics of the violence, and the large-scale civilian participation could be indicators of a wide range of causal factors. The findings could mean that anti-Tutsi hatred was widespread, that there was a "culture of hatred," or that there was widely shared poverty. In other words, the average-ness of the killers and the extent of participation do not necessarily tell us what drove ordinary men to become *génocidaires*. To answer the causal questions, I turn to other evidence, in particular what I will present in the next chapter (as well as what I presented in the chapters 2 and 3). But to cut to the chase, I conclude that the evidence runs contrary to cultural and identity arguments. Rather, the evidence points to situational factors—choices were made in particular contexts—to the importance of fear and uncertainty in an acute war, and to preexisting norms about authority and civilian labor mobilization.

The findings from this chapter also square with what I found in my micro-comparative study. In rural areas, something like the following seems to have occurred: in a period of acute crisis and turmoil—after the assassination, the resumption of war, and national hardliners declared Tutsis as the "enemy"—a core of leaders took the initiative in their communities. The leaders tended to have preexisting social status or were armed, and they worked closely with a small group of very violent individuals—the "thugs." Once this small nucleus of actors consolidated control, they in turn mobilized as many Hutu men as they could to join them, no matter who those Hutu men were. In doing so, the leaders and thugs claimed that participating in the killing was an "obligation" or "law"—it became synonymous with order and authority—and adult Hutu men were required to do their part. From there, the violence snowballed: once a man was incorporated into the killing, he expected the same from his peers. Thus, very quickly large numbers of men came to participate, and the violence spiked. Hence the perpetrators look like a random sample of adult Hutu men—most perpetrators were likely mobilized at random.

The analysis in the chapter does not adequately address three important problems. First, motivation remains an open question, as I have argued. The chapter shows that in the aggregate, perpetrators were not especially deviant, poor, or deprived; they did not have fewer social attachments or belong to particular parties. But clearly we need more precision and more specific information about motivation—points I take up in the next chapter. Second, we still are far from understanding the logic of killing and extermination. What rationales did perpetrators use to justify and support the mass murder of civilians? I will take up that question directly in chapter 6.

Finally, the evidence presented here shows that perpetrators were a minority of adult Rwandan males. The arguments presented so far cannot explain why. If my hypothesis is correct that the majority of perpetrators were mobilized at random and that social pressure and coercion played an important role, then why were there not *more* genocide perpetrators? I have some plausible explanations, but the matter deserves further research. For one, chance might explain why some became perpetrators while others did not: some Rwandan men may simply have been at the wrong place at the wrong time. That is, they might have been at a commercial center when a band of young thugs came there to find others to join in an attack. Others might have been on the path to a Tutsi home. In fact, as we will see in the next chapter, a huge proportion of respondents lived in close proximity to Tutsis. Still others might have lived near a local leader. I have anecdotal reasons to support the claim that luck mattered in who did and did not become a perpetrator, but I did not systematically investigate the question. Again, we need more research in this area.

Another plausible explanation is that in many locations the killing ended very quickly because Tutsis were killed quickly in that area. If we take the example of Kayove commune from the last chapter, the killing ended within seven days there because, it would seem, there remained no Tutsis left to kill. I heard similar accounts in other areas, particularly in Ruhengeri and Byumba Prefectures. Thus, the number of Hutu men who complied with participation in the war effort—through night patrols, especially—was probably greater than the number of perpetrators (those who took an active role in killing or trying to kill other civilians). I will revisit some of these issues in the next chapter, but the question of why some Hutu men became perpetrators while others did not is an important area for future research on this genocide.

5 Why Perpetrators Say They Committed Genocide

I focus in this chapter on the specific reasons why ordinary Rwandan men committed genocide. When I interviewed convicted perpetrators, I asked them a series of direct and indirect questions that would allow me to test several common explanations about participation in the genocide. The perpetrators' answers are valuable in their own right: they further flesh out what happened at the local level both before and during the genocide. But my main objective in analyzing the responses is to test hypotheses about why ordinary Rwandan men took part in mass violence, often against people they knew personally.

The findings are consistent with those in the previous chapters. Overall, I find little evidence to suggest that ethnic hatred, material deprivation, or a culture of obedience were widespread among the perpetrators I interviewed. Rather, two other factors were more salient. First, men participated in the killing because other men encouraged, intimidated, and coerced them to do so in the name of authority and "the law." Many respondents described situations where they believed that they faced a choice between being punished or committing violence, and many chose the latter. Second, men participated in the killing because they were scared and angry. Many respondents said that they feared the advancing Tutsi rebels and were angry about the president's death, which they blamed on the rebels. Those are the chapter's principal findings—in the aggregate. I also present a series of other findings that pertain to common arguments about the genocide's causes, and I discuss throughout explanations for the differences in levels of participation among perpetrators.

Credibility is an obvious concern in this chapter, perhaps more so than anywhere else in this book. Perpetrators are more likely to lie or to reconstruct events in their own self-interest when answering questions about their attitudes and motivations than when discussing their age and education levels. That being the case, I crosscheck the results whenever possible, and I explicitly evaluate the truthfulness of various responses at different points in the chapter. These are measures I take in addition to the sampling criteria discussed in the last chapter. In short, credibility is an important and unavoidable concern in the chapter, but I triangulate the findings as much as possible.

Social Conditions and Destabilization before the Genocide

I start here with a series of questions about life in Rwanda before the genocide. As chapter 1 showed, there were a number of sources of social upheaval in Rwanda before the genocide. There was the civil war with the RPF that started in October 1990, the introduction of multiparty politics, the assassination of Burundi's first Hutu president and the ensuing violence in that country, and general economic malaise. The changes contributed to the radicalization of the hardliners within the ruling party. But did these national-level issues trickle down to the local level? If so, did the events contribute to individuals committing genocide? Many authors claim that they did, and some prominent theories of genocide stress political upheaval as a key causal factor.[1] To get at the issue, I asked perpetrators a series of questions about pre-genocide Rwanda, starting with the 1990 civil war (commonly called the "October War" in Rwanda).

Table 5.1 shows fairly widespread upheaval at the local level. Multipartyism was clearly a significant source of change. Respondents frequently described violent contests for local-level control among parties. They told how party youths threw stones at each other and at opposing party leaders, how men forcibly pressured others to switch parties, how party activists tore down flags and posters of opposing parties, and how political rivalries escalated occasionally into brawls and murder. The overall impression was that political party activity significantly disrupted the local political arena—a result that is consistent with the findings from chapter 3, where I found that multiparty

1. Barbara Harff, "No Lessons Learned from the Holocaust? Assessing Risks of Genocide and Political Mass Murder since 1955," *American Political Science Review* 97, no. 1 (2003), 62; Ervin Staub, *The Roots of Evil: The Origins of Genocide and Other Group Violence* (Cambridge, UK: Cambridge University Press, 1989).

Table 5.1 Opinions about pre-1994 upheaval (weighted results)[a]

	Did the "October War" cause changes in your area? (N = 206)	Before 1994, were you afraid of the RPF? (N = 198)	Did multipartyism cause changes in your area? (N = 205)	Had you heard of political problems in Burundi in 1993? (N = 205)[b]	If so, were you affected by what you heard? (N = 98)
Yes	38.3%	50.3%	63.4%	48.2%	53.1%
No	61.7%	49.7%	36.6%	51.8%	46.9%

[a]All statistical analyses in this chapter are weighted as in chapter 4.
[b]In my initial interviews, I asked respondents if they were disturbed or affected by the problems in Burundi. In several interviews, respondents responded quizzically, saying that they did not understand the question. Thus, I created a two-stage question, asking first if respondents had heard of Burundi's political problems and, second, if what they had heard affected them.

politics helped set the stage for the competition for power among local elites once the genocide began.

Responses about the civil war were mixed. Unsurprisingly, in the areas closest to the war, respondents reported significant war-related changes, including troop movements, fighting, and refugees or internally displaced persons (IDPs).[2] However, in those areas far from the front lines, respondents reported almost no war-related changes.[3] At the same time, about half the respondents countrywide reported being afraid of the rebel Rwandan Patriotic Front (RPF) before the genocide. They said that they had heard that RPF soldiers killed Hutu civilians, that the rebels disemboweled pregnant women, that the rebels were "snakes," and that they had tails. When I asked respondents how they learned this information, most answered radio broadcasts. Similarly, respondents from southern regions bordering Burundi reported the greatest concern about events in that country. But nationwide events in Burundi do not seem to have created deep resentment, fear, and anger among the perpetrators.

What do these results show? The war with the RPF and violence in Burundi clearly worried both Rwanda's national elites and ordinary Rwandans in regions where the effects of these events could be observed directly. But for many Rwandans, especially those engaged in

2. This was the case for respondents in Ruhengeri and Byumba Prefectures and in Bugesera (Kigali-Rural Prefecture).
3. This was the case for respondents in Cyangugu, Gikongoro, Butare, Kibuye, and Gitarama Prefectures.

Table 5.2 Opinions of the Habyarimana government (weighted results)

	What was your opinion of the Habyarimana government? (N = 196)
Opposed[a]	17.9%
No particular opinion[b]	32.1
Ambivalent[c]	1.3
Supported[d]	48.6

[a]The responses included "I didn't support it," "I opposed," "it was not good," "I did not benefit," "it was a dictatorship," "I was unhappy," "I reproached it," "I criticized," "it did nothing for me," "he wanted to stay alone in power," and "I did not benefit."
[b]The responses included in this category were "no problem," "I had no reproach," "OK," "it never bothered me," "it didn't concern me," "I was not interested," "it caused no problem," "there were no complications," "no opinion," "it was like others," "I didn't know anything else," "I obeyed," "I submitted myself," "one followed the law," "I was led," and "it caused nothing bad."
[c]The responses included "it was a good dictatorship," "it started out good and then became bad," and "it was good except for *umuganda* and taxes."
[d]The responses included "I supported it," "it was good," "it was very good," "I liked it," "I fought for him," "it united and developed the country," "it was a secure authority," "I respected," "I was happy," "there was no ethnic problem," "people had security," and "it was positive."

subsistence agriculture and who had low levels of education, these events remained distant concerns. By contrast, multiparty contests happened across the country, thus impacting more Rwandans. Similarly, negative propaganda about the RPF broadcast over the radio reached households across the country and would have been readily understandable to most Rwandans.[4] In short, the main finding here is that the civil war and violence in Burundi created anxiety and fear in Rwanda, but these events are not sufficient to explain why ordinary Rwandans became violent. Similarly, multipartyism disrupted the local landscape nationwide, but it does not emerge as a direct driver of genocide.

I also asked respondents to rate the Habyarimana regime (see table 5.2 for the results). The question does not directly test a hypothesis, but it taps into perpetrators' attitudes before the genocide.

Not all perpetrators supported the regime, although many did. The range of responses, in fact, is itself a reason to have confidence in the credibility of the results. Respondents expressed neither total opposition to the regime (which might indicate that they biased their responses to please current authorities) nor total support (which might

4. The point about education holds up under further statistical analysis. Bivariate regression analyses show that respondents' levels of education correlate positively and in statistically significant ways with concerns about the war, multipartyism, and Burundi.

Table 5.3 Life conditions and the future

	When you look back at your situation before 1994, how was it? (N = 188)	At the time, how did you imagine your future? (N = 175)
Negative	6.5%	21.4%
Fine	31.6	30.3
Positive	61.9	48.3

indicate that they biased their responses to lash out at the current authorities and their living conditions inside prisons). Even the high number of respondents who had no opinion of the government makes sense: respondents with little social power before and during the genocide claimed they were not in a position to comment on high politics.[5]

More significantly, I asked respondents questions about their lives before the genocide. Here I sought to evaluate the argument that frustration caused by deprivation and "difficult life conditions" can lead to aggression and violence. The theory is common in studies of genocide, and since Rwandans are very poor, some scholars apply the argument to Rwanda.[6] I asked respondents two specific questions: how was your life before the genocide and how did you imagine your future at the time (that is, before the genocide what kind of future did respondents imagine for themselves)? The responses varied, but I fit them into three categories in table 5.3: negative, fine, and positive.[7]

These responses are clearly subject to retrospective bias since at the time they answered my questions the respondents were serving jail sentences in overcrowded prisons. Their life conditions before the

5. Indeed, some 92 percent of those expressing no opinion identified themselves as "farmers," while all non-state local elites and all those with post-primary school education had an opinion one way or another.

6. Peter Uvin, *Aiding Violence: The Development Enterprise in Rwanda* (West Hartford, CT: Kumarian Press, 1998); Staub, *The Roots of Evil.*

7. For the question about life conditions, the category of "negative" includes the following responses: *bad, not good, not very good, insecure, fearful of war,* and *poor.* The category of "fine" includes: *OK, no problem, no opinion, fine, fair, middling, sufficient, like others, never bad,* and *very good before 1990.* The category of "positive" includes: *good, very good, well, very well,* and *secure.* For the question about the future, the category of "negative" includes: *bad, not good, fear, insecure, uncertain, no hope, afraid, worse, fear not enough land, no peace, lose power, not survive, war-related fear, problems,* and *no possibility for improvement.* The category of "fine" includes: *didn't think about it, did not know what could happen, same, continue, no change, didn't know, no choice, had reserves, no problem, prepare for it, live together, OK,* and *didn't imagine the future.* The category of "positive" includes: *very good, good, progress, hope for progress, hope, hope for Arusha, better, obtain everything, be rich, gain, buy land, happy, at ease, improve, advance,* and *peace.*

genocide were surely better than they were when the interviews were taking place. Nonetheless, the responses are instructive. Overall, the respondents appear neither dissatisfied with their lives before the genocide nor anxious about the future. Taken together with the findings from previous chapters—namely, that violence did not start in the poorest areas of the country and that the profile of the perpetrators was very similar to that of the adult Hutu male population—the evidence in table 5.3 runs contrary to frustration-aggression theories of genocide. Not only were the Rwandans who became *génocidaires* not comparatively poor, undereducated, or underemployed, they were also not necessarily angry about their station in life before the genocide.

What about degree of participation? Fear of the RPF, concerns about violence in Burundi, and negative life conditions are all statistically significant when degree of participation is regressed on these variables (though in a multivariate context none of the variables proves significant—the regression results are in Appendix table 5.1). In other words, the factors examined above did not drive participation as such, but they help explain which perpetrators instigated and led the violence at the local level. A frustration-aggression theory of participation in genocide is not bunk. It helps explain which perpetrators became most violent, but the theory is not a sufficient explanation of large-scale civilian participation in the genocide.

Interethnic Relations and Genocidal Ideology

I also asked a series of questions about ethnicity, interethnic feelings, and racist beliefs. These are the factors that many assume caused the genocide and participation in it. Because I probed these questions in a number of ways, I divide the answers into a series of tables. I start here with a series of questions about interethnic proximity and intermarriage. One hypothesis might be that Hutus who committed violence were ignorant of Tutsis and thus had little interaction with them. In such a context, stereotypes and myths might flourish. Hence I asked whether respondents had Tutsi neighbors, whether they had a Tutsi family member, and whether they would allow their child to marry a Tutsi (if the respondent himself was married) or if they would marry a Tutsi (if he was unmarried). The responses are striking, as table 5.4 shows.

Almost every single perpetrator I interviewed had a Tutsi neighbor before the genocide. Even more remarkable, nearly 70 percent of the respondents had a Tutsi family member before the genocide. The responses to the question about prospective intermarriage show the

Table 5.4 Hutu-Tutsi proximity and intermarriage (weighted results)

	Before 1994, did you have a Tutsi neighbor? (N = 210)[a]	Before 1994, did you have a Tutsi family member? (N = 205)[b]	Before 1994, would you allow your child to (or would you) marry a Tutsi? (N = 195)[c]
Yes	96.0%	68.8%	98.9%
No	3.6	28.3	1.1
Do not know	0.4	2.9	

[a]All but one respondent was Hutu. This respondent had a Hutu identity card, he said, but his family was considered Tutsi.

[b]Family members include any relation by blood or marriage, from mother and wife to sister-in-law, son-in-law, aunt, grandparent, and cousin.

[c]I asked married men and fathers whether they would allow their child to marry a Tutsi; for unmarried men, I asked if they themselves would marry a Tutsi woman.

same. Nearly all the respondents said that they would have no problem with interethnic marriage for their children or themselves if they were unmarried. Taken together, these findings run squarely against the claims that ethnic distance, ethnic hatred, or widespread dehumanization of Tutsis drove participation in the genocide.

If almost every perpetrator I interviewed lived near a Tutsi before the genocide, how were their relations with their Tutsi neighbors and did those relations change after the war with the RPF started in 1990? I asked respondents both questions; table 5.5 shows the results.

The results again strongly suggest that ethnic antipathy did not drive participation in the genocide. The overwhelming majority of perpetrators in the sample reported positive attitudes toward their Tutsi neighbors before the genocide. The war with the RPF that began in 1990 changed some attitudes—but relatively few. Taken together, the findings in tables 5.4 and 5.5 indicate clearly that something other than ethnic distance and antipathy led a large number of ordinary Rwandans to commit genocide.

That said, the descriptive statistics mask a strong relationship between degree of violence, on the one hand, and social distance and ethnic antipathy, on the other. In bivariate and multivariate regression analyses, three variables—whether respondents had a Tutsi family member, attitudes toward Tutsi neighbors, and changing attitudes after the 1990 war—were statistically significant with the level of violence committed. (The regression results are reported in Appendix table 5.2.) The finding suggests that the Rwandans who responded to

Table 5.5 Respondents' relations with Tutsi neighbors before 1994 (weighted)

	Before 1994, how were your relations with your Tutsi neighbors? (N = 200)		Did relations with your Tutsi neighbors change after the war began in 1990? (N = 185)
Positive[a]	86.5%	No	86.5%
"No problem"	11.2	A little	1.0
Negative[b]	2.4	Yes	12.5

[a]Responses categorized as positive include "good," "very good," "truly good," "more than 100%," "we were friends," "we shared." and "we intermarried."

[b]Responses categorized as negative include "not good," "we were friends before 1990," "not good after 1990," and "they were accomplices."

the hardliners' call, who took the initiative to kill, and who in fact did the most killing were those Rwandans who had fewer preexisting ties with Tutsis and who tended to look unfavorably on them. As with theories of violence that center on deprivation, theories that center on identity cannot explain participation in the genocide as such, but they might explain who drove and led the violence.

Racist Ideology and Propaganda

Many analyses of the genocide emphasize racial ideology and racist propaganda, which, according to various arguments, dehumanized Tutsis and created ethnic hatred. There is no denying that racist ideology was present at the national level and that there was much racist, anti-Tutsi propaganda in the Rwandan media before the genocide. The question is whether that ideology diffused to rural areas and, if so, whether rural Rwandans with little education and limited social status believed that ideology. In other words, was the discourse of ethnic nationalism and racist propaganda an elite phenomenon? Did commitments to nationalism and propaganda drive participation? To get at these questions, I asked respondents a series of questions that below I divide into three tables.

I intended the first question to determine whether "race" was a meaningful concept to respondents. However, "race" does not have an exact translation in Kinyarwanda. The best approximation is *ubwoko* (*amoko* is plural), but *ubwoko* also refers to ethnic groups, clans, the relative quality of a product, and even different car manufacturers. In short, *ubwoko* indicates categories, but not necessarily racial ones. To compensate for this, I also asked respondents how they could tell the difference between a Hutu and a Tutsi. Most commonly, respondents

Table 5.6 Race, nationalism, and the "Hutu Ten Commandments" (weighted)

	In 1994, did you think Hutus and Tutsis were different "amoko"? (N = 201)	Had you heard of the Hutu Ten Commandments? (N = 204)	Was Rwanda a country for Hutus? (N = 181)	I heard in the United States that Hutus have hatred for Tutsis Is that true? (N = 181)
Yes	64.9%	2.8%	5.9%	6.5%
No	34.8%	97.2%	94.1%	93.5%

cited a physical characteristic such as height or skin color. Others cited activity preferences: some respondents said Hutus were generally farmers, while Tutsis tended cattle.

No matter how respondents said they understood the difference between Hutus and Tutsis, the result from the question about *amoko* is significant. Nearly two-thirds of the respondents said that they thought that Hutu and Tutsis were different *amoko*. In other words, awareness of ethnic/racial categories was widespread before the genocide and possibly even more widespread than the respondents reported. Why do I claim this latter point? After the genocide, the RPF-dominated government officially removed ethnic categories from public discourse, and officials frequently lectured prisoners about the unity of the Rwandan population (and thus about the nonexistence of ethnic/racial differences). Moreover, my assistant raised concerns about these answers. In his view, awareness of ethnic/racial categories was more widespread before the genocide than the respondents suggested. In short, while the answers do not necessarily tell us whether or not perpetrators considered Tutsis a different race—because that term does not have an exact translation—the results indicate a widespread belief among perpetrators that Hutus and Tutsis represented different social categories and that those categories could be distinguished by racial criteria.

That said, awareness of difference alone did not cause strife. Here is a typical excerpt from an interview with a perpetrator from Butare Prefecture:

Did you believe that Tutsis were Inkotanyi "accomplices"? I thought the accomplices were in the city. But with my neighbors, I did not think about it. *At the time did you think that Hutus and Tutsis were different* amoko? Yes, but there were no problems with that. *What is the dif-*

ference between the amoko? Even if this was not true for everyone, you looked at the nose.[8]

The excerpt shows how respondents were aware of ethnic difference between Hutus and Tutsis—expressed here in racial terms—but that such difference in and of itself did not produce antipathy. In fact, in this case, the respondent's wife was a Tutsi.

The question about the "Hutu Ten Commandments" refers to a Hutu extremist document many reference as evidence of a genocidal ideology in place before the genocide began (see chapter 1).[9] The document undoubtedly circulated in Kigali and among national elites. However, again, it is unclear whether the "Hutu Ten Commandments" had diffused to rural areas and, if so, whether exposure to the propaganda is sufficient to explain participation. My findings indicate that the answer to both questions is no: only 3 percent of the respondents, all of whom were perpetrators, knew of the document, to say nothing of whether they subscribed to its doctrine. From outside Rwanda, the extreme language of the "Hutu Ten Commandments" looks like evidence of widespread extremist anti-Tutsi sentiment. Closer examination reveals that we cannot make assumptions about whether elite-level propaganda reached rural areas and whether that propaganda drove participation.[10]

I designed the question about the nature of Rwanda—whether it can be described as "a country for Hutus"—to probe ethnic nationalist sentiment among perpetrators. Again, the findings provide little evidence to support the idea that the perpetrators were committed ethnic nationalists: only 6 percent of the sample agreed that Rwanda was "a country for Hutus." Most respondents said Rwanda was a country for all three ethnic groups—Hutu, Tutsi, and Twa—an answer that reflected official discourse under President Habyarimana. In many instances, respondents expressed confusion at the question itself and

8. This excerpt (as well as long chunks of other raw interviews I did with perpetrators) can be found in Robert Lyons and Scott Straus, *Intimate Enemy: Images and Voices of the Rwandan Genocide* (New York: Zone Books, 2006), 47.

9. For examples where the document is cited and featured prominently, see African Rights, *Rwanda: Death, Despair, and Defiance,* rev. ed. (London: African Rights, 1995), 42–44, and Jean-Pierre Chrétien et al., *Rwanda: Les médias du génocide* (Paris: Karthala, 1995), 141–42. Colette Braeckman claims "everyone knew by heart" the Hutu Ten Commandments. Braeckman, *Rwanda: Histoire d'un génocide* (Paris: Fayard, 1994), 139.

10. As I note in the introduction and in chapter 1, Rwanda is overwhelmingly rural, and about 95 percent of my respondents lived in rural areas before and during the genocide.

indicated that for them, of course, Rwanda was a country for all three ethnic groups. Again, this result invites caution in interpreting a large-scale event such as genocide. The fact of a campaign of ethnic annihilation would seem to constitute prima facie evidence of widespread nationalist sentiment. However, these results suggest that even if perpetrators complied with those elites' program, most perpetrators were not ethnic nationalists, at least before the genocide.

The question about hatred is an indirect test of the same idea. If respondents denied having their own negative feelings toward Tutsis, they might admit that Hutus in general hated Tutsis. The question also tests validity. If other responses indicate minimal interethnic enmity, so too should responses to this question. Indeed, they do: only 6.5 percent of the respondents agreed that Hutus had hatred for Tutsis.

I asked still other questions that tested respondents' knowledge of and commitment to anti-Tutsi ideology. One question concerned the "Hamitic Hypothesis"—the idea that Tutsis were Nilotics who centuries before had migrated from the north to dominate Hutus (see chapter 1). Another question concerned propaganda characterizing the RPF as wanting to reintroduce the monarchy and enslave Hutus, as Tutsis had purportedly done in precolonial and colonial times. For both questions, I asked an initial question—if a respondent had heard of the idea—and then followed up with a question about respondents' opinion of that idea if they had heard of it (see table 5.7).

The results are mixed. On the one hand, they indicate that these ideas had reached a fair number of perpetrators. Of the two, the more concrete idea—that the Tutsis planned to reinstall the monarchy—was more prevalent. On the other hand, the results indicate that these ideas did not command widespread support. For instance, many respondents said that while they had heard of Tutsis being called

Table 5.7 The Hamitic Hypothesis and the RPF's monarchist intentions

	Before 1994, had you heard Tutsis were Hamites who came from the Horn of Africa? (N = 204)	Before 1994, had you heard that the Tutsis planned to reinstall the monarchy and make Hutu abagaragu (servants)? (N = 197)
No	58.3%	48.5%
Yes, but did not believe the idea or had no interest	27.7	31.8
Yes, and believed it was true	14.0	19.7

Table 5.8 Hutu *Pawa* and the "Great Majority" (weighted results)

	Before 1994, had you heard the term "rubanda nyamwishi"? (N = 196)	Before 1994, had you heard the term "Hutu Pawa"? (N = 179)
No	32.1%	28.7%
Yes, but meaning unknown or different from extremist propaganda	40.6	58.8
Yes, and meaning similar to extremist propaganda	27.3	8.6
Yes, understood meaning, and supported Hutu *Pawa*	n/a	3.9

Hamites, they did not know what a Hamite was. Others said that they did not understand the idea that Tutsis had come from northern Africa because they (the respondents) had always lived next door to Tutsis. Similarly, many respondents acknowledged hearing that Tutsis planned to reinstall the monarchy. However, many said that they thought this was impossible. In short, certain ideological elements were prevalent, but belief in them appears to have been much less so. Not all perpetrators necessarily heard or believed the racist and nationalist claims made in the extremist media before the genocide.

For other questions about ideology, I initially asked if respondents had heard of a term and then followed up with a question about the term's meaning. The first question concerned the term *"rubanda nyamwishi,"* which means "great majority." Many commentators point to the phrase as evidence of the hardliner's incitement campaign. The connotation was that Hutus were the majority and had to fight the Tutsi minority. The second question was about Hutu *Pawa*, the extremist political party coalition formed in 1993 (discussed in chapter 1).

These results indicate fairly widespread familiarity among perpetrators with certain aspects of racist propaganda, as measured by the terms *"rubanda nyamwishi"* and "Hutu *Pawa.*" However, relatively few respondents appear to have understood these terms in a racist way. Asked what *"rubanda nyamwishi"* meant, many respondents said that they did not know or that it referred to "the population," not necessarily to Hutus. As for Hutu *Pawa*, many respondents said that it referred to an internal split in the MDR party. Others said that *"pawa"* was a foreign word they did not understand, while still others said that "*pawa*" referred to the party with the greatest number of supporters. It is worth noting that only 4 percent of the respondents both understood Hutu *Pawa* to refer to an anti-Tutsi, pro-Hutu coalition of parties and supported it.

Are these results valid? Their internal consistency is one indication that they are: no one finding substantively contradicts another. Another indication is that the results are consistent with the profile of the perpetrators: most respondents were poor farmers who thought in practical terms about their lives. Many had never traveled outside their home region, and many had very limited education. As such, one way to check validity is to correlate the respondents' education levels with their answers about ideology, under the assumption that the most educated respondents had the most knowledge about and therefore potentially the most belief in anti-Tutsi ideology. The results from various regression analyses clearly show this relationship: the better-educated respondents demonstrate greater awareness, understanding, and belief in racist ideology than the less-educated respondents.[11] That finding does not prove that the results are valid, but it is another indication that they are.

Further regression analyses do not indicate that belief in or knowledge of anti-Tutsi ideology and propaganda drove the most violent perpetrators—with one exception. The respondents who said that they had heard of the "Hutu Ten Commandments" were among the most violent in the sample. Even though very few respondents had heard of the document, those that did—presumably those most tuned into the most racist propaganda—were the most prone to initiate and drive the violence.

In sum, my interviews with perpetrators show that most Rwandans did not participate in the genocide because they hated Tutsis as despicable "others," because they adhered to an ethnic nationalist vision of society, or because racist propaganda had instilled racism in them. The perpetrators had an awareness of different ethnic categories, but that awareness did not create ethnic hatred or directly lead to violence. As such, explanations that center on social distance, ethnic antipathy, racist culture, and propaganda are insufficient explanations of participation in genocide. At the same time, the results show that ethnic hatred and distance, as well as exposure to some of the most virulent

11. I ran six bivariate regressions with education levels as the independent variable and answers about ideology as dependent variables. Of the tested relationships, all had positive coefficients and all but one (the question about Hutu Ten Commandments) had a statistically significant result (at the .05 probability level).

propaganda, do explain which perpetrators were the most violent. Theories of genocide that center on racism and propaganda cannot be discarded; rather, they help us understand who responds to the call to violence and who leads it. But such theories do not explain why there was large-scale civilian participation in Rwanda's genocide.

Motivation

What do perpetrators say about why they participated in the genocide? I asked that question at several points in the interview, both directly and indirectly. I asked respondents to describe how the violence started in their community and then I asked how they became involved in that violence. Most often, these questions elicited specific statements about motivation. In other cases, a point made by the respondent led naturally to a follow-up question about motivation. In all cases, I asked respondents for the details of the attack or the attacks in which they participated, and at that point I asked them specifically why they joined each particular attack. Finally, near the end of the interview, I asked respondents to state the most important reason for their participation.

These separate questions, asked at different times in the interview, allowed for triangulation during the interviews and after. Sometimes respondents described different but simultaneous motivations. Other respondents explained how their motivations changed over time. Some entered violent attacks for one reason but continued in them for another. All this presents a coding problem, which I handle first by identifying the main categories of motivation and then, for those cases where respondents expressed distinct motivations, by identifying the primary, secondary, and tertiary motivations.

To account for the fact that some perpetrators cited more than one motivation, I create two separate tables on motivation. The first (table 5.9) summarizes the frequency with which a respondent volunteered any one motive. The categories correspond to ones that the respondents themselves offered. I organize them not according to which was most frequent but according to what I believe should correlate to degree of participation (more on this below). The second table (table 5.10) aggregates motives and, in contrast to table 5.9, assigns only one motive to each respondent.

The categories in table 5.9 require some definition and explication. "Intra-Hutu coercion" refers to those cases where respondents described participating because they feared the negative consequences

Table 5.9 Respondents' stated motivations (weighted results)

Respondents' stated motivations (N = 209)	
Intra-Hutu coercion	64.1%
Obedience	12.9
Protect Tutsi family members or hidden Tutsis	5.2
Copycat	4.8
Accidental integration	6.2
Material gain (looting)	5.2
War-related fear and combativeness	22.0
Anger at or revenge for Habyarimana's death	4.8
Interpersonal revenge	1.0
Claimed no active participation	15.3

from other Hutus of not participating. Those negative consequences included physical harm and death but also property damage and financial penalty. Some said participation was an "obligation" (*agahato*) that "everyone had to" comply with or they would face serious repercussions. By and large, the coercion that respondents described was the result of direct, face-to-face mobilization: individuals, leaders, or groups directly solicited the respondents' participation at commercial centers, on roads and pathways, or at their homes. Sometimes the threat of noncompliance was implied; other times, it was explicit. On occasion, respondents described being beaten before they agreed to participate.

Here is how one respondent described the process:

> Anyone who did not go on a patrol paid a penalty. That is where people were killed. The people who killed first, afterward they obliged others to kill.

Here is another example from a man from Ruhengeri:

> I was in an attack, and this attack killed one person. *How did you find yourself in an attack?* We heard whistles; we went to see; and when we arrived we went with the others. *Why did you go?* When there are whistles, no one stays in the house. *When you arrived, why did you go with the group?* It was necessary, because anyone who did not go with the others was asked for money. *How much?* More than 5,000 FRW [Rwandan Francs, about $35 at the time of the genocide], but if you negotiated, maybe 2,000 or 3,000 FRW. *Why not do that?* It was not possible. *Why?* When you refused, they said you were an accomplice and you hid Tutsis. They could destroy your house, and if you were young [and hence living at home] you created poverty for your parents.

"Obedience" is quite similar to intra-Hutu coercion, with the exception that obedience does not imply direct harm for noncompliance. Here respondents said that they joined attacks because doing so was "the law" (*igeteko*). Others said that they went with murderous groups or killed because they were "obeying" what they had been told to do. Still others said they participated because they had been "authorized" to kill Tutsis. In these accounts, respondents stressed that "the state" or "the authorities" had mandated participation for all able-bodied Hutu men. Killing was "the law." Those who emphasized coercion made similar statements. Indeed, when pressed, respondents who stressed obedience often said that they feared punishment if they did not comply. For coding purposes, however, the difference between these categories is that the former respondents stressed they participated because they feared what would happen to them if they did not take part in the killing, while the latter respondents stressed the general importance of complying with law and authority.

"Protecting Tutsi family members or Tutsis hiding in their house" is somewhat self-explanatory. In these cases, respondents described how they joined attacks in order to avert suspicion or accusations that they were protecting Tutsis. In some cases, the threat was direct: groups showed up at their homes and charged that the respondents were hiding Tutsis or were enemy "accomplices." Knowing that there were Tutsis hiding in their homes, these respondents said that they opted to join attacks to save those they were hiding. In other cases, the threat was indirect: because respondents knew they were hiding Tutsis, they joined attacks in order to prevent suspicion that they were doing so. Some respondents described how a friend had come to their home and warned that a certain group was planning an attack against them and the Tutsis hiding in their home. To prevent such an attack, respondents felt that it was best to join the group.

A "copycat" motivation is one where respondents said that they participated because others were doing so. Typical responses would be, "I went into the attack because I wanted to help others" or "I went to join my colleagues." By the same token, other respondents said they joined attacks because they saw "no consequences" for doing so or because they were "habituated" to the violence around them. Overall, the responses that I have put in this category emphasize some form of mimicking.

"Accidental integration" is similar, but here respondents described hearing a commotion nearby, going to see what was happening, and then finding themselves swept up in a group that was attacking Tutsis. Other respondents described a general state of confusion or "ignorance": they said that they joined attacks without really knowing what they were doing. In short, some type of confusion, uncertainty, or curiosity ties this category of responses together. "Material gain" is self-explanatory: in these cases, respondents said they joined attacks in order to loot property from Tutsis, including household goods and livestock.

"War-related fear and combativeness" is quite different. In these cases, respondents described fearing the RPF or a combination of the RPF and their Tutsi allies after the assassination of President Habyarimana. In these narratives, both the president's assassination and the renewed onset of civil war loomed large, and respondents said that they joined attacks or killed to "protect Hutus," to "win the war," or to "save the country." Others said that they joined attacks to "defend" themselves or their families against attack, while still others said that they joined attacks to prevent the monarchy from returning. The overall image that the respondents conveyed was one of ethnic warfare, whereby "the Tutsis" were attacking "the Hutus" and the respondents were participating in order to preempt attacks against them.

"Anger at or revenge for Habyarimana's death" is similar to war-related fear and combativeness. But here the emphasis is less on wartime fear and more on a specific response to the president's assassination. In these accounts, respondents emphasized that Habyarimana was their "parent" or "father" and that his death had to be avenged. Many respondents used a version of the Kinyarwanda verb *guhora*, which translates as "avenge." In short, these respondents blamed the RPF for killing the president, and they said that a violation of such magnitude required revenge against the RPF's alleged supporters—"the Tutsis."

The respondent from Kayove quoted in chapter 3 expressed the logic of both anger and self-defense quite well. Here he describes his response when he learned of Habyarimana's death:

> In my mind, I understood right away that the Tutsis were responsible. I was angry, and I said to myself, "It is true. The Tutsis are mean." And I said everything people say about them is true. . . . We said . . . we are going to kill them before being killed by them.

"Inter-personal revenge" entails a similar mechanism but in a different context. In these cases, a respondent described how a group had killed a Tutsi family member or friend who had been hiding in his home. Such action, according to the respondents, necessitated re-

Table 5.10 Respondents' aggregated stated motivation (weighted results)

Aggregated motivation (N = 210)	
Intra-Hutu coercion and/or obedience only	45%
Intra-Hutu coercion and/or obedience plus some other motive unrelated to war or anger at Habyarimana's assassination	10.6
Protect Tutsis	0.2
Copycat or accidental integration	3.9
Material gain	0.9
War-related motive or anger at/revenge for Habyarimana's assassination and intra-Hutu coercion or obedience	13.7
War-related motive or anger at/revenge for Habyarimana's death and other noncoercion/obedience motive	2.3
War-related motive and/or anger at/revenge for Habyarimana's death	8.3
Claimed no active participation	15.1

venge. However, because during the genocide killing Hutus was difficult or impossible, said the respondents, they exacted revenge against Tutsis associated with the original attackers. The logic may seem strange to an outsider, but nonetheless a few respondents explained their participation in this way. As I noted above, these categories of motivation were not mutually exclusive. Several respondents voiced various simultaneous or changing motivations. Indeed, by my count some 38.6 percent of the respondents reported two distinct motives, and 9.5 percent reported at least three. To account for this, I combine motives into nine aggregate categories, and I report their frequency in table 5.10.

These results point to two primary motivations to participate in the genocide: in-group pressure and out-group fear or revenge. In the sample, 79.9 percent of the respondents cited either one of these motivations (or both), while 5 percent mentioned neither (15.1 percent claimed that they did not actively participate in the killing). If true, this finding suggests that most perpetrators participated in violence because they feared the consequences of not doing so. Either they feared punishment from other Hutus for not participating, or they feared retribution and attack from Tutsi rebels and their alleged ethnic civilian allies.

The findings support theories of genocide that emphasize obedience and fear in the context of a security dilemma. However, both theories need modification. For Rwandan *génocidaires*, obedience stemmed less from a blind "culture of obedience" or from the legitimacy of au-

thorities. Rather, obedience stemmed from in-group coercion and social pressure: men feared that they would be punished for appearing to
refuse to participate in the genocide. As for fear, the argument about
a "security dilemma" emphasizes that people commit violence in order to preempt violence being committed against them, especially in
the context of anarchy and state collapse. The first part of the claim
fits the evidence from Rwanda. Individuals said that they feared the
RPF in the context of renewed war and after the president's assassination. Hence they attacked their Tutsi neighbors, they said. But the second part of the claim fits the evidence less well. In Rwanda, there was
not total anarchy. State institutions stayed intact, as did norms of
compliance, and both contributed to why so many men participated
in the genocide.

Triangulation

The question remains as to whether these results can be believed.
A perpetrator wanting to minimize his responsibility would naturally
claim that others forced him to participate or that he feared for his security. With less conscious deception, a perpetrator also could retrospectively attribute a motivation even if one never existed or because
the one that did exist was too horrible to admit. Both possibilities exist, and there is no way to prove conclusively what the actual truth
was at the moment when each individual chose to participate in violence or chose to kill. That said, there are ways of triangulating these
results to see if the dynamics that the perpetrators describe did, in fact,
occur. Again, the research goal is not to ascertain perfect validity, but
rather to determine to what extent results are meaningful. I do this in
four ways: (1) by analyzing the internal consistency of the results, (2)
by citing excerpts from the most aggressive perpetrators, (3) by examining other sources, and (4) by interviewing nonperpetrators.

Given the respondents' stated motivations, a reasonable expectation is that those who claimed that they participated because of in-
group pressure would have been less violent than those who claimed
that they participated because of war-related fear or anger at the president's assassination. If the data support that supposition, it would
lend credibility to the respondents' stated motivations. To test the
supposition, I ran bivariate regressions with primary and aggregate
motive as separate independent variables and degree of violence as dependent ones. The regressions show a strong relationship between the
variables (see Appendix table 5.4).

The results have two main implications. First, the results support the supposition that the most violent individuals cited war-related motives (including revenge for the president's assassination) while the least violent individuals cited in-group pressure. That finding does not rule out the possibility that the narratives of some perpetrators were fabricated or biased retrospectively. However, the finding demonstrates a strong internal consistency to the narratives and thus gives reason to have confidence in them. Second, the regression results again point to important differences among perpetrators. The results indicate that war-related fear and anger drove the most aggressive perpetrators, while a fear of in-group punishment motivated the least violent to participate.

Another method for checking the credibility of the respondents is to ask those who identified as leaders of the violence whether they pressured other Hutus to join them. Although I learned the significance of in-group coercion in the field, midway through the survey I began asking individuals who admitted to being leaders of the violence in their communities whether they pressured others to participate. Each readily acknowledged that he did. I reproduce excerpts from four interviews below. The first is from a *cellule* committee member from Gitesi Commune in Kibuye Prefecture. He said that he initially resisted killing Tutsis but then switched after soldiers pressured him to attack Tutsis:

Did you oblige others to join you? Yes. *What was said?* That they [the Tutsis] killed Habyarimana, our parent, that no one could stay [home] without joining the attacks; that the Tutsis were fighting to retake the country as it was before 1959 [i.e. before the revolution] that they [the Tutsis] killed all the Hutus in Byumba [where the RPF held territory]; and that we had been told if we didn't defend ourselves we also would be killed. *Who said that?* Soldiers. . . . *Why was it necessary to oblige others?* The others had to help us because it was a communal activity [*igikorwa rusange*]. *What happened if someone did not participate?* It would be bad. *For example?* He could be killed. *Would you kill a Hutu who did not participate?* And why did they attack me? I was Hutu. *Why was it an activity for everyone?* Because where the *Inkotanyi* attacked, they also did not differentiate. *But if someone did not want to participate, why was it necessary to force him?* They had to go, absolutely! *Why?* Because of the death of Habyarimana. It was understood that the Tutsis were fighting to live alone [that is, without Hutus] in the country. *But why mobilize others?* If there was only one person, there would not be deaths [meaning that to accomplish the goal of killing Tutsis many men were needed].

This particular excerpt demonstrates, among other things, how the rationale for genocide—that the RPF killed Habyarimana, that the RPF wanted to kill Hutus, and thus that all Tutsis had to be killed—became the dominant idea during this period. This respondent described how once others—in this case, soldiers—pressured him to accept this rationale, he then mobilized others in the same way. I will return to this rationale in the next chapter, but the point to stress here is how, for this respondent, obliging others was an almost natural course of action. "They had to go, absolutely!" he said. That kind of thinking was repeated over and over in my interviews.

The second example is the man from Kayove Commune in Gisenyi Prefecture whose testimony I cited above and extensively in chapter 3. I start the excerpt at the point where I asked him how he and other perpetrators located Tutsis to kill during the genocide:

> *How did you find them?* We knew where they lived. We arrived at their place, and when we did not find them, we attacked their neighbors, and they showed us by force where they had gone or where they were hiding. *What do you mean "by force"?* If the neighbor did not show us, we had to kill him. *Did one oblige other Hutus to participate?* Ehhhh! If we found someone at his house, without accompanying us, we hit him. We asked him for money and we went to drink. If he had cows or goats, we took them because he was an accomplice. *If you did not participate, you were considered an accomplice?* Accomplice! Yes! You were considered like a Tutsi. Even if you were Hutu, you were no longer considered Hutu. . . .[12] *Why was it necessary to oblige others to participate?* They had to understand that we were attacked by the Tutsi *ubwoko*. They had to help us fight them because we knew we would finish them and go to the front. *Kill the Tutsis and then go to the front?* Yes.

This is a remarkable statement. As with the previous example, this respondent shows how attacking civilians was part of the war rationale. Killing Tutsis was seen as the first step in a war to defeat the RPF, after which one would "go to the front" to fight soldiers. I will return to this respondent (and this rationale) in the next chapter, but again the point to stress here is that the respondent admits to beating and robbing Hutus who did not participate. This respondent called non-participating Hutus "accomplices," which during the genocide was ef-

---

12. At this point in the interview, the respondent describes how he and his group attacked the Hutu *conseiller* because the latter had not participated. For a description of the attack and the role of the burgomaster in trying to save the *conseiller*, see chapter 3, the section on Kayove Commune.

fectively a death warrant. In fact, the respondent went so far as to say that Hutus who did not participate "were no longer considered Hutu."

The third example comes from a *cellule* committee member who was the leader of a roadblock in Kayonza Commune in Kibungo Prefecture. He did not kill, nor did he order others to kill, he said, but he was responsible for the roadblock where Tutsis were killed. He described how on April 10 a *conseiller* and an army lieutenant came to his house and ordered him, along with other *cellule* committee members, to set up roadblocks throughout the *cellule.* The excerpt below picks up where I ask him to describe how the roadblock worked:

> *Did you recruit people for the roadblock?* Yes, but always with the other members of the *cellule. How did you choose people to go to the roadblock?* We chose men who were strong, not children and not elders. *Every strong man?* All men, except those who were sick, because the purpose was to ensure security and prevent infiltration by the *Inkotanyi. . . . Were peasants ordered to go to the roadblock?* Yes. *And if they refused?* They didn't refuse! *Why not?* They obey the authorities. They said, "What the authorities order, we must accept."

Like the others, this respondent couches mobilization in the language of war: manning roadblocks was a means to protect security and stop the rebels. And, again, the excerpt makes clear that there was pressure for all able-bodied adult men to participate and that compliance amounted to obeying authorities. Authorities mobilized men to kill, and they took anyone they could find.

A last example makes the point. The respondent was a well-educated farmer, whom the local *conseiller* in his commune in Ruhengeri Prefecture had chosen to oversee several roadblocks in his sector. The respondent said that the local *responsable* made a list of men in that area to ensure that all participated:

> *All men had to participate?* Yes, all men. *And if they refused?* It was not possible. He who refused could be killed. *Could you have killed someone who refused?* That was possible, if the person did not give a reason for why he could not go. *What was a good reason?* If he was sick.

Again, the pattern is the same: once genocidal violence began in an area, local Hutus who were in charge used their power and authority to mobilize able-bodied men to participate.

These are examples of Hutus who pressured other Hutus to participate in the genocide. The examples resonate strongly with what many respondents said, namely that they participated because they feared the consequences of not participating. To cite one representative example of a perpetrator who claimed he participated because he was afraid of not doing so:

> All Rwandans who were in the zone controlled by the *Abatabazi* government had to participate—to save his own life.[13] Anyone who did not participate was considered an enemy or accomplice, and the penalty was death.

In short, I find a strong similarity between those who say they pressured other Hutus and those who say they were pressured by other Hutus.

That finding does not rule out other types of biases inherent to the method. For example, the period in which I interviewed may have been one where prisoners across the country had convinced themselves of in-group coercion. Or the style of my questions or my assistants' translations may have unwittingly invited such responses. However unlikely, these are possibilities and thus it becomes important to examine other primary sources to see if there is consistency among the various accounts.

To date, there is no other systematic nationwide study of perpetrators of which I am aware, but there is much informed judgment and anecdotal information about perpetrators in various reports. Close analysis of these documents reveals consistent references to intra-Hutu coercion. For example, the media watchdog group Article 19 reports that "people throughout the country were compelled, under penalty of death, to cooperate with security forces."[14] Bruce Jones argues that "coercive mobilization" characterized popular participation during the genocide.[15] "Everyone had to participate," said a Rwandan Lutheran minister interviewed in August 1994. "To prove that you weren't RPF, you had to walk around with a club."[16]

---

13. The *"abatabazi"* government refers to the interim government led by hardliners that took power after Habyarimana's assassination.

14. Article 19, *Broadcasting Genocide: Censorship, Propaganda, and State-Sponsored Violence in Rwanda, 1990–1994* (New York: Article 19, 1996), 114. Elsewhere the same report notes radio broadcasts that called for punishment of those who did not comply. See 120–21.

15. Bruce Jones, *Peacemaking in Rwanda: The Dynamics of Failure* (Boulder, CO: Lynne Rienner, 2001), 41

16. Raymond Bonner, "Rwandans in Death Squad Say Choice Was Kill or Die," *New York Times,* August 14, 1994, A16. Said a teacher quoted in the same story: "We were forced to move with the killers in order not to be killed." He added, "We risked being killed. They said, 'If you don't come and work with us, you are R.P.F.'"

Several other academic studies, human rights reports, and journalistic accounts cite examples where perpetrators say that they were directly threatened for not participating in the genocide.[17] Indeed, these other sources all indicate that an intra-Hutu coercion narrative was not an artificial product of my research: other sources using information collected in other periods and with other methods report the same dynamic.

All this raises the question of nonparticipation that I broached at the end of the last chapter: if there was significant coercive pressure to participate, how and why did some escape it? That question is critical to any comprehensive analysis of the genocide. However, systematically researching that question when I conducted research in Rwanda was difficult because there was no way to know if randomly sampled Hutu non-detainees were nonperpetrators. To account for this, during the micro-comparative segment of my fieldwork, I interviewed Hutu men who survivors and current authorities agreed had not participated in the genocide.

In total, I interviewed ten nonparticipating Hutu men from four communes. Not only did each describe strong in-group pressure to participate, but several also described in some detail what happened. I asked seven of the group what exactly they did to avoid participating; five said that they escaped only after bribing their attackers or allowing the attackers to take Tutsis hiding in their homes. I quote from all of these interviews below. The first is from a Hutu businessman from Gafunzo Commune. He described how after an initial period of confusion following Habyarimana's death, a core group of attackers formed and consolidated control. They then traversed the sector attacking Tutsis as well as Hutus who were suspected of disobedience or hiding Tutsis. Shortly after the killing began, an attack group of about thirty men came to his home:

17. For examples, see Alison Des Forges, *Leave None to Tell the Story: Genocide in Rwanda* (New York: Human Rights Watch, 1999), 2, 322–24; African Rights, *Rwanda,* 326, 338, 402, 460, 466, and 476; Ephrem Rugiririza, "Bourreaux et victimes: Le face à face," *Diplomatie judiciare,* October 18, 2002; Monthly Report, Internews, November 25, 2002, Kajelijeli trial; Sara Rakita, "Lasting Wounds: Consequences of Genocide and War for Rwanda's Children," Human Rights Watch, March 2003, 13–14; Bill Berkeley, *The Graves Are Not Yet Full: Race, Tribe and Power in the Heart of Africa* (New York: Basic Books, 2001), 1; and André Sibomana, *Hope for Rwanda: Conversations with Laure Guilbert and Hervé Deguine,* trans. Carina Tertsakian (London: Pluto Press, 1999), 104–5. Alan Zarembo describes the way that Hutu men were mobilized face to face, but he interprets participation as an outcome of Rwanda's culture of obedience and "upholding the standards of good citizenship." Zarembo, "Judgment Day," *Harper's,* April 1997, esp. 70, 80.

They found me there. They began to call me an accomplice. They said
they even would eat my cows. . . . *Did they try to forcibly take you?*
They tried and I refused. They said if I didn't go with them, they would
cut me, but I refused. *It was possible to refuse?* Yes, if you were not
afraid. They threatened with their machetes.

At this point in the interview, the respondent showed me how his attackers menacingly brandished their machetes at him. Asked why he
was not afraid, he said, "I knew that those who were killed had done
nothing [wrong]," and "I said, 'If they kill me, it would be like the others who were killed.'"

However, when asked, the respondent also acknowledged that he
had to pay off the attackers, and his occupation as a businessman
meant that he had the means to do so. Whatever the ultimate reason
for why this man did not join the attack, his testimony is consistent
with what we have seen up to now: coercive pressure to participate
and threats by Hutus who already had been violent against those who
had not been.

The second example comes from a young Hutu man from Musambira Commune who had been a student during the genocide. When I
interviewed him, he had recently been elected president of the *Gacaca*
courts in his district. He described how during the genocide, the attackers came around and recruited all Hutu men to join the patrols:

> The chance we had is that we were children. We were students. They
> did not require someone from our house to go. *People did not come to
> your place?* They came. We had [Tutsi] women we hid because their
> houses had been destroyed. We hid the boys too. They came to take these
> women and they took them and they killed them. *Did they ask you to
> go?* No.

This testimony again demonstrates the pressure for able-bodied Hutu
men of a certain age to participate. This respondent escaped because
he was considered a child.

The third example also comes from Musambira Commune, this
time from a Hutu man who during the genocide was a farmer and afterwards was appointed *conseiller:*

> *Was there an obligation to participate?* Yes. Some were afraid of being
> killed. There was a moment when we learned that people who hid oth-
> ers [Tutsis] would have to kill them and then, and after having killed
> them, they too would be killed. There were many who hid others. . . .
> *Did that happen here?* I was told of a youth who had hidden his brother-

in-law and who refused to kill him and who was killed also. There was a certain [name withheld] who had hidden someone, a sister-in-law, and he was told to kill this girl. He tried to refuse. They began to hit him. They gave him the machete and he used the machete on this girl.

Even if this respondent did not witness these events, that he believed them indicates that in-group threats for noncompliance were credible. In other words, those who did choose to participate may not have been directly beaten or threatened, but based on these and other stories, it would have seemed reasonable for them to expect serious negative consequences for not complying.

The fourth example is from a Hutu man from Kayove Commune who was a teacher during the genocide and was appointed headmaster of a school afterwards.[18] He described the behavior of a violent group during the genocide:

One day they came to my place. I didn't know anyone. They said, "You will give us money. If not, you will help us." . . . Many people gave money to avoid the situation. If you refused, you were badly beaten.[19]

The excerpt again shows, at the very least, that it was credible for Hutu men to fear negative consequences for not participating. Some Hutu men had the means to bribe, and did so; others who became perpetrators told me that they did not have money to pay off the attackers.

The fifth example is again from Kayove, but this time from a former MRND official in the commune who subsequently was elected president of the *Gacaca* courts in his district. In this excerpt, he describes how shortly after the news of Habyarimana's death reached the commune, gangs of youths went on a rampage:

[They] passed everywhere. If they found you, no matter whom they found, they took you to go with them by force. They were crazy in the head. . . . They took people by force, by force! To resist, you had to pay.[20]

The testimony continues to point to a pattern of in-group coercion during the genocide.

All the information above—the statistical analyses linking motivation to degree of participation, the narratives of genocide leaders, other

18. This respondent was cited in chapter 3.
19. I did not ask if he bribed his way out of participating.
20. Again, I did not ask if he paid.

sources on the genocide, and the narratives of Hutu nonperpetrators—
it all consistently corroborates perpetrator accounts of intra-ethnic coercion to commit violence. There appears to have been widespread
pressure for Hutu men of a certain age to participate and a credible
threat of punishment if they did not comply. Moreover, the pressure
to participate was equated with authority. In short, *intra-ethnic* coercion and pressure appears to have been a central factor driving mass
participation in the genocide; based on the evidence seen so far, intra-
ethnic coercion and pressure appear to have been greater determinants
of genocidal participation than interethnic enmity.

Motivation Continued

In the survey, I asked another series of questions that pertain to motivation: whether the radio motivated perpetrators, whether they
looted, whether they were drunk, and whether participating in the
genocide was equivalent to working for the country. Given my findings about coercion and social pressure, I also began asking respondents if they had ever disobeyed the authorities (see table 5.11).

The responses to the question about the effect of the radio are important. Common wisdom and much commentary on the genocide
stress the major role that radio played in inciting Rwandans to kill.[21]
While the radio undoubtedly did play a critical role, particularly in tipping the balance of power toward violence in some communities by
signaling who had power and in linking genocidal violence to authority, the overwhelming majority of respondents said that the radio on
its own did not cause them to participate. Rather, most said they
joined the attacks because of face-to-face mobilization. They complied
after encountering groups or individuals on roads, in commercial centers, or at their homes. In short, the respondents said they chose to par-

21. For examples where radio is emphasized, see Frank Chalk, "Hate Radio in
Rwanda," in *The Path of a Genocide: The Rwanda Crisis from Uganda to Zaire,* ed.
Howard Adelman and Astri Suhrke (New Brunswick: Transaction, 1999), 93–99; Alain
Destexhe, *Rwanda and Genocide in the Twentieth Century,* trans. Alison Marschner
(New York: New York University Press, 1995), 30; Christine Kellow and H. Leslie
Steeves, "The Role of Radio in the Rwandan Genocide," *Journal of Communication* 48:3
(1998), 107–28; and Darryl Li, "Echoes of Violence," in *The New Killing Fields: Massacre and the Politics of Intervention,* ed. Nicolaus Mills and Kira Brunner (New York:
Basic Books, 2002), 117–28. Some of these studies are careful not to overestimate the radio's role, but reductionist claims about the radio's impact, in general, abound. For example, Kellow and Steeves quote a journalist who asserts, "When the radio said it was
time to kill people . . . the masses slid off a dark edge into insanity." (124). Li asserts that
"hundreds of thousands heeded" the calls of RTLM broadcasts by taking part in the
genocide (118).

Table 5.11 Other possible motivations (weighted results)

	Did the radio lead you to go into the attacks? (N = 176)	Did you take any property during the genocide (including food)? (N = 170)	Were you given/did you drink alcohol during killing? (N = 122)	Did you think you were working for the country? (N = 120)	Have you ever disobeyed the authorities? (N = 115)
No	85%	77.3%	84.8%	57.5%	90.9%
Yes	15%	22.7%	15.2%	42.5%	9.1%

ticipate not principally because of being told to do so over the radio—although that undoubtedly contributed indirectly—but because a person or persons directly solicited their participation.

The finding about looting is also significant. In my interviews with non-perpetrators, Rwandans often said that peasants participated to steal property because they are poor. However, the survey results challenge that assumption. During the genocide, there was undoubtedly a great deal of looting. Those who said they stole said that they took food, tiles, and other pieces of property or tried to take over a plot after a house or the land was empty. However, very few said that they killed or originally took part in the violence for material reasons. For most, the looting came later, after the killing was done.

The respondents also said that they tended not to be drunk while committing violence, which challenges another common claim found in and outside Rwanda. The responses to the question about working for the country are hard to interpret. Many respondents readily answered "yes" and said that participation was a way to save the nation from external attack or was a "law" high-level authorities had decreed. But many answered "no" and said that those leading the violence were elites, peasants, youth, or "delinquents" who did not represent the country. Thus, the question seems to show partly whether respondents thought government officials were responsible and partly whether respondents were convinced of the violence's legitimacy.

Finally, the result from the obedience question is striking and is consistent with other findings. Recall that about 88 percent of the sample said that they did weekly community labor programs called *umuganda,* a figure that is in keeping with the response to the obedience question. Both results indicate that the Rwandan state could command a great deal of compliance from the citizenry before the genocide, and the findings above indicate that the pattern was reproduced during the genocide. I return to the point in greater detail in chapter 8.

Regression analyses again show that while some of these factors do not explain the behavior of the majority of perpetrators, they predict which perpetrators were most violent. In bivariate regressions, radio incitement, looting, and the idea that men were "working for the country" all proved statistically significant. However, in a multivariate context only the latter variable proved significant (see Appendix table 5.5 for regression results). Here again we see a bifurcated sample, with the most violent perpetrators saying that they killed for expected reasons (looting, radio incitement, and working for the country), while most respondents said that these factors did not matter.

Comprehensive Regression Analyses

In this chapter and the previous one, I ran a number of bivariate and multivariate regression analyses. Several indicated statistically significant results. However, of all the variables I cited, it remains unclear which ones have the strongest relationship with degree of participation. To answer that question, I ran a series of multivariate regression analyses, including all of the variables that proved meaningful in previous regressions (see Appendix table 5.6 for one representative table of results).

In every multivariate regression I ran, the variable for combined motivation had the strongest relationship with degree of participation. In other words, those respondents who claimed that war-related anger and fear drove them were consistently the most violent. The most violent perpetrators claimed that Hutus had to fight for the country and they mobilized the less violent to join them. Several multivariate regressions I ran also show significant relationships between age and degree of violence (with the youngest being most violent) and between preexisting relations with Tutsi neighbors and degree of violence (with those reporting the worst relations being the most violent).

———————

This chapter has three major findings. First, the chapter shows that many common hypotheses about participation in genocide are both accurate and misleading. On the one hand, the survey results run contrary to various theories linking violence to preexisting ethnic antipathy and distance, to frustration from poverty, and to material incentives. Most perpetrators did not report hostile relations with Tutsis, social distance with Tutsis, deep belief in racist culture, brainwashing or other extensive manipulation from propaganda, general deprivation before the genocide, or looting as a primary motive to commit genocide. Clearly there were dynamics other than these that drove large-scale participation in Rwanda's genocide. On the other hand, the results show that some of these variables are correlated with degree of participation in a statistically significant way—with preexisting relations with Tutsis as especially important. In other words, these theories explain, at least in part, the behavior of the most violent perpetrators.

Second, the chapter demonstrates that there was strong intra-Hutu pressure to participate in the genocide, that the pressure was associated with authority, and that this pressure, in all likelihood, contributed heavily to rapid, large-scale civilian mobilization. This chapter and the last also present evidence of high levels of civilian compliance with state authorities before the genocide: the interviewees regularly participated in obligatory state-induced labor projects and in nighttime patrols *before* the genocide. But the mechanism during the genocide appears less Rwanda's often-claimed "culture of obedience" and more intra-ethnic enforcement and coercion. In dry terms, there was a credible threat of sanction for noncompliance. In less dry terms, during the genocide, many Hutu men felt their choice was either participate in the genocide or be punished, and many chose the former.

Third, the chapter again points to the importance of the war. Many perpetrators said that they committed genocide because they wanted to protect themselves from the RPF and because they were enraged at Habyarimana's death and wanted revenge. The most powerful predictor of why one perpetrator committed more violence than another was whether a respondent described himself as motivated by war-related fear or anger. The qualitative testimony briefly presented above also showed how killing Tutsis was inseparable from the language of war. Killing Tutsis in fact was equated with fighting the enemy. These findings all support theories that claim that men kill to protect themselves and avenge those who killed their own; the findings are also further evidence that war is an essential part of the causal story of why genocide happened in Rwanda.

The findings from this chapter are consistent with the picture of genocide that emerged from previous chapters. After Habyarimana's assassination and the resumption of war, national hardliners declared war on Tutsis. At the local level, in the context of crisis and emergency, local actors jostled for control until those promoting violence against Tutsis won the upper hand. Once they did, they in turn mobilized as many people as they could, claiming that killing Tutsis was self-defense and authorized by the state. This chapter shows that downstream, many men experienced a choice between compliance and the risk of punishment, and many opted to join the attacks. This chapter also shows that those who were the most aggressive during the genocide had the fewest ties to Tutsis, had the most deprivation, and, above all, were angry and fearful after Habyarimana's assassination and the renewed onset of war. Their mindset was one of rage and revenge, of killing before being killed, of organizing society categorically into an ethnic "us" and "them." Once these men wielded a plurality of force, once a tipping point was reached, mass mobilization and violence spiked, and from that point forward—in the context of continuing calls for violence from the national authorities and the continuing advance of the Tutsis—killing dominated local life. Genocide became the new order of the day.

6   The Logic of Genocide

So far, I have focused on the patterns and dynamics of violence as well as the characteristics, attitudes, and motivations of perpetrators. But there is one big question that remains unexamined: why genocide? What was the logic of extermination in Rwanda? At different points in my interviews, I asked respondents to explain what they thought the purpose of the violence was. I asked them to describe the language they used, and I asked them to explain how they rationalized killing children and other obviously unthreatening civilians. Their answers are below. While they do not conclusively resolve why genocide happened, they do provide insight into the overall logic of extermination.

The Meta-Rationale for Genocide

The main rationale that perpetrators consistently gave for genocidal violence is the following: the RPF killed President Habyarimana; RPF soldiers had invaded to kill Hutus; all Tutsis were RPF supporters or potential supporters; ergo, Hutus had to kill Tutsis to prevent being attacked by them. A range of perpetrators explained the logic of the genocide in this way, no matter what reason they gave for their individual participation. What follows are some representative excerpts, chosen from respondents in different parts of the country. (I identify each respondent's prefecture of origin below.) Most excerpts come from responses to the question, "How did the violence start in your area?"

> After Habyarimana's plane was shot down, people began saying that Tutsis had attacked Byumba and Ruhengeri [prefectures the RPF attacked before 1994], that they had killed the president, and that meant Tutsis were going to finish off Hutus. The war began in this way. (Kibuye)

> After the crash, people said our parent was dead. . . . Since he loved us and we loved him, when he was dead, everyone was affected, and we thought we were finished. People said the enemy had attacked us and that we had to defend ourselves. (Gisenyi)

> I do not remember the date. But people said the president was dead, and he was our parent. Then the Tutsis immediately fled. We saw houses burned here and there. We were angry after the death of our parent. The war began. The Tutsis were killed. (Gikongoro)

> I learned in the morning that the plane crashed. People said. . . . Tutsis did it. We were told, "The Tutsis are the ones who killed the president. They also are going to kill you. You must kill them before they kill you." That is how the killings started. (Kigali-Rural)

The remainder of the chapter will unpack these ideas and demonstrate their prevalence among the perpetrators I interviewed. But what I hope is clear right off the bat is the central importance of security and, to a lesser extent, revenge. Perpetrators frame the logic of violence as self-defense in war or as retaliation for the death of the president. Tutsi civilians were killed, perpetrators say, because Tutsis killed the president and represented a dangerous threat.

How representative were these ideas? I coded each interview by the predominant rationale for the violence expressed in each interview (usually in response to the question, "What was the goal of the killing?"). Table 6.1 reports the results.

There are various rationales here, but the most common concerned security and revenge in war. The importance of war was an unexpected result, and, once I realized its importance, I began to ask respondents whether they thought killing Tutsi civilians was "an act of war" and whether they thought "revenge" for the president's death in general played a role in the genocide. About 81 percent answered affirmatively to the first question (N=106, weighted) and 48 percent to the second (N=99, weighted). The results are consistent: respondents overwhelmingly frame the logic of violence against civilians as war and, to a lesser extent, as revenge. Why perpetrators thought this way, however, is a key question—one that requires closer analysis of the various perpetrator testimonies.

Table 6.1 Main rationales for killing (weighted results)

What was the main reason for killing?	N = 171
Insecurity; "war"; "kill the Tutsis before they kill the Hutus"[a]	47.9%
Revenge for Habyarimana's death[b]	21.1
So authorities could stay in power	3.7
To get rid of the Tutsis	3.5
It was the work of "Satan" or of "meanness"	1.8
It was the law/an order	1.5
To prevent Tutsi monarchy from returning	1.2
Don't know	4.5
Unclear response	13.7

[a]The responses in this category varied, but some typical examples were "the Tutsis killed the president and must be killed otherwise the Hutus will be killed," "the President who kept the peace had been killed and Tutsis must be killed to protect oneself," "kill Tutsis who will exterminate Hutus," "one had to kill the accomplices of the Inkotanyi before they killed us," "fight for the country," "kill the enemy who attacked the country," "win the war," "have security," and "destroy the supporters of the RPF who were the enemy."

[b]Typical examples were statements such as, "the Tutsis killed Habyarimana so they had to be killed," "because the Inkotanyi killed the President, the Tutsis were the enemy," "we had to eliminate the ethnic group (ubwoko) because the Tutsis killed Habyarimana," and "Tutsis had to be killed because they supported those who killed the president."

The Habyarimana Assassination

Many respondents emphasize the importance of President Habyarimana's assassination. In particular, they claim that the president's death signaled that they—as low-level Hutus—were at risk. This is a puzzling idea: it is not immediately obvious why a president's assassination would cause ordinary Hutu men in rural areas around the country to feel that they were in danger. To understand the logic, I reproduce some representative excerpts below and then analyze them.

> When Habyarimana was killed, people said, "It's over. Since they killed Habyarimana, now all the Hutus will be killed." (Gitarama)

> We were told that the plane carrying Habyarimana and Burundi's president had been shot down. That is when the killings began. People understood that if the head of state is killed first, then the peasants would be next—in other words, that the Tutsi regime was coming back. (Ruhengeri)

> With Habyarimana's death, I thought that Tutsis were the enemy. . . . Why? Because, during the war, when the Inkotanyi attacked, they only killed Hutus. Before Habyarimana died, did you think that Tutsis were the enemy? With the 1990 war, I began to think that Tutsis were the enemy because during this period I saw that Hutus were killed. This idea stayed in my head until the period when Habyarimana died. Could you

have killed a Tutsi before the death of the president? No. *Even if Tutsis were the enemy?* No. *Why not?* With the war, we heard that [Fred] Rwigema [the former RPF leader] wanted to take power and we did not think all Tutsis were enemies, but with the death of Habyarimana, we thought that we would be killed next. *Why?* With the attack [before 1994], the elders said that they [the RPF] might bring back the monarchy, but when the *Inkotanyi* spoke, you saw they wanted to take power, not bring back the monarchy. Because of this, I had no conflict with my Tutsi neighbors, but all the same the idea was in my head with the beginning of the war. But with the death of Habyarimana, we saw they were the enemy. . . . We were truly affected. There was even calm. Nothing was heard on the hills. Everyone was affected. *Describe your mood.* I saw that my parents and my neighbors had no peace. They asked themselves, "The Tutsis will take power, where will we go?" (Ruhengeri)

With Habyarimana's death, our leader had been killed. That means we also would be killed. That is why people killed others. . . . On RTLM [the extremist radio station] people said to look for the enemy; the enemy is the Tutsi. We took weapons and we fought them. *You heard the radio, you took a weapon, and you went to look for Tutsis?* Because Habyarimana had just been killed, we thought we were finished and we decided to protect ourselves before they arrived where we lived. (Cyangugu)

The morning that I heard Habyarimana was dead, I asked the person who told me, "Where are we going to flee to?" In each person, there was a derangement. Heads became hot. Thursday afternoon [the day after the president died], we heard the *ibihembe* [a horn made from antelope bone]. It was known that when you heard that instrument people had to meet at the place where the instrument was used. We went there. One among the people there asked others, "Do you know that Habyarimana is dead?" We responded that we knew that. He asked us, "Do you know what we are going to do now?" We answered, "No." He said, "You must kill the Tutsis and the people who opposed Habyarimana and you must loot their goods." It was like that that the killings started. (Kibungo)

Habyarimana's death is central in these excerpts: his assassination signaled war and danger. Respondents claim that President Habyarimana guaranteed their safety as the head of state, and they describe an affectionate relationship to the president. Habyarimana was their "father" or "parent." Perpetrators identified with the president as their own; he seemed to symbolize Hutus. By extension, according to the perpetrators' logic, if the rebels killed Habyarimana, then their next targets would be ordinary Hutus. Ordinary Hutus would suffer the same fate as the president, the reasoning went, and were more vulnerable than the president. As one respondent said, "People understood that if the head of state is killed first, then the peasants would

Table 6.2 Respondent's opinion about the genocide's main cause (weighted)

What was the most important reason for the genocide?	N = 176
Habyarimana's death (attributed to the RPF)	65.4%
"Desire for power," "big bellies," or "egoism"	14.1
Killing by the RPF, "the enemy," or "the Tutsis"	8.4
War	2.4
Government manipulation	1.8
"Satan"	0.2
Looting	0.2
Don't know	7.6

be next." Or, as another said: "Our leader had been killed. That means we also would be killed." What comes through here is a sense of acute insecurity, even panic, in the face of the president's death and the advancing Tutsi rebels.

It is unclear from the excerpts to what degree individuals came to these conclusions on their own or to what degree direct pressure mattered. The latter two excerpts suggest direct encouragement. In one case, there was an informal meeting, and a local leader told the assembled group that because the president had been killed, the time had come to kill Tutsis. In the other case, the respondent describes how radio broadcasts helped convince him of the need to attack Tutsis. But others describe how they themselves concluded and how "people understood" that Hutus were in danger and that Tutsis had to be killed. I interpret these common perceptions as evidence of the tipping point described in chapter 3. In most communities, there came a point when many people understood that killing Tutsis was the new consensus and one that the new authorities backed. I will return to the point. First, I want to give a sense of how representative these excerpts are by reporting results to the question "What was the most important reason for the genocide?" Table 6.2 shows the results.

Nearly two-thirds of the respondents claimed that the president's assassination was the most important cause of the genocide. They gave other reasons, such as elites' "desire for power" and evil "satanic" forces, but the president's death is the top reason the respondents gave for the genocide.

The Language of Killing

I want to turn now to the language of killing. When outside observers comment on the language of the genocide, they often stress

Table 6.3 The language of violence during the genocide (weighted results)

What were these activities called?	N = 146
Fight the enemy (*umwanzi*)[a]	27.4%
War[b]	5.6
Kill the Tutsis[c]	13.2
Kill the *Inyenzi*[d]	0.6
"Kill," "killing," or "massacres"	7.5
"Annihilate" or "exterminate" (*gutsembasemba* or *gutsembaubwoko*)	7.3
"Revenge" for Habyarimana's death	3.4
"Work"	0.6
"Fighting between Hutus and Tutsis"	3.0
"End the conflict between ethnic groups"	0.4
"*Pawa*"	0.2
Mix of the above	4.6
No name	26.0

[a]The key noun that distinguishes the responses in this category was "enemy." Thus, responses included "fight the enemy," "kill the enemy," "combat the enemy," "chase the enemy," and "search for the enemy."

[b]The key idea here is that the violence was part of a broader national conflict. Thus, responses included "war," "fight for the country," "go to the front," "save the country," "assure security," "defend ourselves," and "assure security."

[c]The key noun here is "the Tutsi." The responses included "chase the Tutsi," "search for the Tutsi," "remove the Tutsi," "kill the Tutsi," and "sweep the Tutsi."

[d]The key noun here is *Inyenzi.* The responses include "combat the *Inyenzi*," "kill the *Inyenzi*," or "combat/kill the *Inyenzi* and their accomplices."

that extremist propaganda dehumanized Tutsis. Many observers make much of the fact that during the genocide Tutsis were called "*inyenzi*," which literally means "cockroaches."[1] Hardliners undoubtedly used dehumanizing language both before and during the genocide, and some perpetrators I interviewed used dehumanizing language to describe Tutsis. Sometimes Tutsis were likened to "rats" or "snakes." But in my interviews, the language of threat, danger, and war was far more prevalent than any subhuman metaphors. Many respondents equated Tutsis with the "enemy" (*umwanzi*) or with "accomplices" (*ibiyitso*) of "the enemy." Table 6.3 shows aggregate responses to the question, "What were these activities called?" It was clear that respondents were to describe the terminology surrounding the killings.

Table 6.3 shows that many respondents frame the genocide in terms of threat and security—as "fighting the enemy," as "war," or just as "killing." Some cite the Kinyarwanda word "*gutsembasemba*," which means "total destruction" or "annihilation"; others cite "*gut-*

1. For an example, see Alain Destexhe, *Rwanda and Genocide in the Twentieth Century,* trans. Alison Marschner (New York: New York University Press, 1995), 28.

sembaubwoko," which means "destruction of an ethnic group" or "extermination." A few recall hearing *"inyenzi,"* but the word has a double meaning that should be acknowledged. It does mean "cockroach," but it also is a pejorative synonym for Tutsi rebels. The term was first used in the 1960s when Tutsi rebels attacked Rwanda (more on this in chapter 7); in the 1990s, hardliners recycled the term as a way of denigrating RPF soldiers. Calling Tutsis *"inyenzi"* during the genocide was thus sometimes a nasty way of labeling them as rebels (or potential rebels).

The Kinyarwanda word *"umwanzi"* was so prevalent in my early interviews that I began to ask respondents if they had heard the expression "The Tutsi is the enemy" during the genocide. Of those I asked, 75 percent answered "yes" (N=137, weighted).[2] Again, respondents framed and understood the violence in a security paradigm. The panel of excerpts below shows the same:

> The authorities said our president had just been killed, that he was liked by many people, that you have to kill the Tutsis, that they are our enemies. (Gitarama)

> What pushed us to kill the Tutsis was the death of Habyarimana because we never had a problem with the Tutsis. *How does one go from hearing of the death of the president to killing a neighbor?* I don't know how to explain. You could say his death made everyone crazy; it was like a poison that spread in the population. *Why did you join the group?* I will tell you: the president who maintained peace had just died, so it was said that the enemy was the Tutsi. (Kigali-Rural)

> When we found [Tutsi civilians hiding], because the law said the Tutsi is the enemy, we took them to the sector office, where we gave them to a *cellule* [committee] member who was at a roadblock. . . . *The law said, "The Tutsi is the enemy"?* That was said after the death of Habyarimana, and it spread. *Did local authorities spread that?* Yes, they traveled around the *cellules.* The radio also said it. (Kigali-Rural)

> [A soldier who arrived by car] said, "Guard your own security." I asked, "What security?" He said, "I don't know what your problem is. You know that the *Inkotanyi* have multiplied in the country, and you know that the *Inkotanyi* are Tutsis. There are many of them, and they have killed Habyarimana. You have to protect yourself because they will infiltrate [and hide] amongst their own. . . . You know your Tutsi neighbors. You have to kill them because they are accomplices [of the RPF].

---

2. I included a positive reply if respondents said they heard either this expression or "The enemy is one, it is the Tutsi." The phrases in Kinyarwanda are *"umwanzi ni umwe ni umutusi"* and *"umwanzi ni umutusi."*

You have to kill them. You have to eat their cows. You have to destroy their homes. To combat those outside, you have to first fight those inside. If I come back and if I don't find a body here and the cows are still here, I will make an example out of you." (Butare)

I was at my house. An attack came. . . . This attack took me. . . . *What did they say?* "Others look for the enemy, and you, you, are just sitting here. Come, we will go together." I left like that. *Why did you go?* If I did not go, they would have beaten me because others were beaten in this way. (Gisenyi)

There are a number of important ideas embedded in these excerpts. The key theme is that Tutsis had become "enemies" after the president's assassination and in the context of war. Again, we see the importance of Habyarimana's death. As one respondent said, "The president who maintained peace had just died, so it was said that the enemy was the Tutsi." But these excerpts in particular also show the way in which killing Tutsis became what respondents believed authorities expected of them. Sometimes the communication was direct: in the last two excerpts, a soldier and a group of attackers respectively ordered the respondents to participate in the genocide. But in some of the other excerpts, we see how there was a common perception that killing Tutsis had become the "law" or an activity sanctioned by the authorities.

Killing Civilians

If killing was couched in the language of war, why did perpetrators attack all Tutsi civilians, including those who posed no immediate danger? That question actually resolves itself into two distinct issues: violence against nonthreatening civilians and violence against an entire ethnic group. I examine the questions in turn, through two separate panels of excerpts:

It was understood that if the Tutsis were killed the war would succeed. *Why?* It was said that all Tutsis were accomplices of the *Inkotanyi* and that the *Inkotanyi* came to defend their Tutsis. *And if one kills them, what would that accomplish?* That the *Inkotanyi* could not win battles. (Cyangugu)

Did you think you were working for the nation? I would say we had become crazy. We just learned that the Tutsis were the enemy, and we thought that if we killed them all, they would not have the power to kill us. We believed that if the *Inyenzi* arrived they would find no one, that they would no longer have the force to kill us or to take power. (Ruhengeri)

I was told, "Habyarimana is dead. He was killed by the *Inkotanyi*. Come! We are going to look for the Tutsis. If you do not come, you die." Those are the three [sic] things they told me. . . . *Why were civilians targeted for actions done by [RPF] soldiers?* We could not fight with the soldiers. We fought with those we could fight. . . . *Certainly your neighbors did not kill Habyarimana?* The *Inkotanyi*, they were Tutsis; they were Tutsis so we believed the solution was to kill the Tutsis. *Why was that the solution?* The solution was to kill the Tutsis like Habyarimana was killed. *If they were killed, what did that accomplish?* Nothing. We said we were defending against the enemy. (Ruhengeri)

Why did you join? No man could stay at home. *Why?* The majority went because you would have to pay beer if you did not go. Where could you find this money? *When you heard for the first time that Tutsis had to be killed, what did you think?* I believed it because it was said that people in Umutara [i.e. RPF soldiers] kill people, including women, so when the President died, we believed that was true. *If the plane was shot down by soldiers, why kill all the Tutsis?* To avoid infiltration of the *Inkotanyi* in the area. If one gets rid of all Tutsis, the *Inkotanyi*, if they arrived, they would not find any accomplices. (Kigali-Rural)

In May, things changed. The soldiers came to the countryside . . . and refugees arrived. . . . They gave information about what happened in their communes of origin, that it was the Tutsis from the RPF who made them leave and who had killed Hutus. With this information, we expected death and we knew who the enemy was. It was then that the population was unhappy and that there were divisions [between Hutus and Tutsis]. With all this information, the Hutus decided to get together to combat their enemy who was the Tutsi. . . . *How did you become involved?* I was at my home. I heard whistles and noise. I left the house. I went, as a youth, to see what happened. When I arrived, I found they had a Tutsi child and he was asked where his colleagues were. He was sitting on the ground, and many people were surrounding him. He explained that he did not know where his colleagues were. Someone took him and brought him to the valley, near the river. When they got there, he was hit and asked to reveal RPF secrets. He said he knew nothing. Two boys took him, and tied him. They hit him with a club in the head and he passed directly into the stage of agony, just before dying. My colleague asked me to tie him well with strong rope. I asked my colleagues, "Why kill this child who is my neighbor?" My colleague said he was an *Inyenzi* and they had exterminated our families in Umutara. I asked this youth, "When did he become an *Inyenzi*?" We had learned that the *Inyenzi* had trained in Kimihira [in northern Rwanda], but he had not gone. One among these two others then went to cut a branch; he made a cross and put it in his shirt, so that God would welcome him. (Kigali-Rural)

These excerpts are rich with detail about the genocide, but I want to focus on how perpetrators collapse the difference between a Tutsi civilian and a Tutsi rebel. The respondents call civilians rebel "accomplices," "colleagues," or "supporters." Or perpetrators use the same noun—*inyenzi,* for example—to refer to both rebel soldiers and their alleged civilian supporters. This is most evident in the last excerpt, where an aggressive perpetrator insistently refers to a Tutsi child as an *"inyenzi"* despite what appears to be good reason to doubt that the child was a soldier in civilian clothing.

The mechanism behind the collapsing of civilian and combatant is collective ethnic categorization. Each individual Tutsi stands in for the Tutsis as a collective. Thus, respondents blame all Tutsis for the rebels' alleged assassination of the president. Collective ethnic categorization allowed events occurring at the national level (the assassination and war) to transpose to the local level. With the president's death and the resumption of war, by this logic, "the Tutsis" had attacked "the Hutus."

Another related theme in the excerpts is explicitly strategic: some respondents describe how killing Tutsi civilians was a tactic to weaken, if not defeat, the rebels. By the perpetrators' logic, killing Tutsis would deplete the rebel ranks, stymie infiltration, and deter the rebels. Killing civilians was also expedient. Since Hutu civilians could not realistically fight the rebels, the civilians attacked the rebels' presumed supporters. In other testimony (for an example, see below), perpetrators claimed that Tutsi civilians collected milk and other foodstuffs for the rebels. Killing Tutsi civilians then became a way to weaken the rebels' supply and intelligence lines.

Sexual Violence

I did not focus on sexual violence in my interviews with perpetrators. Very few Rwandan men in fact confessed to raping women—an offense that, under Rwandan law, could carry the death penalty. However, in certain interviews, particularly with the most articulate respondents, I asked about the prevalence of sexual violence. Almost all said that they did not witness rapes; they mostly said that the rule was to kill women, not rape them. A few said that they had heard that women were raped. Others described how women were taken as "wives." By and large, then, very little detail emerged from these interviews about sexual violence.

Below are three excerpts. The first offers some, albeit limited, insight into what happened; the second describes how men forcibly took women as "wives," but how at a certain point the authorities said all Tutsi women had to be killed; the third excerpt is more typical of my interviews in which the respondent said raping of women did not happen in his area.

> *Was there rape?* Yes. *By whom?* Youth. . . . *What happened?* They would find women who were hidden, take them to their place, and then chase them out after a day or two, after having done what he wanted to do. *And you?* No. *Why not?* I was not interested by that. I looked for money. (Kigali-Rural)

> Four days later [after a large attack on Tutsis] the prefect and the burgomaster said that he who sweeps must get rid of the waste, instead of bringing it in the house. They said this because there remained girls who had been taken by young men and were found at their places as wives. It was to say that these women that had been left at the youths' places also had to be killed. We went back, and the next day we went to look for these women because it was known where they were. In our sector, we divided into several groups; the group I was in found three women in three homes. We took them all to a place where they would be killed, and I was ordered to kill one of them. (Butare).

> *Were women raped?* No. Rapes did not happen in our area. (Kibuye)

The Rationales for Extermination

In the excerpts above, an exterminatory rationale is evident: "the Tutsis"—all Tutsis—were called "enemies" and thus categorized as legitimate targets for violence. But why was this the case? Given that many perpetrators invoked war and threat to explain the killing, it would be reasonable to expect that only soldiers or possible soldiers— men of fighting age—would be targets. In most interviews, I broached this question by asking respondents how they explained to themselves the killing of women and children. In other words, if many cited security fears to explain the overall logic of genocide, then why kill those who did not pose an immediate threat? Below are some responses:

> *What was the goal?* Terminate the Tutsis. *Why?* Because it was said that the Tutsis wanted to take back power. *How did one explain to oneself the killing of women and children?* That they were Tutsis. That Kagame had left as a child. (Cyangugu)

How does one explain killing women and children? These women and children, people said they brought food to those who were hiding. (Kigali-Rural)

What was the goal of the killings? To prevent the RPF from taking power. *How could killing accomplish that?* The *Inkotanyi* would no longer receive information from the interior. *Why were women and children considered enemies?* The children and women would reproduce. *And if they reproduced?* They would kill us again as they killed before, as is said in history. (Ruhengeri)

What was the goal? Exterminate the Tutsis. *And then what do people get?* It was said that if the Tutsis were exterminated, then the Hutus would occupy their land. (Ruhengeri)

How does one explain to oneself the killing of women and children? If the women and children remained, they could claim the goods that had been looted. (Kigali)

What was the goal? Kill the Tutsis and all persons who opposed Habyarimana. *And then what?* I don't know if in your country, there are people who know nothing. What happened in Rwanda was the loss of intelligence. I told you that it had been decided that we had to kill Tutsis; we did not differentiate age or sex. (Kibungo)

Before the death of Habyarimana, we had no problem. With the death of Habyarimana, the Hutus, all Hutus, felt threatened by the Tutsis who attacked the country. . . . You understand the distrust between two ethnic groups. A president killed by another ethnic group? *But why kill all Tutsis?* That, no! Ehhh! That is the reasoning of an American. People are created like that. If you do something bad to me, will I have good intentions for your children? This is the logic of Africans. (Gitarama)

In these excerpts, there are five somewhat distinct rationales perpetrators give to explain and justify killing all Tutsi civilians. First, killing all Tutsis would prevent a future threat: children were killed so that they would not become rebels in the future, and women were killed so they would not give birth to children who would become future rebels. That is what the perpetrator from Cyangugu means when he says that, "Kagame had left as a child." The reference is to Paul Kagame, then the RPF rebel leader, who had been a child when his parents left for exile in the early 1960s. The implication is that since Kagame was spared in the past and ultimately grew up to be a rebel, all Tutsis should be killed this time.

Second, women and children were seen as a fifth column of support for the rebels. Thus, killing them was a way to weaken the soldiers' fighting force and more generally a way to defeat the rebels. In short, women and children aided combatants and therefore were considered akin to combatants.

Third, there is a rationale of material gain: if all the Tutsis were killed, then their property could be taken. The rationale here is that if some Tutsi family members survived, then they could make a claim to that property or they could identify who had stolen property.

Fourth, killing all Tutsis was seen as what the authorities had ordered, as what was expected of people—the new order of genocide. Thus, when asked why women and children were killed, individual perpetrators said, for example, "It was decided that we had to kill Tutsis." Others used different constructions, but the basic rationale was that all Tutsis were killed because "the Tutsis"—all Tutsis—had been declared the enemy. As we shall see in a moment, this type of response was the most common.

Fifth, there is again the rationale of collective ethnic categorization. Why were Tutsi women and children killed? Because, said the respondent from Gitarama—who was a sub-prefect (and thus a comparatively high level civilian official) at the time of the genocide—that is what happens in Africa: a whole category of people is blamed for the actions of one or a few.

To probe these questions in more detail, I asked respondents how they explained to themselves the killing of women and children. Their aggregate answers are given in table 6.4.

There is a range of reasons that respondents offered as to why Tutsi women and children were killed. But the most frequent was that during this period there was a common understanding that all Tutsis had to be killed. As some said, "the law" was to kill Tutsis.

Local Leaders and Killers

To examine further the rationale for extermination—a critical question for the study of genocide—I turn now to those respondents who admitted to the highest degree of participation. These are the local-level leaders and "thugs" whose actions I discussed in chapters 3, 4, and 5. I begin here with excerpts from two local elites. The first is from the man from a well-connected family in Kayove quoted at length in chapter 3.

> I told you it was anger. When one is angry, one does not think. . . . We believed that the Tutsis would come to kill us so we had to kill them first instead of waiting for them to kill us. Me, I saw on television how they kill and I saw it was extreme meanness. *What is difficult for me to*

Table 6.4 The rationale for extermination (weighted results)[a]

How did one explain to oneself the killing of women and children?	N = 140
All Tutsis had to be killed[b]	24.4%
Win the war[c]	12.9
Prevent survivors from avenging, identifying killers, or reclaiming property	6.7
The RPF or "enemy" also killed women and children	3.7
If one family member is killed, the whole family must be killed (including a metaphor about rats)[d]	5.1
Prevent the RPF from taking power/prevent monarchy from returning	2.3
Take property	1.3
It was the work of "Satan" or of "meanness"	1.4
Collective revenge for Habyarimana's death	1.0
Authorities benefited	0.4
Women not killed	9.8
Don't know	22.3
No reason/unclear response	5.9

[a]I coded answers by identifying the most prominent or main rationale given for killing women and children, thus attributing only one rationale per respondent even though some offered multiple rationales in the course of the interview.

[b]Responses included "one killed the *ubwoko*," "all Tutsi were targeted," "the ubwoko was targeted/chased," "that was the law," "it was like that," "there was no differentiation," and "they were killed without exception."

[c]In addition to simply "it was to win the war," responses in this category include "to have peace," "to resolve the problem," "women and children supported the enemy," and "so Hutus could be alone."

[d]The "rat metaphor" refers to a Rwandan proverb that some respondents cited. They said if a rat is killed, then the unborn baby rat in the adult rat's belly also had to be killed.

understand is, if you were afraid of being killed, why kill women and children? When we look back at what happened, we too do not understand how this happened because we no longer had pardon in this period. Even if there was someone among us who had pitied someone, we killed him immediately with the other. *If the Tutsis were terminated, what did that accomplish?* You terminate them and go to the front. The *Inkotanyi* were very strong and they pushed us. . . . *If you terminated them, was that a way of having peace?* Yes, that's true. We thought that if we could terminate them that would give us peace because they would not live with us. . . . *Why were [your neighbors] killed?* Because some among them sent contributions to the *Inkotanyi* to buy weapons, and others sent children. . . . *How did you explain to yourself the killing of women and children?* Is the wife not happy for her children who were in the *Inkotanyi* who would come to rule? *And the children?* Would he not grow up to join his colleagues? *According to you, were these killings an act of war?* Yes, and they also killed our children. Did you not see those who fled Byumba [that is, those who fled in fear of the RPF]? Were they not women and children? That is why we were angry. (Gisenyi)

What was the goal of these killings? I explained it to you, that the *Inkotanyi* attacked to terminate the Hutus, that is why it was necessary for the Hutus to kill the Tutsis. *How did you explain to yourself the killing of women and children?* We were given information that said those who were attacking were those who had fled before. That is why there was no separation [among men, women, and children]. *You said before you had good relations with your Tutsi neighbors, that they were not accomplices. Why all of a sudden did they become the same as the Inkotanyi?* Rwandans, we very much like to respect laws. That is why a Rwandan will never refuse what he is told to do. *I don't understand.* It is understandable! Starting with the information of the soldiers that I spoke of, that is the way to make Rwandans understand. *But you accepted?* Yes, I accepted. That is the secret of the soldiers. They could inform someone here and word would spread to everyone in the enclosure [entire prison]. (Kibuye)

These are the themes we saw above. To explain the violence, the respondent from Gisenyi cites (1) anger at Habyarimana's death, (2) fear that the Tutsis in general represented a threat to all Hutus, (3) outrage that civilians were a fifth column of military support who supplied and financed the rebels, (4) a desire to punish civilians for supposedly supporting the rebels, (5) the notion that children could grow up and attack later, and, relevantly, (6) a lack of self-understanding about the killings. That so many themes can be present in a single narrative—albeit from one of the most articulate respondents I interviewed—suggests that all these emotions, fears, and myths were involved in the violence. However, the dominant theme in this narrative is that the Hutus were fighting a defensive war against the Tutsis.

The Kibuye interviewee articulates some similar themes, but his account is particularly interesting for the way in which he describes how killing was synonymous with authority during the genocide. "We were given information" by soldiers, he insisted when pressed to explain why all Tutsi civilians were killed. And Rwandans, he continued, "like to respect laws."

The most aggressive killers strike similar themes. I quote two excerpts below:

Were there many deaths this day? About 300. . . . *What was your spirit like? Were you angry?* After having seen what happened, I would say I was no longer a person. My heart was no longer open, and I thought what just happened would also happen to me. *What does that mean exactly?* We were told the enemy was near us, and that if the enemy arrived, we too would be killed. *Why kill people?* It was said the enemy was the

Tutsi who had to be killed. *And you believed it?* How can you not accept things said by the high authorities while you are a peasant? *Did you kill this day?* Yes. I cut a person. *Did you change after killing a person?* After we continued, I did not think of what happened until I came here in this prison, after returning from Congo [a two-year period]. *Did you loot something this day?* We looted at Nyamata. *Why?* If you killed someone, you must take his things; you can't leave his things without owners. *Did you kill to take things?* No, we killed these people because we were told they were the enemy. . . . *Why was it necessary to kill children?* I don't know. Maybe it was that the *ubwoko* [the ethnic category] was hunted in this period. *Did it occur to you that it was wrong to kill a child?* I told you in this period I did not reflect any more to say this is a person. (Kigali-Rural)

Why were children targeted? It was said that the people who had left were children, and they were attacking the country [the RPF]. . . . *Why target the women?* In these massacres, Tutsis were targeted, without taking account of their age, sex, education, or even handicap. *Why?* Because each was an enemy, even a woman. *Why?* I explained. What don't you understand? *A woman is not threatening.* Even if she is not threatening, but how can you leave her if you have killed her children and her husband, how can you live with her? *And the elderly?* The one who killed the woman could not leave the elder. *What does that mean?* Because it was said there was a moment when the Tutsis must bring someone with whom he had to stand up using a sword, that the elder knew how to do it and they had done it. (Ruhengeri)

Again, the themes of war and order dominate these excerpts. Both respondents say that killing Tutsis were acts of war *and* that it was what the authorities had decreed.

But the passages point to other important dynamics. The first respondent, for instance, says he was "no longer a person" and that his heart was "no longer open." This resonates with the quote from the Gisenyi man above in which he said he "no longer had pardon." Both constructions suggest that witnessing violence and killing hardened and intensified the angry determination of the most violent perpetrators. Other interviewees describe how some perpetrators changed their demeanor after having killed. As one respondent quoted above said, some people became "crazy in the head" during this period.

On reflection, this makes sense, especially because these perpetrators were not professional soldiers and had no prior experience with killing. Whatever the emotions and feelings they experienced after killing another person in close proximity—anxiety, horror, shame, guilt, hysteria, fear, satisfaction, or all of these—one common outward response was to become more aggressive, to close off "pardon" and "openness," and to demand others kill as they had killed. Here we see how in the context of official encouragement and instructions to kill, the violence had a momentum of its own. Having killed, the most aggressive perpetrators and local leaders hardened and engendered others to do as they had done, thereby extending and spreading the violence that had already started.

There is one last theme worthy of explication: the myth of Tutsi viciousness. We see this in the excerpt from the Ruhengeri perpetrator. When pressed to explain why elders were killed, he raised the specter of a gruesome legend. He said that during monarchical times, Tutsis supposedly stood up using a sword—a reference to how the Tutsi queen mother supposedly got out of bed every morning by plunging a sword into a Hutu and standing up. Several respondents mentioned the myth in my interviews. It captures the fears of Tutsi cruelty during the monarchy, fears that the Hutu hardliners stoked before and during the genocide. It is clear that for some perpetrators, especially the most violent, the fear of historical Tutsi viciousness played a role.

Cross-Referencing the Interviews

When considering after-the-fact perpetrator testimony, there is a critical question that must be asked: are their claims, especially those about fear, war, and orders from above, post-hoc rationalizations used to mask other dynamics? It is difficult to know for certain, but I check by comparing statements made during or very close in time to the actual violence with the testimony above. Below is a panel of excerpts from radio broadcasts, letters, and other interviews with perpetrators during or just after the genocide. I begin with the radio broadcasts:

> You must truly stand firm, combat these enemies, truly destroy them, in short, defend yourself. (RTLM broadcast, April 10, 1994)[3]

> Soldiers, gendarmes, and all Rwandans have decided to fight their common enemy. . . . The enemy is still the same. He is the one who has always been trying to return the monarch who was overthrown. . . . The Ministry of Defense asks Rwandans, soldiers and gendarmes the following: citizens are asked to act together, carry out patrols, and fight the enemy. (Radio Rwanda broadcast, April 12, 1994)[4]

3. My translation of French broadcast reported in Article 19, *Broadcasting Genocide: Censorship, Propaganda, and State-Sponsored Violence in Rwanda, 1990–1994* (London: Article 19, 1996), note 16, 147.
4. Alison Des Forges, *Leave None to Tell the Story: Genocide in Rwanda* (New York: Human Rights Watch, 1999), 203.

What is happening in Rwanda has never been seen elsewhere. . . . Nowhere else in the world has one seen a minority ethnic group take up arms and try to defy the majority ethnic group in trying to exterminate them. (RTLM broadcast, April 13, 1994)[5]

This war that we bring is a very important war. . . . They can call it what they want, but it's a war of extermination, a war unleashed by the *Inkotanyi,* because it was they who unleashed it in order to exterminate the Hutu. (RTLM broadcast, May 14, 1994)[6]

Some moments ago, I was late due to a small *Inkotanyi* captured in Kimisagara . . . aged 14 . . . this small dirty *Inkotanyi* with big ears who would come with a jerrican pretending to go to fetch water but he was observing the guns of our soldiers. (RTLM broadcast June 5, 1994)[7]

Our enemy is one/We know him/It is the Tutsi (song heard in the streets of Kigali)[8]

Communal administrators: please maintain roadblocks, [night patrols], barriers. Please distribute weapons to the population to defend themselves. . . . If a farmer hears shooting let him stop cultivating and go to fight. . . . That is guerilla warfare. . . . Rather than fleeing, go and search for the enemy and fight back. (RTLM broadcast, genocide period, 1994)[9]

If you see deserters, arrest them wherever they are. . . . Let them save their country. They ought not to escape. Beat them up, refuse them food, drinks, take them to the authorities so that they can go back to the battlefield. . . . They have to fight and fight the enemy. (RTLM broadcast, genocide period, 1994)[10]

This selection of excerpts demonstrates that the themes heard from my interviewees are similar to those on the radio during the genocide. The central notions in these excerpts are that Tutsis have attacked Hutus, that Tutsis seek to destroy Hutus, and that the Hutus must defend themselves against "the enemy." In some instances, Hutus are implored to wage war against the rebel troops and their civilian base

5. My translation based on the French in Jean-Pierre Chrétien et al., *Les médias du génocide* (Paris: Karthala, 1994), 196–97.
6. My translation based on the French in Chrétien et al., *Les médias du génocide,* 202–3. For similar statements, see International Criminal Tribunal for Rwanda, "The Prosecutor v. Ferdinand Nahimana, Jean-Bosco Barayagwiza, Hassan Ngeze," Case No. ICTR–99–52–T, Judgement and Sentence, December 3, 2003, 136, 146.
7. ICTR, "The Prosecutor v. Ferdinand Nahimana," 140.
8. Des Forges, *Leave None,* 203.
9. African Rights, *Rwanda: Death, Despair, and Defiance,* rev. ed. (London: African Rights, 1995), 80–81. The book does not cite a specific date for the broadcast but rather says that this broadcast (and others) happened in "April and May 1994."
10. African Rights, *Rwanda,* 82.

of support. Moreover, the radio broadcasts call on all Hutus, under penalty of punishment, to participate.

Other statements, this time from high-level officials implicated in the genocide, reveal the same themes.

> All of us, together, must wage this war. . . . It is a final war, it must be finished. (Interim Prime Minister Jean Kambanda on Radio Rwanda, April 21, 1994)[11]

> During these difficult periods, our wish is that the [security] forces be assisted by all able-bodied members of the population; all, all of us. Let no one say "This does not concern me." . . . Security is not a matter for the gendarmes alone. (Interim President Theodore Sindikubwabo, April 21, 1994)[12]

> Whoever does not have his identity card should be arrested and maybe lose his head there. . . . One should have his identity card with him, showing that he is Rwandan and that he is the son of [a] cultivator, that he is not an enemy or an accomplice, that he is not an *Inkotanyi*. (CDR Militia leader on RTLM, May 1994)[13]

> The President was Hutu. When he was killed, in the Hutu mind, they thought the Tutsis were going to bring back their regime and that we the Hutus were going to work for them again. (François Karera, former prefect, interviewed August 14, 1994)[14]

> The message was a simple one—all Tutsis were supporters of the Patriotic Front and if the Front won the war, all Hutu would be killed. (Journalist's summary of statements by perpetrators interviewed in August 1994)[15]

> The destruction of the presidential [plane] . . . is the straw that broke the camel's back. . . . For four years, the RPF has used the gun, the grenade, mines, rope, the hoe, the mortar and I don't know what else to sow desolation and terror. The ripping open of pregnant women and the massacres of innocent civilians by a blow of the hoe to the head. . . . Isn't it evident that the RPF had put everything in place to implement an ethnic purge from the [moment of the] assassination of the President? (Interim Minister of Health Casimir Bizimungu, writing to African Rights on October 7, 1994)[16]

11. Article 19, *Broadcasting Genocide*, 140
12. Article 19, *Broadcasting Genocide*, 141.
13. Article 19, *Broadcasting Genocide*, 116.
14. Jane Perlez, "Under the Bougainvillea, A Litany of Past Wrongs," *New York Times*, August 15, 1994.
15. Raymond Bonner, "Rwandans in Death Squad Say Choice Was Kill or Die," *New York Times*, August 14, 1994, A16.
16. African Rights, *Rwanda*, 167.

The themes in these excerpts are consistent with the others.[17] The language of the violence is war—a "final war," as the interim prime minister said—and the aim of the violence is "security," as the interim president said. The difference between "the Tutsis" and the RPF or "*Inkotanyi*" is collapsed, as the militia leader's statement and the journalist's summary show. Both terms become synonymous with "enemy." Moreover, several respondents display an acute fear of being killed by the RPF, in light of the rebels' alleged assassination of President Habyarimana, in light of the rebels' alleged killing of civilians during the war, and in light of "the Tutsis'" alleged harsh treatment of Hutus during monarchical times. And, finally, as the interim president makes clear, "security" was the responsibility of all: there was pressure for all able-bodied men to participate. These are precisely the themes that perpetrators cited in my interviews with them.

Overall, the chapter shows that there were many variations on how perpetrators explain the logic of genocide. But the testimony above reinforces the importance of three themes that appear throughout this book. First, the language and logic of war dominates these narratives. Killing is called "war"; the victims are called "enemies" and enemy "accomplices." Inflammatory radio broadcasts likely contributed to this perception, but so did the actual circumstances of war and the legends of rebel violence against civilians during the war. So too did historical myths about the ruthlessness of the Tutsi monarchy toward Hutus. But especially critical was the president's assassination. In narrative after narrative, perpetrators describe how the president's death crystallized an abstract fear, which in turn gave wartime propaganda a new resonance and saliency. Tutsi neighbors rapidly transformed into nascent threats, into rebel supporters whose ultimate goal was Hutu extermination. The Hutus' task became very basic: attack first. There is a cluster of emotions and mechanisms at work here. They include fear, anger, revenge, self-defense, and security. Men killed because they thought they were in combat. They killed to win the war, to avenge the death of their leader, and to protect themselves. The aim was "security" in a context of acute insecurity.

17. See, for example, the statements by hardliners in Ruhengeri Prefecture, where the killing of Habyarimana was said to justify the extermination of the Tutsi: International Criminal Tribunal for Rwanda, "The Prosecutor v. Juvénal Kajelijeli," Case No. ICTR-98-44A-T, 96–98, 106. For other examples of similar themes, see Alan Zarembo, "Judgment Day," *Harper's*, April 1997, 68–80.

But why kill all Tutsis, combatants and noncombatants? Why exterminate? Here we see the second major theme: collective ethnic categorization or what I also refer to as "race." Over and over again,
perpetrators speak of the Tutsis as a unit, as "one." Over and over
again, Tutsis stop being neighbors, friends, and a disparate population:
they become a single entity with identical—and permanent—intentions. And over and over again in these narratives, the category—"the
Tutsi"—substitutes for the individual. As many said, "*Umwanzi ni
umwe ni umutusi*" ("The enemy is one, it is the Tutsi"). Embedded in
this phrase is the foundation for genocide. That all Tutsis could become "one" and more specifically "one enemy" is what allowed a security rationale to become a rationale for extermination. This was not
a war against an army, but against "the Tutsis."

Is this evidence of preexisting ethnic hatred? Did widespread prejudice lead to Tutsis being called the "enemy"? My research suggests
that the answer is no. In Rwanda, in most times and places, Hutus and
Tutsis lived side by side throughout the country and intermarried
without deep underlying animosity or tension. Yet there was widespread awareness in Rwandan society that "Hutu" and "Tutsi" represented different ethnic categories, even different "races"—even if
such differentiation did not usually give rise to deep antipathy. What
the evidence suggests is that acute insecurity and orders from above
ignited a categorical logic of race and ethnicity. In a defensive battle,
after a presidential assassination, and in the context of orders to kill,
Tutsis became "the enemy." In short, neighbors became enemies in
war and under the authorities' direction.

Hence the third major theme of these narratives: authorization. Perpetrator after perpetrator describes how killing Tutsis was considered
de facto policy. The authorities had ordered and legitimized killing;
the idea that "Tutsi is the enemy" came from the top. Perpetrators interpret killing then as a "law," as what the authorities had decreed,
that required participation from the population. In this sense, killing
Tutsis became a mandatory, state-sanctioned project, and, as such, a
basis for authority. As we saw in chapter 3, local elites and killers
claimed power and legitimacy on the basis of adhering to the order to
fight the enemy decreed from above. As we see here, many ordinary
men believed that "the law" required that they participate in the extermination of Tutsis.

In sum, we see in this chapter, through close analysis of perpetrator
rationales for killing, the central three dynamics that drove genocide:
war, race, and power. War—and its attendant dynamics of fear, inse-

curity, rage, revenge, and self-defense—ignited the rationale for killing. Race—and its attendant dynamic of collective categorization—ignited the rationale for making Tutsis, all Tutsis, the enemy. Power—that is, the hardliners' ability to control a plurality of force in government-controlled Rwanda and to issue instructions to fight the Tutsi enemy—authorized the killing. These dimensions were all in play; they are difficult to disentangle. But together they combined to make genocide the order of the day in Rwanda during the hundred days between the president's assassination and the RPF victory.

7 Historical Patterns of Violence

It is time for a historical turn. The 1994 genocide was by far the most intense episode of violence in Rwanda's recent history, but it is not the first. Violence broke out in 1959, in the early 1960s, in 1973, and at several points in the early 1990s. In each case, the violence had a similar character to the 1994 genocide. In each case, civilians—almost always Tutsi civilians—were attacked and, on some occasions, massacred (though, again, the episodes were considerably less intense than the 1994 genocide). By the same token, anti-Tutsi killing in Rwanda was by no means constant across time; during most of the forty years of Rwandan history preceding the genocide, ethnic peace or an absence of ethnic violence was more common than ethnic killing. The same is true for ethnic ideologies: public calls for Hutu nationalism emerged and receded in different periods.

One interpretation of Rwanda's history of anti-Tutsi violence is that killing Tutsis was a routine, even legitimate, practice in Rwandan society. In my interviews with perpetrators, I tried to test the theory. The overwhelming majority of respondents said they considering killing *un*common. The question I asked was: "There have been other massacres in Rwandan history. At the time of the killing, did you think about this or was this remarked?" Only 8.6 percent answered some version of "yes" (N=99, weighted). If they had heard of pre-1990 episodes of violence, respondents said that in the past Tutsi homes had been burned and Tutsis chased off their land but not killed in large numbers. Overall, then, my interviews with perpetrators did not support the idea that Rwandan men were, before the genocide, habituated to killing Tutsis or that massacring Tutsis was part of a standard repertoire of violence.

That being the case, my approach to the historical episodes of violence is slightly different. Rather than seeing prior violence as teleological precursors to genocide or as evidence of a norm of anti-Tutsi killing in Rwandan society, I examine the past as comparative points of reference. In theory, whatever dynamics were at work during the genocide should be at work during prior episodes of violence, though on a smaller scale. I examine prior episodes of violence, then, not as genocide "rehearsals" but as less intense versions of a similar type of violence. The point is not to equate prior episodes with the genocide; much changed in Rwandan history between 1959 and 1994, and the genocide was on a very different scale in the earlier episodes. Yet the comparative historical analysis (of one country across time) can reveal commonalities that in turn can provide more analytic leverage on the findings in previous chapters. In other words, this chapter's historical analysis is another way to triangulate evidence—another way to examine the conditions and mechanisms that precipitate ethnic violence in Rwanda.

All told, I find that violence against Tutsi civilians consistently occurs during periods of imminent political change when political power is unsettled and the country is destabilized. The violence also tends to follow an armed attack. By contrast, violence is largely absent when political control is clearly established. These findings lead to some deceptively simple arguments: (1) the central mechanisms driving violence are uncertainty and acute insecurity, and (2) violence is a means to assert power when power is most threatened. The findings also have some surprising implications for modeling the dynamics of genocide and for explaining why the violence in 1994 was so intense, as we shall see.

The chapter is laid out in five main sections. The first four are close analyses of episodes of anti-Tutsi violence before the genocide. Though I have tried to simplify Rwanda's complex history, the discussion is still quite detailed, and I ask readers unfamiliar with the history to be patient with the many names and places. The details are essential to understand the dynamics that ultimately resulted in violence. The fifth section is a close analysis of one of the most notorious pre-genocide speeches by a MRND hardliner, Léon Mugesera. In the 1992 screed, Mugesera warned ominously of extermination and sending Tutsis "home" to Ethiopia. Many observers now point to the speech as evidence of a genocidal mentality well before the actual events of 1994. The analysis here reveals that Mugesera's obsessions resonate with the earlier episodes of anti-Tutsi violence. Violence is a response to uncertainty and threat in periods of unsettled authority, imminent change, and war.

The Rwandan Revolution: 1957–62

The first major episode of violence in Rwanda occurred during the terminal colonial period. On the eve of independence, there were four principal political actors: (1) the Belgian colonial authorities, who, having initially backed the Tutsi aristocracy, now came under international pressure to prepare Rwanda for independence, which led to reforms that benefited Hutus; (2) an emergent Hutu counter-elite, which, with Catholic Church support, decried Hutu oppression under the Tutsi-led monarchy and claimed democratization meant an ethnic redistribution of power;[1] (3) Tutsi traditionalists, who argued that ethnicity was not a relevant political factor and that democracy meant independence from European rule;[2] and (4) Tutsi and Hutu moderates, who called for political compromise and gradual change.

The year 1959 was critical. In January, Belgium declared its intention to grant independence to the Congo, making the same seem inevitable for Rwanda. Then on July 25, the Rwandan king died unexpectedly and mysteriously. He had traveled to Usumbura, the Burundi capital, to see a film. The king had an aperitif at a hotel; he asked to see his Belgian doctor, who administered a penicillin-based injection. The king collapsed and then died. The cause remains unclear: some argue suicide, some argue Belgian poisoning, some argue a bad reaction to the injection, and still others argue murder by Tutsi elites.[3]

At the time, however, the king's sudden death created a serious crisis in Rwanda.[4] Some Hutu politicians called for a republic. Tutsi traditionalists, however, quickly installed a successor monarch—but

1. The clearest manifestation of the Hutu elites' political position is the 1957 "Bahutu Manifesto." An English version is found in Trusteeship Council, "Report of the United Nations Visiting Mission to Trust Territories in East Africa, 1957, on Ruanda-Urundi," UN document T/1346, New York, 1958, 39–42 (hereafter *1957 Report*).

2. The clearest manifestation of the Tutsi traditionalists' political position is found in the 1957 "Statement of Views," available in English in Trusteeship Council, *1957 Report*, 42–46.

3. For a review of these hypotheses, see Filip Reyntjens, *Pouvoir et droit au Rwanda* (Tervuren, Belgium: Musée Royale de L'Afrique Centrale, 1985), 239–41; and Jean-Paul Harroy, *Rwanda: Souvenirs d'un compagnon de la marche du Rwanda vers la démocratie et l'independence* (Brussels: Hayez. 1984), 269–70.

4. See Trusteeship Council, "United Nations Visiting Mission to Trust Territories in East Africa, 1960: Report on Ruanda-Urundi," United Nations Document T/1538, 1960, 20–22 (hereafter *1960 Report*).

without first consulting the Belgian authorities. The appointment was widely interpreted as a "coup d'état," and it worsened already strained relations with Belgium.[5] Shortly thereafter, political parties legally formed in Rwanda for the first time. There were four main parties: the Party of the Movement for Hutu Emancipation (PARMEHUTU) and the Association for the Social Promotion of the Masses (APROSOMA), both of which represented the Hutu counter-elite; the Rwandan National Union (UNAR), which represented the Tutsi traditionalists; and the Rwandan Democratic Assembly (RADER), which represented the moderates.[6]

In this context—the king's death, the formation of political parties, impending decolonization, and rapidly deteriorating relations with the Belgian authorities—UNAR resorted to violence.[7] Party activists intimidated both Hutu and Tutsi opponents, calling them, in one instance, "traitors," "enemies," and "snakes" whom the population should "exterminate."[8] UNAR leaders also denounced the Belgians and the Catholic hierarchy.[9]

On November 1, young Tutsi militants associated with UNAR went one step further by roughing up Dominique Mbonyumutwa, a leading Hutu politician who at the time was one of only ten Hutu sub-chiefs in the country.[10] UNAR partisans had previously threatened to kill Mbonyumutwa and his supporters, and, indeed, after the attack rumors circulated that UNAR party members had killed him.[11] Later that day, another Hutu political leader was attacked.[12]

5. Trusteeship Council, *1960 Report*, 20–22; Harroy, *Rwanda*, 261–78; René Lemarchand, *Rwanda and Burundi* (London: Pall Mall, 1970), 156–58; Fidèle Nkundabagenzi, *Rwanda politique, 1958–1960* (Brussels: Centre de recherche et d'information sociopolitique, 1961), 87–92; and Reyntjens, *Pouvoir et droit*, 241–50.

6. For more details on the parties and their representatives, see Nkundabagenzi, *Rwanda politique*, 92–103, 113–23, 125–37; Reyntjens, *Pouvoir et droit*, 250–60; and Trusteeship Council, *1960 Report*, 24, 37–40.

7. On the perception of crisis, see Trusteeship Council, *1960 Report*, 20–27; Reyntjens, *Pouvoir et droit*, 250–60; and Harroy, *Rwanda*, 282–89, 301.

8. Trusteeship Council, *1960 Report*, 25; Harroy, *Rwanda*, 284–94; Jean Hubert, *La touissant rwandaise et sa répression* (Brussels: Academie royale des sciences d'outremer, 1965), 29, 62.

9. Trusteeship Council, *1960 Report*, 25.

10. Accounts differ as to whether he was in PARMEHUTU or in APROSOMA. For the former, see Trusteeship Council, *1960 Report*, 27; for the latter, see Hubert, *La toussaint rwandaise*, 62. That he was one of ten Hutu subchiefs comes from Reyntjens, *Pouvoir et droit*, 260.

11. Hubert, *La toussaint rwandaise*, 62; Harroy, *Rwanda*, 301.

12. See the Commission of Inquiry report on the events in November in Nkundabagenzi, *Rwanda politique*, 149.

The attacks triggered a wave of counterattacks against UNAR activists.[13] On November 3, a Tutsi chief in the area convened a security meeting, which prompted PARMEHUTU politicians to lead a crowd of about one hundred Hutus to the chief's doorstep. Around that time, according to a Belgian investigation, a Tutsi sub-chief arrived to attend the meeting, and the crowd hurled rocks at him. The sub-chief later emerged from the meeting, allegedly threatening and insulting the assembled crowd, and eventually wielding a bow and arrow. The crowd responded by invading the house, killing the Tutsi chief as well as three other Tutsis.[14]

For the next ten days, Rwanda roiled in violence. There were mainly two kinds of attacks. The first consisted of Hutu crowds, usually of young men, attacking Tutsis and property owned by Tutsis. In general, these attacks were limited to the looting and burning of Tutsi dwellings, but the violence was sometimes fatal.[15] The second kind of attacks consisted of UNAR partisans and/or supporters of the monarchy—both Hutus and Tutsis—beating, arresting, torturing, or assassinating political leaders from the main opposition parties.[16]

The Hutu attacks against Tutsis spread quickly: first to several areas in Gitarama and Kigali the night of the third of November, then to Gisenyi, Ruhengeri and Kibuye on the sixth, to Byumba and other areas in Gisenyi on the seventh, to other areas in Ruhengeri on the eighth, and finally to other areas in Gitarama and Kigali on the ninth and tenth. The attacks did not reach Astrida (Butare), Cyangugu, or Kibungo, and they ended around the twelfth of November.[17] In total, an estimated five thousand dwellings were burnt, and seven to ten thousand refugees fled the country.[18] A Belgian investigation found that thirteen Tutsi men had been killed, mostly while defending their homes.[19]

The attackers were primarily bands of youths. As in the genocide,

13. Trusteeship Council, *1960 Report*, 27.

14. This account is based on Hubert, *La toussaint rwandaise*, 63–64. For another description of the events of November 3, see Trusteeship Council, *1960 Report*, 27.

15. Hubert, *La toussaint rwandaise*, 65; Trusteeship Council, *1960 Report*, 28.

16. For this period, in addition to the documents cited below, see Nkundabagenzi, *Rwanda politique*, 141–58.

17. Trusteeship Council, *1960 Report*, 27–28; Hubert, *La toussaint rwandaise*, 31–32; and Harroy, *Rwanda*, 304.

18. Trusteeship Council, *1960 Report*, 32; Harroy, *Rwanda*, 304–5; Reyntjens, *Pouvoir et droit*, 261.

19. Hubert, *La toussaint rwandaise*, 34, 40; Belgian Government Commission of Inquiry quoted in Nkundabagenzi, *Rwanda politique*, 149; and Harroy, *Rwanda*, 304–5.

many also compelled others to participate.[20] A United Nations investigating team described the attacks this way:

> The operations were generally carried out by a fairly similar process. Incendiaries set off in bands of ten. Armed with matches and paraffin, which the indigenous inhabitants used in large quantities for their lamps, they pillaged the Tutsi houses they passed on their way and set fire to them. On their way they would enlist other incendiaries to follow in the procession while the first recruits, too exhausted to continue, would give up and return home. Thus, day after day fires spread from hill to hill.[21]

As René Lemarchand argues in his detailed study of the period, the November Hutu attacks were akin to a *jacquerie,* to "rural riots."[22]

The official Belgian interpretation was that the attacks constituted revolutionary violence, the "exteriorization of several generations of anger."[23] However, there is substantial evidence to the contrary. Many Hutu arsonists apparently thought the king had ordered Tutsi homes to be destroyed because Tutsis were supposedly holding the king prisoner.[24] Other arsonists thought they were acting on behalf of the Belgian administration. On one occasion, attackers followed a Belgian military reconnaissance plane, thinking that the aircraft indicated the direction in which the king and the authorities wanted them to travel. Some sought paraffin from Belgian administrators to help with the burning.[25]

By contrast, the violence initiated by UNAR and the monarchy targeted politicians, mostly Hutu ones. On November 5, the king's representatives summoned all Rwandans—Hutu, Tutsi, and Twa—to the seat of the royal court in Nyanza. Drums were beaten, costumes donned, men told to bring their weapons to defend the monarchy

20. On this point and the previous one, see the notes from a missionary in Gitarama quoted in Lemarchand, *Rwanda and Burundi,* 163–64; and Jean-Claude Willame, *Aux sources de l'hécatombe rwandaise* (Brussels: CEDAF, 1995), 53.

21. Trusteeship Council, *1960 Report,* 28.

22. Hubert, *La toussaint rwandaise,* 32; Lemarchand, *Rwanda and Burundi,* 168; and Willame, *Aux sources,* 53.

23. Harroy, *Rwanda,* 304; Hubert, *La toussaint rwandaise,* 65.

24. Belgian Government Commission of Inquiry quoted in Nkundabagenzi, *Rwanda politique,* 150; Trusteeship Council, *1960 Report,* 28; Hubert, *La toussaint rwandaise,* 32, 95–97; Willame, *Aux sources,* 56; Lemarchand, *Rwanda and Burundi,* 164; and Harroy, *Rwanda,* 303.

25. Trusteeship Council, *1960 Report,* 28; Hubert, *La toussaint rwandaise,* 32–33; Belgian Government Commission of Inquiry quoted in Nkundabagenzi, *Rwanda politique,* 150.

against "enemies"—and participation was required. The king in turn asked Belgian Governor Jean-Paul Harroy for permission to restore order. Harroy refused and then found himself surrounded by a threatening crowd as he left the king's residence. The next day—despite Harroy's refusal—the monarchy launched a counteroffensive. Speaking on the king's veranda, a UNAR leader instructed the crowd to arrest Hutu political leaders, prompting a wave of assassinations, attacks, and house burnings. Tutsi politicians seen as no longer loyal to the monarchy also were attacked.[26] According to the Belgian investigation, the monarchy/UNAR counteroffensive killed thirty-seven people in all.[27]

Belgium, however, sealed Rwanda's political fate. After a year of tense relations with Tutsi political authorities, the Belgians backed what they considered a Hutu insurgency. Starting on November 7, Belgian officials launched a military operation to stop the violence. Two days later Colonel Guy Logiest took control of the operation and on November 11 introduced a state of emergency.[28] A day later, the violence ended.[29]

Like other Belgian colonial administrators, Logiest saw events strictly in ethnic terms.[30] And Logiest clearly sided with the Hutus.[31] After he quelled the violence, Logiest massively restructured the ethnic composition of Rwanda's local administration. On November 1, 1959, every chief in Rwanda was Tutsi, as were all but ten of the 559 sub-chiefs. During the November violence, some of these Tutsi authorities were killed; others were arrested for crimes they had allegedly committed; still others went into exile for fear of being arrested. Af-

26. This account is based on Hubert, *La toussaint rwandaise,* 34–38, 66–75; the Belgian Government Commission of Inquiry quoted in Nkundabagenzi, *Rwanda politique,* 152–56; Trusteeship Council, *1960 Report,* 29–30; Willame, *Aux sources,* 54; Lemarchand, *Rwanda and Burundi,* 164–66; and Harroy, *Rwanda,* 305–9.

27. Hubert, *La toussaint rwandaise,* 34–35. Of the 1,986 crimes during this period that the Belgians labeled as having either a "Tutsi motive" or a "Hutu motive," 52 percent were classified in the former category, though many Hutu persons committed so-called Tutsi-motivated crimes (*La toussaint rwandaise,* 156). As for total number killed, for the entire early November period (including deaths from the Tutsi counteroffensive), estimates vary: from 100 to 370 (Nkundabagenzi, *Rwanda politique,* 156); 200 killed (Trusteeship Council, *1960 Report,* 31); and 300 deaths (Willame, *Aux sources,* 59).

28. Hubert, *La toussaint rwandaise,* 42; Harroy, *Rwanda,* 309; and Reyntjens, *Pouvoir et droit,* 261.

29. Guy Logiest, *Mission au Rwanda* (Brussels: Didier Hatier, 1988), 46.

30. Trusteeship Council, *1960 Report,* 33.

31. Reyntjens, *Pouvoir et droit,* 268–72; Harroy, *Rwanda,* 356; and Catharine Newbury, *The Cohesion of Oppression: Clientship and Ethnicity in Rwanda, 1860–1960* (New York: Columbia University Press, 1988), 197.

ter Logiest's intervention, there were twenty-two Hutu and twenty-two Tutsi chiefs (with one post vacant) and 297 Hutu sub-chiefs and 217 Tutsi sub-chiefs (with seventeen positions vacant).[32] The most active UNAR supporters were dismissed.[33] The restructuring abruptly and significantly weakened the monarchy and UNAR and strengthened the Hutu nationalist movement.[34]

National elections were called for June and July. With UNAR boycotting, PARMEHUTU won an overwhelming victory.[35] The following year, in January 1961, Logiest and Hutu party leaders met in Gitarama, not far from where the violence had started in November 1959. A newly appointed Hutu official announced an end to "feudalism" and to the monarchy, and Rwanda was declared a republic. Mbonyumutwa, the first victim of the 1959 violence, was declared president, and Grégoire Kayibanda, the PARMEHUTU leader, was named prime minister (later that year he became president). The announcements sealed Rwanda's political transformation from a Tutsi-dominated monarchy to a republic founded on Hutu rule, though formal independence was not granted until July 1962 and limited violence continued until then.[36] As one UN report put it, a "one-party racial dictatorship" had replaced an oppressive regime.[37]

What does this brief analysis of the Revolution period (1957–62) teach us about patterns of violence in Rwandan history? First, violence and the rise of ethnic nationalism were embedded in a process of imminent change and intense contestation for political power. From 1957 to 1962, Rwanda was in a colonial endgame. An old order was ending, but a new one had not yet been fashioned. The resulting uncertainty, upheaval, instability, and political maneuvering—and

32. The dates are as of March 1, 1960. Reyntjens, *Pouvoir et droit*, 269; Trusteeship Council, *1960 Report*, 33.

33. Reyntjens, *Pouvoir et droit*, 269.

34. Reyntjens, *Pouvoir et droit*, 271.

35. The party won 70.4 percent of the vote. APROSOMA won 7.4 percent, RADER 6.6 percent, joint PARMEHUTU-APROSOMA candidates 6.0 percent, and UNAR 1.8 percent. Reyntjens, *Pouvoir et droit*, 283–84. For a detailed micro-level examination of electoral votes in southwest Rwanda, see Newbury, *The Cohesion of Oppression*, 198–206.

36. For further details on this period, see Hubert, *La toussaint rwandaise*, 55, 103–11; Lemarchand, *Rwanda and Burundi*, 179–80, 188–96; Reyntjens, *Pouvoir et droit*, 289–91; and Trusteeship Council, *1960 Report*, 31. For a remarkable ethnographic study of one commune in Kibungo during this period, where a newly elected Hutu official initiated violence to consolidate power in the areas he now ruled, see Pierre Gavel, *Remera: A Community in Eastern Ruanda* (The Hague: Mouton, 1968), 191–95.

37. Willame, *Aux sources*, 64.

the broad perception of a window of political opportunity—were all integral to the appearance and spread of violence.

Second, the Revolution period reveals a pattern of retaliation and escalation. In 1959, Tutsis initially used violence to maintain the status quo, to protect their power when their power was eroding and threatened. But from that point forward, violence was always committed in response to violence that already had been committed. Violence became part of a cycle of retaliation, in which one side tried to assert power and respond to threats induced by the other side. The political upheaval and uncertainty intensified these dynamics.

Third, the Hutu counter-elites' ideological emphasis on ethnicity cannot be divorced from the particularities of the Rwandan political arena. Belgium established a system of rule fundamentally based on ethnicity: "race" was the primary marker of status and power in the colonial system. As decolonization approached, as the political arena opened, Hutu elites insisted on ethnicity in order to recognize and change an unequal distribution of power. They also likely calculated that with Hutus being 85 percent of the population, insisting on ethnic majoritarian rule would be a strategy for political success. The insistence deepened as their main rivals for political power—old guard Tutsis mostly associated with the monarchy and representing ethnic minority interests—denied the relevance of ethnicity.

One final point: much commentary on the Rwandan Revolution refers to an abrupt Belgian switch from the Tutsis to the Hutus. Many observers root the policy change in the context of the cold war: the Hutu political movement was seen as pro-West and UNAR as pro-communist.[38] However, the historical analysis above shows that the Belgian switch was also a gradual shift rooted in local dynamics. Belgium initially supported change. UNAR resisted, denied the relevance of ethnicity, took anti-Belgian stands, launched a campaign of intimidation, and, critically, tried to restore order violently in November 1959. These and other acts alienated the Belgian administration, pushing the European rulers toward favoring the Hutu parties. But the Belgians always framed the Rwandan political arena in ethnic terms, which reinforced the ethnic revolt and the political salience of ethnic categories. The Revolution became a "Hutu Revolution." The Belgians' critical role in the events of the period thus further consolidated the political relevance of ethnicity.

38. Reyntjens, *Pouvoir et droit*, 263; Lemarchand, *Rwanda and Burundi*, 176.

Ethnic Massacres: 1962–64

In two distinct episodes in 1962 and in 1963–64, ethnic massacres broke out in Rwanda. "Ethnic massacre" here refers to the large-scale killing of civilians—men, women, and children—who were targeted on the basis of their categorical identity, because they were Tutsi. Very little is known about the first episode, and the picture is only marginally clearer with regard to the second. But in both cases there was a dynamic of reprisal and escalation, whereby an attack by Tutsi exiles led to the categorical killing of Tutsi civilians inside the country. The second episode also came in the context of political divisions and eroding control within the Kayibanda regime.

As early as 1961, UNAR leaders in exile began developing plans for armed opposition. They initiated scattered, small attacks in 1961 and then launched more substantial raids in February and March 1962 in northern Rwanda, in Byumba. The raids killed a handful of Hutu policemen and civil servants but resulted in little territorial gain. Because they attacked at night, the raiders were called "*inyenzi*" or "cockroaches"—a term that hardliners in the 1990s used to insult the RPF and Tutsis in general, as we saw in the last two chapters and as we shall see again below. It is unclear whether the attackers themselves or the Kayibanda regime coined the term in the 1960s. Most written sources from this period refer to "*inyenzi*" attackers in a non-pejorative sense, as a label for the attackers.[39]

But for reasons that remain unclear, the March 1962 raids triggered an ethnic massacre. The violence began a day after the UNAR raid and lasted for two days, and it claimed one to two thousand Tutsi civilian lives. Details are scant; who organized the killing (if such a group can even be isolated), how the violence stopped, why this particular raid spawned reprisals, what role the Belgians played (Rwanda was then not yet independent), and where the killing was concentrated remain open questions.[40]

39. Luc de Heusch, "Massacres collectifs au Rwanda?" *Syntheses* 221 (October 1964), 422; Lemarchand, *Rwanda and Burundi,* 198; Reyntjens, *Pouvoir et droit,* 461; and Aaron Segal, "Massacre in Rwanda," Fabian Research Series 240, London, April 1964, 11.

40. According to Lemarchand, who has the only specific account, the killing of civilians took place in Byumba; see Lemarchand, *Rwanda and Burundi,* 217–19. Hubert refers to an episode during which Tutsi raids attacked Hutu burgomasters and judges, some of whom were assassinated. Hubert writes that "Hutus" in turn massacred entire Tutsi families, leaving 1,000 to 3,000 dead. It is likely that this was the same event to which Lemarchand makes reference, though Hubert claims that the violence took place in Kibungo. See Hubert, *La toussaint rwandaise,* 58–59. There is also evidence of a raid

More is known about the 1963–64 massacres. By late 1963, PARME-
HUTU officials had become increasingly fearful of the now 150,000
Tutsi refugees living abroad. The Rwandan armed forces only had one
thousand men, while the *"inyenzi"* were thought to have 10,000 rebel
recruits who, the authorities feared, could link up with Tutsi civilians
in the country.[41] This threat was exaggerated. UNAR was factional-
ized, and the rebels may have numbered only a few hundred. But the
perception of a threat was real.[42] Internal, intra-Hutu divisions within
the Kayibanda regime also were beginning to show, in particular
during commune elections in August 1963.[43] Finally, the production
of coffee—the main cash-earning export—declined significantly in
1963, and relations between the Rwandan and Burundian governments soured over trade and monetary issues.[44] In late 1963, in short,
newly independent Rwanda faced a multifaceted crisis.[45]

In this context, on the morning of December 21, 1963, a band of
Rwandan Tutsi exiles armed with bows, arrows, and homemade rifles
invaded from Burundi. They first rallied hundreds of Tutsi men to
their cause, and then they seized the Gako military camp located in
what later became Kigali-Rural Prefecture. They killed a handful of
government soldiers, commandeered several vehicles, and seized a
cache of weapons. The attackers continued to recruit men to their
cause and numbered 1,000 to 7,000 men by the time they began
marching toward Kigali.[46]

The initial reaction on the part of Rwandan military officials was a
"paralyzing panic."[47] They feared a several-pronged attack aimed at
overthrowing the regime and restoring the monarchy—all with Burundi's support.[48] The newly trained National Guard leader handed

---

the night of July 4–5, 1962, but that attack appears not to have prompted reprisal
killings. See de Heusch, "Massacres collectifs," 422.

41. De Heusch, "Massacres collectifs," 423; Segal, "Massacre in Rwanda," 14.

42. De Heusch, "Massacres collectifs," 423; Reyntjens, *Pouvoir et droit,* 456–57;
Lemarchand, *Rwanda and Burundi,* 198–206; and Willame, *Aux sources,* 67–69.

43. Lemarchand, *Rwanda and Burundi,* 219.

44. Segal, "Massacre in Rwanda," 12–13; Lemarchand, *Rwanda and Burundi,* 221.

45. One official told Lemarchand that "the government was on the point of collapse"
in 1963. Lemarchand, *Rwanda and Burundi,* 227.

46. For the smaller estimate, see Lemarchand, *Rwanda and Burundi,* 223; for the
larger estimate, see Segal, "Massacre in Rwanda," 13.

47. Segal, "Massacre in Rwanda," 13–14.

48. On fear of Burundi's support, see Segal, "Massacre in Rwanda," 14; on fear of a
multi-pronged attack, see Lemarchand, *Rwanda and Burundi,* 222. Indeed, there were
other attacks during the following six days, but they were either thwarted by neighboring governments or repulsed in Rwanda. On these, see Lemarchand, *Rwanda and Burundi,* 223; Segal, "Massacre in Rwanda," 16; and Willame, *Aux sources,* 72.

over command to a Belgian military adviser, who rallied the "panic-stricken" soldiers.[49] Government soldiers then intercepted and routed the Tutsi attackers as they crossed the Nyarabongo River sixteen miles outside of Kigali.[50]

The government then turned on civilians, first arresting prominent Tutsi political leaders in UNAR and RADER and some Hutu opponents of the regime. Many of those arrested were executed; others were beaten and released. Among those executed, according to government accounts, were those whom the rebels wanted to install as Rwanda's new leaders after overthrowing the Kayibanda regime; the list was supposedly carried by one of the rebels.[51] Whether the list was a government fabrication is unclear.[52]

What happened next was devastating for Tutsi civilians. President Kayibanda called on his ministers to organize local self-defense committees. The ministers then met with prefects, sub-prefects, and burgomasters, who in turn mobilized civilian self-defense committees at the local level. Hutu civilians hastily set up and manned roadblocks throughout the country.[53] Government officials also broadcast messages urging the population to defend themselves against the "Tutsi terrorists."[54]

Violence against Tutsi civilians did not break out everywhere, but in several locations, it did—particularly in Gikongoro Prefecture. On December 23, the Gikongoro prefect called a meeting of burgomasters and party activists. In it, he declared that the only effective means of self-defense was to paralyze the Tutsis completely, and the only way to achieve that was to kill them.[55] The killing of Tutsi civilians began on Christmas Day.[56] The estimated number of deaths in Gikongoro varies from 5,000 to 10,000.[57] There also was violence against Tutsi ci-

49. Segal, "Massacre in Rwanda," 13.

50. The paragraph is based on accounts in Segal, "Massacre in Rwanda," 13; Lemarchand, *Rwanda and Burundi*, 222–23; Reyntjens, *Pouvoir et droit*, 461; and Willame, *Aux sources*, 71.

51. Lemarchand, *Rwanda and Burundi*, 222; Reyntjens, *Pouvoir et droit*, 461; Segal, "Massacre in Rwanda," 15; and Willame, *Aux sources*, 71.

52. Reyntjens, *Pouvoir et droit*, 462.

53. Lemarchand, *Rwanda and Burundi*, 223; Reyntjens, *Pouvoir et droit*, 464; and Segal, "Massacre in Rwanda," 14.

54. Lemarchand, *Rwanda and Burundi*, 223; Willame, *Aux sources*, 72.

55. Lemarchand, *Rwanda and Burundi*, 223–24; Reyntjens, *Pouvoir et droit*, 465; and Willame, *Aux sources*, 73.

56. "Massacres au Ruanda: Des chrétiens compromis," *Témoignage Chrétien* 1022, February 6, 1964, 8.

57. For the low-end estimate, see Lemarchand, *Rwanda and Burundi*, 224. For the higher estimate, see Segal, "Massacre in Rwanda," 15; Segal estimates 10,000 to 14,000

vilians in Bugesera, Kibungo, and Cyangugu, though on a much smaller scale.[58] In all, the violence lasted for one to three weeks.[59]

Why was the violence greatest in Gikongoro? Many accounts blame a particular government minister and the prefect from Gikongoro.[60] But there are other reasons, ones related to perceptions of threat and control, that may also explain the variation (and the officials' disproportionate actions). First, Gikongoro Prefecture incorporated parts of the old monarchy's heartland, which was the core area of Tutsi opposition to the Kayibanda regime.[61] The massacres were concentrated in areas that were either in or bordered this heartland—including the only commune UNAR won in the 1963 elections.[62] Second, Gikongoro incorporated Nyungwe Forest, a dense uninhabited area that bordered Burundi, from where the rebels attacked. Third, the Rwandan armed forces did not have a sizeable troop presence in Gikongoro, if any. In short, the violence may have been greatest in Gikongoro because government officials perceived the greatest threat and the least control there.

Indeed, most accounts stress that fear, panic, and rumor in a context of insecurity and uncertainty drove the violence.[63] "The raid caused panicky terror at the heart of the government," said one report.[64] "The worst incidents were the results of fear and panic," said another.[65] Max Dorsinville, the UN Secretary-General's Special Representative, who investigated the incident, wrote:

> These brutal acts were in no sense dictated by the government in Kigali, but rather took place in areas over which the government had little con-

---

killed, though he does not specify how many of those were killed in Gikongoro. Reyntjens estimates 5,000 to 8,000 Tutsi victims, which he says would have equaled 10 to 20 percent of the Tutsi population in Gikongoro. Reyntjens, *Pouvoir et droit*, 465.

58. Lemarchand, *Rwanda and Burundi*, 222; Reyntjens, *Pouvoir et droit*, 466; Willame, *Aux sources*, 76; and "Massacres au Ruanda," 8.

59. For the one-week claim, see Reyntjens, *Pouvoir et droit*, 464. By contrast, according to Segal, the reprisal killing lasted until mid-January 1964. Segal, "Massacre in Rwanda," 17.

60. Lemarchand, *Rwanda and Burundi*, 225; Reynjtens, *Pouvoir et droit*, 467; and Segal, "Massacre in Rwanda," 15–16.

61. Lemarchand, *Rwanda and Burundi*, 224; Reyntjens, *Pouvoir et droit*, 465.

62. The two areas in the prefecture mentioned as massacre sites are Kaduha and Cyanika (see "Massacres au Ruanda," 8). Both are in communes that border Nyabisundu, which was the one commune that UNAR won in the August 1963 elections.

63. Lemarchand, *Rwanda and Burundi*, 223; Reyntjens, *Pouvoir et droit*, 467; Segal, "Massacre in Rwanda," 16; and Willame, *Aux sources*, 82.

64. "Massacres au Ruanda," 8.

65. Segal, "Massacre in Rwanda," 16.

trol, due to lack of troops. In such areas a popular militia took reprisals on some of the Batutsi populations as a result of the raids of December 20–21 and the fear and panic which they inspired in the Bahutu population.[66]

Still, the character of the violence closely resembles the 1994 geno-cide, as this description in a Catholic missionary publication makes clear:

> The entire Hutu population, Christian and pagans, catechists and cate-chumens, attacked the unfortunate Tutsi, in bands of about a hundred people, led by Party "propagandists" and with the authorities' blessing. This time, the objective was not to loot, but to kill, to exterminate all who had the name "Tutsi." . . . The massacre was horrifying: except for a few notables or Party propagandists who carried guns, the mass of killers only had large knives and indigenous billhooks. The families who did not want to leave their huts were barricaded inside and burned alive. Some had their necks or limbs slashed on the spot and were left to suf-fer for days. . . . They call it "to wage war": *ni intambara!*[67]

As in 1994, local elites instigated the violence and led large bands of peasant men wielding ordinary farm tools to attack Tutsi homes. The violence was called "self-defense" and "war."

As in 1959, the violence in the early 1960s took place in a climate of political uncertainty. Kayibanda was the leader of a newly inde-pendent nation, and he faced internal political divisions, souring rela-tions with neighboring Burundi, and threats from abroad. But the 1963 violence also took place immediately after a military attack, which, in the broader context of eroding control and crisis, triggered fear and panic, which in turn ignited a massacre. Here, as elsewhere, threat-ened authorities used violence to keep power when their power was most unsettled and at risk.

The 1973 Purges

From the mid-1960s to the early 1970s, the Kayibanda regime ap-pears to have ruled securely, and there is no evidence of ethnic killing. "*Inyenzi*" attacks continued from 1964 through 1967.[68] But after the 1963–64 violence, Rwanda became a de facto one-party state, and the

---

66. Quoted in Lemarchand, *Rwanda and Burundi*, 225.
67. "Massacres au Ruanda," 8.
68. Reyntjens, *Pouvoir et droit*, 471.

Rwandan armed forces became more confident and better organized.[69] The attacks were easily repulsed and did not provoke killings. There were personal rivalries, regional favoritism, and some factionalism within the party, and in 1968 there was a weak coup attempt.[70] But there is no evidence of acute uncertainty or deep divisions within the regime.

The perception of political stability began changing in the early 1970s, for three main reasons. First, presidential and parliamentary elections were scheduled for September 1973, but the constitution precluded President Kayibanda from serving another term.[71] Second, military officers from the northwest began preparations for an ultimately successful coup (more on this below). Third, mass violence broke out in Burundi. Unlike Rwanda, Burundi did not undergo an ethnic reversal of power at independence. Rather, Tutsis—Tutsis from a particular region—dominated the state, the military, and the economy. In 1972, Burundian Hutu dissidents launched a rebellion, which triggered a wave of military-led massacres against educated Hutus and other Hutu elites; 100,000 to 200,000 Hutu civilians were killed.[72] The violence led to a Hutu refugee influx into Rwanda and to anger and insecurity, particularly among Rwandan Hutu elites.[73]

In January 1973 violence in Rwanda began, seemingly without a specific trigger. The violence did not initially involve killing but rather purging: Hutu students descended on secondary schools, teaching colleges, and the national university with lists of Tutsi students to expel. In some cases, party and government officials backed the students publicly. In all cases, previously unheard-of "Public Safety Committees" and "Student Movement Committees" signed and authorized the lists. The raids forced out large numbers of Tutsis from

---

69. Reyntjens, *Pouvoir et droit*, 471.

70. Reyntjens, *Pouvoir et droit*, 478–95; Baudouin Paternostre de la Mairieu, *"Pour vous mes frères!" Vie de Grégoire Kayibanda, premier président du Rwanda* (Paris: Pierre Téqui, 1994), 221–23; Claudine Vidal, *Sociologie des passions (Côte d'Ivoire, Rwanda)* (Paris: Karthala, 1991), 38; and Willame, *Aux sources*, 83–85. On the coup attempt, see Reyntjens, *Pouvoir et droit*, 500–501.

71. Reyntjens, *Pouvoir et droit*, 505–6; Paternostre de la Mairieu, *"Pour vous mes frères!"* 221–23.

72. René Lemarchand, *Burundi: Ethnic Conflict and Genocide* (New York: Woodrow Wilson Center Press and Cambridge University Press, 1996), esp. 76–105. See also Stanley Meisler, "Holocaust in Burundi, 1972," in *The History and Sociology of Genocide: Analyses and Case Studies*, ed. Frank Chalk and Kurt Jonassohn (New Haven: Yale University Press, 1990), 384–93.

73. Paternostre de la Mairieu, *"Pour vous mes frères!"* 221; and Reyntjens, *Pouvoir et droit*, 501.

secondary school and from the university. The purges then spread to the public and private sectors. Notices were posted, declaring that such and such a person was no longer allowed to set foot in a particular establishment.[74]

Rwandan officials and government supporters called the actions "ethnic rebalancing," "clearing off" (*déguerpir*), and removing a Tutsi "surplus."[75] The issue to which they referred was "ethnic proportionality." After independence Kayibanda had supported ethnic quotas; proportional to their demographics, Tutsis were supposed to occupy between 10 and 20 percent of posts in government, in secondary school, and in higher education.[76] But by the early 1970s, about half the teachers and about half of the students in secondary schools and in higher education were Tutsi.[77] Tutsis were also particularly successful in the private sector.[78]

The purging to create "ethnic proportionality," however, evolved into an occasion for expressing political and regional frustration. In several areas, the homes and businesses of Hutu officials in the Kayibanda regime were attacked, as were homes of southern Hutus living in northern areas—the Kayibanda regime was widely perceived as favoring southern Hutus.[79] Some accounts suggest that the violence turned into attacks against Tutsi homes in rural areas, as it did in 1959.[80] But, according to a researcher then in Rwanda, ethnic violence never took hold in rural areas.[81] Whatever the truth, the violence led to another large exodus of Tutsi civilians to neighboring countries. Together with the refugees who fled in 1959 and the 1960s, these new refugees and their children formed the core of the RPF that later invaded from Uganda in 1990 (see below).

Even though Kayibanda, or those close to him, may have initially fomented the purging, the violence led to the end of his regime.[82] On

74. The account is based on Valens Kajeguhakwa, *Rwanda: De la terre de paix à la terre de sang et après?* (Paris: Éditions Remi Perrin, 2001), 137–46; Reyntjens, *Pouvoir et droit,* 502–3; Vidal, *Sociologie des passions,* 38–39; and Willame, *Aux sources,* 87.

75. Willame, *Aux sources,* 89–90 and Paternostre de la Mairieu, *"Pour vous mes frères!"* 225.

76. For the higher percentage, see Paternostre de a Mairieu, *"Pour vous mes frères!"* 180. For the lower one, see Vidal, *Sociologie des passions,* 37.

77. Reyntjens, *Pouvoir et droit,* 501.

78. Vidale, *Sociologie des passions,* 37.

79. Reyntjens, *Pouvoir et droit,* 503; and Vidal, *Sociologie des passions,* 38–39.

80. Reyntjens, *Pouvoir et droit,* 503; and Willame, *Aux sources,* 90. The main locations for rural violence were, by these accounts, Gitarama and Kibuye.

81. Vidal, *Sociologie des passions,* 39.

82. For accounts that implicate Kayibanda and key members of his regime, see Ka-

July 5, Rwandan military officers, primarily from the northwest region, staged a coup led by thirty-six-year-old Juvénal Habyarimana. The officers' stated objectives were to end ethnic division and regional favoritism and to restore national unity. Nonetheless, those Tutsis who had been chased from their posts were not allowed to return to their previous positions. Kayibanda was arrested and died under house arrest in 1976. Meanwhile, the new authorities arrested key figures from the Kayibanda regime and, in 1974, executed about fifty-five of them.[83] By one account, the executions amounted to the "extermination of the Southern political elite."[84]

How then do we understand the purges? As in 1959, the purges took place in a context of impending regime transition and, as in 1963, intra-Hutu political divisions. Unlike 1963, there was no Tutsi attack within Rwanda, but the violence in neighboring Burundi created insecurity among Hutu authorities in Rwanda. Burundi shows that changes outside Rwanda can intensify uncertainty and insecurity already present inside Rwanda. We will see the same happen again in 1993 when Tutsi soldiers assassinated Burundi's first Hutu president, thereby adding to the uncertainty and insecurity that civil war and multipartyism already had caused (as discussed in chapter 1). In both 1973 and 1994, violence in Rwanda was not a direct response to events in Burundi, but the latter contributed to the escalation of tension that ultimately led to violence. In sum, the dynamics of the 1973 purges in Rwanda were similar to those of prior periods, on a smaller scale. Threatened authorities used violence to assert power in a period of uncertainty and insecurity. The authorities still predicated the rationale for violence on security—this was ethnic "balancing" done by "Public Safety Committees"—but the idea was to relegate Tutsis to their supposed rightful place of minority status, not to kill them in large numbers.

---

jeguhakwa, *Rwanda*, 147; Reyntjens, *Pouvoir et droit*, 508; and Vidal, *Sociologies des passions*, 38–39. To be sure, other interpretations are possible, in particular that the coup leaders launched the violence to destabilize the regime and thereby create a pretext for taking power. For this interpretation, see Willame, *Aux sources*, 85.

83. James Gasana, *Rwanda: Du parti-état à l'état-garnison* (Paris: L'Harmattan, 2002), 27–28; Kajeguhakwa, *Rwanda*, 150–52; Paternostre de la Mairieu, *"Pour vous mes frères!"* 226–35; and Reyntjens, *Pouvoir et droit*, 506–8.

84. Gasana, *Rwanda*, 29.

1990–94 Violence

Prior to 1990, the Habyarimana regime did not instigate or authorize killings against Tutsis or other civilians.[85] From 1973 to the late 1980s, the regime presided over a period of economic growth, infrastructure improvement, diplomatic opening, international support, and general economic and political stability. Outsiders viewed the regime as a model in a troubled region. There were regional and economic inequalities and cleavages, but ethnic divisions narrowed. This was true even if, under the rubric of ethnic and regional quotas, the Habyarimana regime kept the Tutsi presence in government and education to a minimum.[86] As we saw in chapter 1, change began in the late 1980s and early 1990s, with the end of one-party rule and the RPF invasion on October 1, 1990. The first major instance of violence took place after a night of gunfire in Kigali on October 5. The following day, Habyarimana blamed the RPF for the shooting, claiming that the rebels had infiltrated the capital. The RPF and their "accomplices" posed a risk, the president said. Mass arrests followed. Between 6,000 and 13,000 civilians were arrested; most of them were Tutsi, but the group also included Hutu opponents of the regime. Some were tortured; most were kept in deplorable conditions.[87]

A week later, in Kibilira Commune in Gisenyi Prefecture, there was a massacre of Tutsi civilians. The following account is based on two detailed human rights reports.[88] Ten days after the initial RPF attack, a sub-prefect summoned Kibilira's *conseillers* to a meeting and there displayed two bodies of Hutus killed, he said, by Tutsis. He ordered the *conseillers* to teach their respective populations how to "assure

85. Reyntjens, *L'Afriques des grands lacs en crise. Rwanda, Burundi: 1988–1994* (Paris: Karthala, 1994), 35.

86. Reyntjens, *L'Afriques des grands lacs*, 31–36; Peter Uvin, *Aiding Violence: The Development Enterprise in Rwanda* (West Hartford, CT: Kumarian Press, 1998).

87. The estimate of 13,000 arrested is found in Alison Des Forges, *Leave None to Tell the Story: Genocide in Rwanda* (New York: Human Rights Watch, 1999), 49; another estimate is of 8,000 to 10,000 comes from FIDH et al., *Rapport de la commission internationale d'enquête sur les violations des droits de l'homme au Rwanda depuis le 1er octobre 1990 (7–21 janvier 1993)*, March 1993, 14; and the low-end estimate of 6,000 to 7,000 comes from Reyntjens, *L'Afriques des grands lacs*, 94. Most accounts claim the shooting in Kigali was fabricated in order to create a pretext for arresting Tutsis. See, for example, Des Forges, *Leave None*, 49. Interviews I conducted with a senior military officer not implicated in the genocide suggest otherwise—that they were the outcome of a panicky soldier firing. At this stage, there is no way to know the truth for certain.

88. FIDH et al., *Rapport de la commission internationale d'enquête*, 18–22; Association Rwandaise pour la defense des droits de la personne et des libertés publiques (ADL), *Rapport sur les droits de l'homme au Rwanda, Septembre 1991–Septembre 1992*, Kigali, Rwanda, December 1992, 101–16.

their security." The *conseillers* then convened meetings the same day in their communities. One *conseiller* instructed the population to burn *"inyenzi"* homes because the *"inyenzi"* wanted to exterminate the Hutus. In another area, officials announced that Tutsis were killing Hutu children.

Violence against Tutsi civilians swiftly followed in seven of the commune's ten sectors. Local authorities, party leaders, teachers, and technical officers—the rural elite—led attacks and encouraged the population to attack too. In two days, 348 people were killed and 550 houses burned. In those sectors with little or no violence, either the local officials preached peace or Tutsis resisted. The violence ended after Kigali officials pressured Kibilira's burgomaster to stop the killing and after Gisenyi's prefect arrived in the commune with five gendarmes, who reportedly told the attackers to stop. The sub-prefect and the burgomaster were later fired and briefly imprisoned. About 280 others were arrested and later released.

The next massacre took place in Ruhengeri Prefecture the following January. In this case, the killing broke out after the RPF made a January 23 lightning strike on Ruhengeri town, briefly seizing the town and freeing inmates from a local prison. Two days later, communal authorities—apparently acting on instructions from soldiers—organized the killing of Tutsi pastoralists, called the Bagogwe, as RPF "accomplices" who had helped the rebels briefly take Ruhengeri.

The exact pattern of violence varied from commune to commune in the prefecture. In Mukingo Commune, the burgomaster dispatched the communal police, forest guards, and *conseillers* who mobilized other rural elites and peasants. In Gaseke Commune, a national minister and the prefect instructed the population to do a "special *umuganda*" consisting of "destroying the bush and all *inkotanyi* hiding there," thus removing the "roots." Both instructions were interpreted as warrants for killing, the latter as a warrant for attacking children. In another instance, a burgomaster told the population that the RPF was about to launch a massive attack against Hutus. He insisted that Hutu civilians find weapons and help the soldiers to attack the RPF and its accomplices. The attacks lasted until mid-March, and, in sum, took between 300 and 1,000 lives. They ended only after authorities in Kigali sent soldiers and gendarmes to stop the killing.[89]

The third major massacre in this period took place in March 1992

---

89. This account is based on FIDH et al., *Rapport de la commission internationale d'enquête*, 27–42; and ADL, *Rapport sur les droits de l'homme au Rwanda*, 117–34.

in the Bugesera region of Kigali-Rural. The main trigger was a March 3 radio broadcast warning that the RPF was about to assassinate twenty-two leading Hutu figures with the help of the Tutsi-dominated Parti Libéral (PL) opposition party.[90] Two days earlier, PL activists had held a meeting in Kanzenze, Bugesera, in which they had denounced the burgomaster. In response, the commune's official truck distributed a tract calling on Hutus to punish Tutsis because the PL had insulted the burgomaster.

Apparently instigated by a businessman close to the burgomaster and to Hassan Ngeze, the editor of the extremist *Kangura* magazine, the attacks started on March 4; the attackers pillaged, burned houses, butchered cattle, and killed Tutsis as "accomplices." By March 7, the violence had spread to the entire commune, finally ending on the ninth after a troop deployment from Kigali. The five days of violence took an estimated 300 lives and was most intense in those sectors where the *conseillers* were most allied to the burgomaster.[91]

The Bugesera region had been particularly tense prior to the March massacre. With a very large Tutsi population and sharing a border with Burundi, Bugesera was an area of active RPF recruitment. Prior to the killings, the local authorities established civilian patrols and roadblocks to stem the outflow of RPF recruits. Those caught were arrested, and some disappeared. The burgomaster defended these actions as legitimate security measures in the face of RPF infiltration. In February 1992, anti-tank mines exploded in Bugesera, although who planted the explosives is unclear.[92]

But Bugesera was not the only region where violence broke out in the aftermath of the March 3 broadcast. Hutu civilians attacked and killed Tutsis on a lesser scale in Kibuye and Gisenyi Prefectures during the second week of March. The rationale was much the same as in Bugesera: Hutus explained their aggression as being motivated by fears of an impending RPF attack that would depend on rebel infiltration and Tutsi civilian support. In several cases, communal authorities actively sought to prevent violence but were overwhelmed.[93]

90. Sections of the broadcast are reprinted in André Guichaoua, ed., *Les crises politiques au Burundi et au Rwanda (1993–1994)*, 2nd ed. (Paris: Karthala, 1995), 611.

91. ADL, *Rapport sur les droits de l'homme au Rwanda*, 203–32; FIDH et al., *Rapport de la commission internationale d'enquête*, 42–47.

92. The information on Bugesera in this paragraph is drawn principally from ADL, *Rapport sur les droits de l'homme au Rwanda*, 196–200; and secondarily from FIDH et al., *Rapport de la commission internationale d'enquête*, 42–43.

93. See ADL, *Rapport sur les droits de l'homme au Rwanda*, 237–44; and FIDH et al., *Rapport de la commission internationale d'enquête*, 22.

As in other periods of Rwandan history, in the early 1990s violence broke out in a climate of impending regime change and acute levels of tension as well as in response to an armed attack (or rumors of an impending armed attack). In the previous periods, impending regime change came in the form of decolonization and the end of Kayibanda's rule; here impending regime change came in the form of the end of one-party rule. In each period, the impending change created a period of political uncertainty, jostling for power, and divisions within the ruling elite. Whereas in previous periods violence intensified after an armed attack from representatives of the monarchy (first inside the country, then outside), here the RPF attacks triggered a dynamic of retaliation and escalation. In short, the broad patterns are the same: violence occurs in periods of imminent political change, in periods of intense contestation for power, and after an armed attack. In a context of uncertainty and insecurity, violence is a means to assert power.

The Mugesera Speech

Many of these themes are evident in one of the most notorious hardliner speeches prior to the genocide. Delivered in Gisenyi Prefecture on November 22, 1992, by Léon Mugesera, a senior MRND ideologue, many observers see the speech as the clearest example of the hardliner thinking within the Habyarimana regime that ultimately precipitated the genocide.[94] The speech is notorious because in it Mugesera threatened to send Tutsis to their "home" in Ethiopia via the Nyabarongo River, thereby invoking violence and the Hutu nationalist claim that Tutsis were foreigners in Rwanda.[95] But a close reading of the speech reveals more.

Mugesera's main message to his audience is "to not let yourselves be invaded." In the speech, the first invasion to which Mugesera refers is by opposition parties, chiefly the MDR, which was the strongest domestic challenger to the ruling party and a Hutu-led party. Urging the audience to fight, Mugesera vows that the MDR will never again have

---

94. See, for example, International Criminal Tribunal for Rwanda, "The Prosecutor Versus Jean-Paul Akayesu," Case No. ICTR–96–4–T, Arusha, Tanzania, September 2, 1998, 19; and Des Forges, *Leave None*, 83–86.

95. The most complete translated version of the speech can be found in a Canadian court case in which Mugesera fought against extradition. The case was initially decided in Mugesera's favor and then reversed. See J. A. Décary, "The Minister of Citizenship and Immigration and Léon Mugesera, Gemma Uwamariya, Irenée Rutema, Yves Rusi, Carmen Non, Mireille Urumuri, and Marie-Grâce Hoho," Dockets A–316–01, A–317–01, Ottawa, Canada, September 8, 2003, 17–25.

a presence in Gisenyi. He refers to the way in which a MDR politician recently became minister of education, and how she later removed MRND supporters from government posts, replacing them with MDR supporters. Mugesera promises revenge: the same will happen to opposition supporters in ministries controlled by the MRND. But he also urges the audience to remove forcibly any nationally appointed education officials and to send them back to the minister's home area of Butare in the south. "We must take decisions," says Mugesera. "We cannot let ourselves be invaded."

Mugesera then turns to the RPF, which he calls "*inyenzi.*" "These people called *inyenzis* are on their way to attack us," Mugesera says. The opposition parties, he insists, helped the "*inyenzis*" gain territory in northern Rwanda, an act of betrayal Mugesera says should be punished by the death penalty. Returning to his main message of "not letting yourselves be invaded," Mugesera warns that throughout the country the "*inyenzis*" actively recruited fighters. Parents too sent their children to fight, he claims. Anyone who recruits rebel soldiers should also be subject to the death sentence, Mugesera continues, and the parents should be arrested and exterminated:

> Are we really waiting till they come to exterminate us? I should like to tell you that we are now asking that these people be placed on a list and be taken to court to be tried in our presence. If they [the judges] refuse, it is written in the Constitution that "Justice is rendered in the people's name." If justice is no longer serving the people, as written in our Constitution which we voted for ourselves, this means at that point we who also make up the population whom it is supposed to serve, we must do something ourselves to exterminate this rabble.

Mugesera continues by relating the following story: two days earlier, a group of armed men entered a bar and demanded that patrons show cards showing to which party they belonged. When an MRND member showed his card, the armed men shot him. Mugesera then vows:

> I do not think we are going to allow them to shoot us! Let no more local representatives of the MDR live in this commune or in this prefecture, because they are accomplices! . . . They only want to exterminate us. . . . My brothers, militants of our movement, what I am telling you is no joke, I am actually telling you the complete truth, so that if one day someone attacks you with a gun, you will not come to tell us that we who represent the party did not warn you of it! So now, I am telling you so you will know. If anyone sends a child to the *inyenzis*, let him

go back with his family and his wife while there is still time, as the time has come when we will also be defending ourselves, so that . . . we will never agree to die because the law refuses to act!

"Unite!" Mugesera urges his audience. "Come together," "rise up," and "crush" any infiltrators. He continues:

Recently, I told someone who came to brag to me that he belonged to the PL. I told him, "The mistake we made in 1959, when I was still a child, is to let you leave." I asked him if he had not heard the story of the Falasha, who returned home to Israel from Ethiopia? He replied he knew nothing about it! I told him. "So don't you know how to listen or read? I am telling you that your home is in Ethiopia, that we will send you by the Nyabarongo so you can get there quickly."

Working to his conclusion, Mugesera again invokes the threats to the MRND. He relates a story of how MDR youth had recently taken over in a southern commune by force. Here are his closing points:

To conclude, I would remind you of all the important things I have just spoken to you about: the most essential is that we should not allow our- selves to be invaded. . . . Do not be afraid, know that anyone whose neck you do not cut is the one who will cut your neck. . . . We must all rise, we must rise as one man.

The Mugesera speech is frighteningly virulent, a window into the an- gry, paranoid, and radical mindset that ultimately led the hardliners to unleash the genocide in April 1994.

But on further reflection, his themes resonate with the other episodes of violence examined above and with the themes developed in previous chapters. Mugesera's main point is that the ruling party is under attack externally and internally. To respond, he urges reprisal, unity, and self-defense. "Are we really waiting for them to come and exterminate us?" he asks provocatively. He invokes violence or the threat of violence as retaliation, as self-protection, and as deterrence. His advice of "not letting yourself be invaded" is, on balance, a call for the population to take the law into its own hands and to defend the territory from internal and external threat. Violence, for him, is a means to assert power when power and control are deeply threatened. These are precisely the ideas and dynamics that we see in each of Rwanda's periods of violence.

Table 7.1 Historical patterns of violence

Date	Sources of instability and insecurity	Violence
1959	Decolonization; death of the king; registration of political parties; forthcoming elections	Monarchists attack Hutu politicians. Hutu crowds burn Tutsi homes and force Tutsis to flee. Belgians intervene, backing Hutus.
1962–1964	Armed attacks by Tutsi exiles; Hutu dissent within the Kayibanda regime (1963)	State-instigated massacre of Tutsi civilians; thousands killed. Hutu dissidents arrested.
1973	Forthcoming elections that President Kayibanda cannot contest; 1972 violence in Burundi; preparations for a military coup inside Rwanda	Tutsis purged from schools, government, and businesses. Some crowd violence against Tutsi civilians. After the coup, officials from former regime assassinated.
1990–1994	War with RPF; multipartyism; Arusha peace accords; violence in neighboring Burundi	Massacres and arrests of Tutsis; brawls and occasional assassination among political party rivals.
April–July 1994	President Habyarimana assassinated; top Hutu opposition leaders assassinated; war with RPF resumes	Genocide and political assassinations of Hutu opposition leaders.

The main finding from examining the pre-1994 episodes of violence is that every case occurred in a period of imminent political change, intense contestation for power, and divisions within ruling coalitions. The most deadly episodes also appear after an armed attack, in periods of perceived threat. Table 7.1 shows the different periods of change and the corresponding violence, including the 1994 genocide.

The chief mechanisms underlying the violence in these various episodes appear to be uncertainty and insecurity. In each case, ruling and local elites initiated violence to assert control when they perceived themselves or their power at risk. Violence was a means to assert dominance, "assure security," and "not be exterminated." The language of violence followed from this logic. Violence appeared as self-defense, retaliation, deterrent, and ethnic "rebalancing." Violence was a means to power and security when power and security were threatened. By the same token, violence ended when power and security were firmly reestablished—that is, when pockets of uncertainty and rupture closed.

Why then were civilians targeted? More specifically, why were there ethnic massacres? The evidence suggests that in most cases the perpetrators linked Tutsi civilians to that which they perceived to be causing the threat. Such a rationale, as we saw in the last chapter, rested on collective ethnic categorization: all Tutsis stood in for the actions of a few. Perpetrators attacked "Tutsis" because "Tutsis" had attacked or otherwise posed an attack threat. Such a rationale depended on an awareness of ethnic/racial categories, but the mechanisms driving the categorization and violence appear to have been insecurity and uncertainty.

This analysis has surprisingly significant implications for understanding the 1994 genocide. If violence is embedded in a dynamic relationship between security and insecurity, then the greater the perception of insecurity, the greater the intensity of violence. Recall the conditions in which the genocide occurred. Before 1994, the country experienced nearly four years of destabilization due to civil war and multiparty politics. The country was in the midst of an unfinished transition. Then on April 6, the president was assassinated, causing a major shock in Rwandan society. Hardliners, who were already weakened in the transition and who had already invested in loyalist institutions such as militias, developed assassination plans, and exhibited angry, paranoid, and vengeful frames of mind (as per Mugesera above), filled the power vacuum left by the president's death. They ordered the prime minister and other leading opposition politicians to be assassinated. Combat with the RPF resumed, and the hardliners declared war on the "Tutsi enemy." During the next three months, the hardliners progressively lost ground to the rebels, and violence against Tutsi civilians intensified in government-held territories.

The dynamics of violence here are not that different from the previous episodes of violence—but the scale is. In a climate of acute uncertainty and insecurity—in the midst of an unfinished political transition, after a presidential assassination, and during a war— threatened elites resorted to violence in the name of self-defense, retaliation, and "security." As in previous episodes, they collectively categorized "Tutsis" as the source of threat and danger and called for their destruction. But unlike previous episodes, when the broad national politics stabilized and violence petered out, this time the national hardliners lost ground and power to the rebels. And unlike previous episodes, when national authorities ultimately salved the violence, in 1994 they encouraged and even ordered it. In so doing, the hardliners threw the full weight of the state behind the killings, and the violence, rather than ending as a limited massacre, totalized. It became genocide.

There are two major implications of this analysis, ones that tie together central themes in this book and the study of genocide. First, if ethnic violence is in dynamic relationship to security and control, then genocide was not necessarily "meticulously planned" well in advance of the actual annihilation campaign. Rather, extermination was ethnic massacring without end. The dynamics driving the killing did not fizzle; they intensified, as did the massacring. The model of extermination, then, is more contingent than the "meticulous planning" model would suggest. Genocide was the outcome of the specific circumstances and dynamics facing the threatened elites in mid-1994.

But—and this is the second major implication—even if the genocide may not have been meticulously planned well in advance, we can see more clearly how *responsible* the hardliners were. In various episodes of pre-1994 violence, the national authorities ultimately acted to deflate the violence. But in 1994, the opposite happened. The national hardliners who took control of Rwanda after Habyarimana's death authorized killing. In response to their eroding control over the country, they chose to stoke the violence. They instructed the population to murder.

With the national authorities' blessing and encouragement, the dynamics of violence in 1994 gathered momentum and rapidly swept across the areas of the country not yet in rebel hands. Opposition to the killing was quickly overwhelmed, and Tutsis were killed in massive numbers over a relative short time, as we have seen. There were different tipping points—the dynamics of violence took longer to materialize in areas where the political opposition initially held sway—but once the tipping points were reached, the killing was swift and devastating. Throughout this process, the role of the national state, then under the hardliners' control, was critical. Rather than serving to calm tension and stand between conflicting parties, the state bore down on the side of the violent. The state stoked, reinforced, and legitimized the massacres. The state made killing Tutsis synonymous with authority and "law." The state made killing Tutsis the order of the day.

8   Rwanda's Leviathan

The state made the difference in Rwanda. The state turned what could have ended as limited ethnic killing and crowd violence into genocide. The state unleashed the force of the military and the civilian administration on Tutsi civilians. The state, in short, threw its considerable weight behind a policy of killing Tutsis and instructed the Hutu population to hunt down their Tutsi neighbors. The state authorized extermination.

The effect, as we have seen, was dramatic. Within days in some areas and weeks in others, genocidal violence swept across Rwanda. The violence ultimately overwhelmed Hutu opposition to it; it incorporated hundreds of thousands of participants; and it came crashing down on the resident Tutsi population. None of this—the force, the speed, the extent of the violence, the mass mobilization—would have been possible had the state been absent from the massacres.

Recall too how central notions of authority and obligation were to how perpetrators explained the violence around them and their participation in it. Many perpetrators equated killing Tutsis with the "law," as a policy the state had decreed. Moreover, many said that they chose to participate not because they were blindly obedient. Rather, they said that they complied with what they considered the authorities' orders because they felt they would be punished if they refused. The perpetrators calculated that compliance was a less risky strategy than disobedience. By their accounts, the state coercively pressured them to participate, *and* the threat of coercion was credible.

The state's presence and power during the Rwandan genocide, how-ever, cannot be taken for granted, for a number of reasons. First, most African states are weak. The literature on African politics treats state weakness and a disconnect between local rural populations and urban elites as virtual articles of faith. Yet during the genocide, hundreds of thousands of civilians in rural areas in Rwanda complied with na-tional officials' orders to kill Tutsis: the state proved remarkably ef-fective. Why? Second, perpetrators' accounts should not be accepted uncritically. In earlier chapters, I presented some evidence that cor-roborates perpetrator claims that intra-ethnic intimidation was a ma-jor factor in the large-scale civilian mobilization during the genocide. But there is more analytical work to be done. In particular, where did the idea and power to mass mobilize originate? For the coercion claims to withstand scrutiny, there should be some evidence that the state can command compliance in the countryside and that large-scale civilian mobilization was a preexisting practice.

The chapter investigates these questions. The chapter seeks to un-derstand why the idea of authority was so resonant in Rwandan soci-ety and why the hardliners who took control of the state were so effective in gaining the compliance of so many citizens in such a short period. The argument I ultimately make is both historical and geo-graphical. Rwanda, I will argue, has a high degree of national and institutional continuity from the precolonial to the postcolonial peri-ods, *and* the country has a long institutional history of mandatory la-bor mobilization. The patterns of mobilization during the genocide strongly resonated with the preexisting practices of labor conscrip-tion. Rwanda also is densely settled, and the country's topography is cultivated rolling hills with little uninhabited open space. The effect is to make the citizenry visible with few options to hide or exit, which in turn increases the effectiveness of the Rwandan state's ability to garner large-scale civilian compliance rapidly.

State Power in Rwanda

The Rwandan state is not powerful in the conventional sense. In 1994, Rwanda was one of the poorest countries in the world with an economy overwhelmingly dependent on smallholder agriculture pro-duction. Infrastructure was rudimentary, and the communication sys-tem was weak.[1] Yet in other ways the Rwandan state demonstrated comparatively strong capacity to govern.

---

1. According to the World Bank, there was one phone line for every thousand per-

Consider two unpaid mandatory labor programs discussed in previous chapters: *umuganda* and the *amarondo*. On a weekly basis, the government obligated Rwandan adults to participate in *umuganda*. The practice entailed everything from digging irrigation ditches to repairing roads to sloganeering for the ruling party. The obligation most frequently was for one person from every household to perform *umuganda*, and participation was high. Though national participation rates are not available, some 87.5 percent of the respondents in my sample said that they did *umuganda* regularly before the genocide.

Amarondo were the night patrols undertaken by able-bodied men in areas of the country near the civil war fighting. The *amarondo* (or "rounds" in Kinyarwanda) were part of the civil defense program that the military introduced in the early 1990s, after hostilities with the RPF began. Although according to the data I collected, the program was not national—some 35 percent of my respondents said they did *amarondo* before the genocide—the percentage was high in areas where the program existed. But its very existence is further evidence of state presence and of large-scale labor mobilization at the local level in Rwanda before the genocide.

Consider too the centralized, hierarchical, and extensive structure of Rwanda's state. Rwanda had five levels of administration before the genocide: the national government, the prefectures, the communes, the sectors, and the *cellules*. In addition, in some areas, there was a sub-*cellule* stratum called *nyumbakumi*, which refers to a semi-formal policy of having one (unpaid) official for every ten households.[2] Figure 8.1 depicts the Rwandan state hierarchy.

What the display of Rwanda's administrative structure shows is that the state had an extensive presence at the local level. In some areas, there was an official responsible for every ten houses; all areas had a five-member *cellule* committee with a strong, local presence. In official conversations, Rwandans typically identify their commune, sector, and *cellules* of origin. State structures are, in other words, meaningful and resonant in Rwandan society.

The scholarship on Rwanda reflects the idea that the country's state is powerful, hierarchical, and quite effective at controlling the population.[3] For example, one recent study concluded that "Rwandese so-

---

sons in Rwanda. World Bank, *World Development Report 1994: Infrastructure for Development* (New York: Oxford University Press, 1994), 224.

2. For a reference to them, see Alison Des Forges, *Leave None to Tell the Story: Genocide in Rwanda* (New York: Human Rights Watch, 1999), 42.

3. Catharine Newbury summarizes two dominant images of the Rwandan state in the 1980s and early 1990s as, on the one hand, a "well-organized state successfully de-

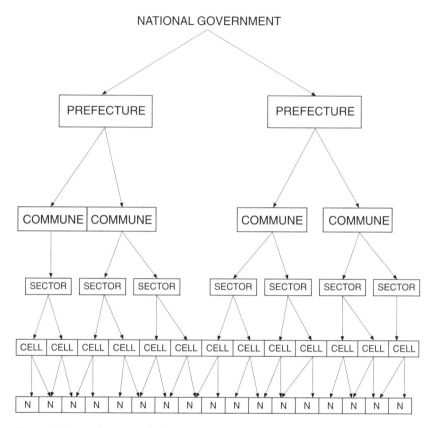

Figure 8.1 Rwandan state administration

---

veloping its economy" and, on the other hand, an "authoritarian, repressive apparatus."
Catharine Newbury, "Rwanda: Recent Debates over Governance and Rural Development," in *Governance and Politics in Africa,* ed. Goran Hyden and Michael Bratton
(Boulder, CO: Lynne Rienner, 1992), 215. Des Forges argues Rwanda has an "intensive
administration" designed for "control and mobilization." *Leave None,* 42. Even the
World Bank refers to the Rwanda's pre-genocide local government as "fairly well developed." World Bank, *Rwanda: Poverty Reduction and Sustainable Growth,* Report No.
12465–RW, May 16, 1994, 36. Gérard Prunier claims that there was "an almost monstrous degree of social control" in Rwanda: Prunier, *The Rwanda Crisis: History of a
Genocide* (New York: Columbia University Press, 1995), 3. See also the Joint Evaluation
of Emergency Assistance to Rwanda, *The International Response to Conflict and Genocide: Lessons from the Rwanda Experience,* vol. 1 (Copenhagen: Steering Committee of
the Joint Evaluation of Emergency Assistance to Rwanda, 1996), 10.

ciety developed over the centuries into a remarkably organized state, with a high degree of authoritarian control from the centre."[4] Several writers go so far as to describe the Rwandan state as "totalitarian."[5] That idea is undoubtedly too strong, but it reflects the perception among outside observers of the extent and power of Rwanda's state.

It is also a cliché about Rwanda that the country has a strong "tradition" or "culture" of obedience.[6] For example, historian Gérard Prunier, a longstanding observer of the region, writes:

> There had always been a strong tradition of unquestioning obedience to authority in the precolonial kingdom of Rwanda. This tradition was of course reinforced by both the German and Belgian colonial administrations. And since independence the country had lived under a well-organized tightly-controlled state. When the highest authorities in that state told you to do something you did it, even if it included killing.[7]

Or, as another observer put it, "Obedience to the orders of the authorities was something that had inculcated [*sic*] in the population for centuries."[8] Recall too that some 91 percent of my respondents said that they had never disobeyed the authorities. Even if many respondents had disobeyed the authorities at some point, which seems likely,

---

4. Joint Evaluation of Emergency Assistance to Rwanda, *The International Response*, 10. The study also notes that "the political culture of centralized social control has facilitated policies aiming at mobilization or manipulation of the Rwandese rural people."

5. Linda Melvern, *A People Betrayed: The Role of the West in Rwanda's Genocide* (London: Zed Books, 2000), 24. According to Melvern, with the exception of communist countries, "Rwanda was probably the most controlled state in the world" (25). On Rwanda's "totalitarian" state, see also Christian Scherrer, *Genocide and Crisis in Central Africa: Conflict Roots, Mass Violence, and Regional War* (Westport, CT: Praeger, 2002), 109.

6. In addition to the references in the next two notes, see the International Criminal Tribunal for Rwanda, "The Prosecutor Versus Jean-Paul Akayesu, Case No. ICTR–96–4–T: Judgement," 17; Bill Berkeley, *The Graves Are Not Yet Full: Race, Tribe, and Power in the Heart of Africa* (New York: Basic Books, 2001), 256; Philip Gourevitch, *We Wish To Inform You that Tomorrow We Will Be Killed with Our Families* (New York: Picador, 1998), 243; and Shaharyar Khan, *The Shallow Graves of Rwanda* (London and New York: I. B. Tauris, 2001), 67. The latter work mentions "hypnotic compliance" and the "extraordinary docility and compliance to command of the Rwandan people." Finally, see Regina Andersen, "How Multilateral Development Assistance Triggered the Conflict in Rwanda," *Third World Quarterly* 21, no. 3 (2000), 445: "The deeply ingrained obedience to authority is one factor contributing to the explanation of the unthinkable."

7. Prunier, *The Rwanda Crisis*, 245. Prunier compares this to the "Prussian tradition of the German state."

8. Scherrer, *Genocide and Crisis in Central Africa*, 113.

that so many said they had not demonstrates the importance of the perception of compliance with the state.

At a minimum, then, it seems clear that there is something distinctive about the Rwandan state outside the context of the genocide. Rwandan and scholarly opinion alike suggest that the Rwandan state was centralized and effective at gaining compliance from the citizenry throughout the country. Rwandan state power in these respects is noteworthy—but especially so in comparison to most other African states. Scholars often refer to the modal African state as organizationally "weak," as a "lame leviathan," as "suspended in 'mid-air' over society," or as "collapsed."[9] The widespread expectation in the scholarly literature is that African states cannot "capture" or otherwise effectively govern the peasantry.[10] As Joel Migdal writes, "The rule of state leaders [in Africa] has extended beyond the capital city or the main port only in the most tenuous and intermittent ways."[11] Migdal's characterization certainly does not fit Rwanda: Rwanda's state was not a "lame leviathan"; it was the real thing. But why?

Institutional Continuity

A central, recurring theme about the origins of state weakness in Africa concerns the newness and foreign-ness of the institutions. Indeed, most contemporary states in Africa are direct legacies of insti-

9. On weak state organization and capacity, see William Tordoff, *Government and Politics in Africa*, 4th ed. (Bloomington and Indianapolis: Indiana University Press, 2002), 22. On Rwandan states being "suspended," see Goran Hyden, *No Shortcuts to Progress: African Development Management in Perspective* (Berkeley and Los Angeles: University of California Press, 1983), 7. On "collapsed" states, see I. William Zartman, "Introduction: Posing the Problem of State Collapse," in *Collapsed States: The Disintegration and Restoration of Legitimate Authority*, ed. I. William Zartman (Boulder, CO: Lynne Rienner, 1995), 1–11. On the idea of a lame Leviathan, see Thomas Callaghy, "Politics and Vision in Africa: The Interplay of Domination, Equality, and Liberty," in *Political Domination in Africa: Reflections on the Limits of Power*, ed. Patrick Chabal (Cambridge, UK: Cambridge University Press, 1986), 36.

10. The "capture" metaphor comes from Goran Hyden, *Beyond Ujamaa in Tanzania: Underdevelopment and an Uncaptured Peasantry* (Berkeley: University of California Press, 1980), esp. 9–34. Note also Michael Bratton's statement: "At the heart of the contemporary crisis in sub-Saharan Africa lies a deep estrangement between state and society. State elites and peasant producers . . . have yet to engage each other. . . . Neither has succeeded in capturing the other." Bratton, "Peasant-State Relations in Postcolonial Africa: Patterns of Engagement and Disengagement," in *State Power and Social Forces: Domination and Transformation in the Third World*, ed. Joel Migdal, Atul Kohli, and Vivienne Shue (New York: Cambridge University Press, 1994), 231.

11. Joel Migdal, *Strong Societies and Weak States: State-Society Relations and State Capabilities in the Third World* (Princeton: Princeton University Press, 1988), 7.

tutions created under European colonialism in the late nineteenth and early twentieth centuries. During the "scramble for Africa," Europeans carved up Sub-Saharan Africa into a series of new administrative entities. The Europeans drew sometimes arbitrary boundaries, bisecting ethnic and language groups into different territories, and cobbling together preexisting rivals who had no previous history of cooperation, administrative or otherwise. The results were often new multilingual units whose national borders had little relationship to preexisting political communities. Many observers of African politics consider the colonial origins of African states a fundamental and persistent problem for establishing political legitimacy and hence for creating capable, administratively strong states with national loyalty, depth, and resonance.[12]

Rwanda, however, does not fit this mold. Contemporary Rwanda is the legacy of an old state, a precolonial kingdom. The boundaries of contemporary Rwanda are largely, though not uniformly, consistent with the kingdom the Europeans found at the end of the nineteenth century. The Europeans incorporated, and in some instances reinforced, Rwanda's precolonial institutions into the colonial state, and versions of those institutions persisted into the postcolonial state. Moreover, contemporary Rwanda has only one major national language besides French and Swahili: Kinyarwanda. To be sure, colonialism changed much, including and especially the salience and meaning of ethnic identity (as we shall see). But Rwanda's institutional history is broadly a story of continuity and integration. Unlike most contemporary African states, Rwanda is not a new, arbitrary, or foreign invention. And, moreover, as we shall see, the precolonial Rwandan state itself was well developed.

To give a feel for the institutional continuity, I want to examine briefly some colonial writings. Germany was Rwanda's first colonial ruler, and, impressed with the monarchical institutions they found, Germany opted to reinforce, rather than destroy, the precolonial system of rule. For example, a senior German official, writing in 1906, remarked:

---

12. The observation is one of the most consistent in the scholarship on African politics. For some examples, see Peter Ekeh, "Colonialism and the Two Publics in Africa: A Theoretical Statement," *Comparative Studies in Society and History* 17, no. 1 (1975), 91–112; Tordoff, *Government and Politics in Africa,* 81; Nicolas van de Walle, *African Economies and the Politics of Permanent Crisis, 1979–1999* (New York: Cambridge University Press, 2001), 115–16; and Pierre Englebert, *State Legitimacy and Development in Africa* (Boulder, CO: Lynne Rienner, 2001), especially 74–75.

> I am convinced . . . that it would be mistaken to try now to break up the great and well established sultanates. . . . The present tightly organized political structure of the sultanates offers a favourable opportunity to administer and develop culturally the natives through their traditional rulers.[13]

Other German colonial authorities characterized Rwanda's governing system similarly. They described Rwanda's "native" authority as "strong and effective" and worth reinforcing.[14] Thus, even from the point of early European contact, Rwanda's precolonial state was considered well organized and well established.[15]

During the course of Germany's brief rule over Rwanda (and neighboring Burundi), the German physical presence was minimal. Germany nominally gained control over Rwanda in 1890; however, seventeen years later an anthropologist traveling in the region described Germany's impact as perfunctory.[16] By 1913, Rwanda was host to only five German administrators and forty-one missionaries.[17]

Where Germany did play a direct role, the effects were to consolidate and expand the monarchy's territory and control in previously peripheral regions. In 1909, for example, German troops put down resistance from a challenger to the central Rwandan court; in 1912, the Germans suppressed a different rebel movement.[18] Both interventions were in the Rwandan north and northwest, where prior to colonialism the Rwandan monarch's authority had been tenuous, as the monarchy's base was in south central Rwanda. In pursuing these interventions, the Germans' explicit goal was to strengthen the king's authority.[19]

Deploying relatively limited resources to Rwanda was undoubtedly

---

13. William Roger Louis, *Ruanda-Urundi, 1884–1919* (Oxford: Clarendon Press, 1963), 129. The sultanates in question here are kingdoms of Rwanda and Burundi. The German colonial unit was called "Ruanda-Urundi." Thus, in name the two kingdoms formed a single European colonial entity; in practice, the two were administered independently and in each the monarchies were left intact.

14. Louis, *Ruanda-Urundi, 1884–1919*, 115.

15. As one historian of the period noted, "No doubt . . . that this was an 'uncommonly complicated' society. From the beginning the Germans had no intention of changing it." See Louis, *Ruanda-Urundi, 1884–1919*, 146–47.

16. Jan Czekanowski, *Carnets de route au coeur de l'Afrique,* trans. Lidia Meschy (Montricher, Switzerland: Éditions noir sur blanc, 2001), 11.

17. David Newbury and Catharine Newbury, "Bringing the Peasants Back In: Agrarian Themes in the Construction and Corrosion of Statist Historiography in Rwanda," *American Historical Review* 105, no. 3 (2000), 845.

18. Louis, *Ruanda-Urundi, 1884–1919*, 147–49, 153–56.

19. Louis, *Ruanda-Urundi, 1884–1919*, 153, 157.

an expedient and cost-effective strategy that served German interests. But in pursuing it, Germany did not eviscerate the preexisting institutions of governing. To the contrary, Germany's principal effect was to reinforce and strengthen the monarchy. Not only did Rwanda's core territory stay intact under German colonialism, but the monarchy even expanded to regions where its control previously had been more contested.

After Germany's defeat in World War I, Belgium assumed control of Rwanda and Burundi as part of a "trust territory." Like the Germans before them, the Belgians initially chose to reinforce Rwanda's monarchy, which the new colonialists also considered remarkably well developed. Consider, for example, the language of the Belgian minister of colonies shortly after the war:

> I have decided that in Ruanda and in Urundi [sic], where there exists an indigenous organization that is highly developed [fortement échafaudée] with an authority powerfully well-established [puissamment assise], relations between the metropole and its territories will be indirect administration.[20]

Later the same year, he wrote:

> We will practice in Ruanda and Urundi a colonial protectorate policy.
>   The basis of this policy is the maintenance of indigenous institutions. . . . This is perfectly realizable in these countries where the organization is ancient and remarkable and whose ruling class shows evident political talents . . .
>   Our administration will maintain royal authority and reinforce it.[21]

Or, as one influential Belgian colonial administrator, Pierre Ryckmans, wrote:

> Among all the problems, one finds a major factor for progress: hierarchy; an authority that is orderly and strong enough to attain, with more or less efficacy, all the elements of social order [corps social]. . . . Since we

---

20. Minister of Colonies Franck to the Governor General, "Politique indigène. Administration indirecte," January 6, 1920, found in the colonial archives at the Ministry of Foreign Affairs, dossier AI 4370, number VII–B.1.B, 1, Brussels, Belgium. Note that the minister says that a similar system might be tried in Congo but that there are only a few "native" societies where such a system could work. However, he notes that such a system would be met with "enormous difficulties" (2).

21. Minister Franck, "Memorandum," June 17, 1920, Belgian colonial archives, Ministry of Foreign Affairs, dossier AI 4370, number VII–B.1.B, 1, 8, Brussels, Belgium.

need chiefs, let's make the most of the authority of those that exist; let us hasten to put them at our service.[22]

Judging from these documents, it is clear that senior Belgian colonial officials considered Rwanda's political system unusually well developed with a strong social hierarchy. The Belgians in turn endorsed a policy of continuity: they opted to develop a colonial administration on the basis of Rwanda's preexisting institutions.

To be sure, change was afoot: the Belgian goal was not to replicate the existing system but to modernize and "civilize" it.[23] In many areas of Rwanda, the king had three representatives, but in the mid-1920s the Belgians abolished this trinitarian system in favor of a single "chief" to govern "chiefdoms." In addition, the Belgians established "subchiefs" who presided over "subchiefdoms." The new authorities were sent for Western education, governing tasks were delineated, "chiefdom" boundaries were demarcated, and the authorities were paid.[24]

Scholarship on this period of Belgian rule emphasizes that the changes increased the state's arbitrary power. In precolonial times, Rwandans could play authorities off one other and thus deflect outright coercion. But the changes under the Belgians streamlined state power. They also reduced the king's authority and elevated Rwanda's aristocracy—exclusively Tutsi chiefs and subchiefs under colonialism.[25] As one keen analyst of the period, Catharine Newbury, concluded, "The impact of colonial statebuilding in Rwanda was thus to elaborate and intensify a system of political oppression."[26] The result

22. Pierre Ryckmans, "Le Problème politique au Ruanda-Urundi," *Société Belge d'études et d'expansion* 23, no. 49 (1925), 60. For a similar statement, see the *Rapport sur l'administration belge,* which claimed that "The first concern for the Belgian administration was to recognize the existing chiefs, indispensable intermediaries with the mass of people, so that their intervention is efficient." Ministère des Colonies, Rapport sur l'administration belge du Ruanda-Urundi pendant l'année 1925, 62.

23. Reyntjens calls this tension between maintaining the existing system and reforming it the "fundamental contradiction" that imbued the Belgian colonial experience. See Reyntjens, *Pouvoir et droit au rwanda* (Tervuren, Belgium: Musée royal de l'afrique centrale, 1985), 112. For a colonial statement on the policy of endorsing existing political institutions, but trying to modernize them, see Ministère des Colonies, *Rapport sur l'administration belge du Ruanda-Urundi pendant l'année 1938,* 72.

24. On these and similar reforms, see Reyntjens, *Pouvoir et droit,* 111.

25. This is the central thesis in Jean Rumiya, *Le Rwanda sous le régime du mandat belge 1916–1931* (Paris: L'Harmattan, 1992).

26. Catharine Newbury, *The Cohesion of Oppression: Clientship and Ethnicity in Rwanda, 1860–1960* (New York: Columbia University Press, 1988), 207.

was that Rwandan men became "susceptible to harassment all the time without the possibility of slipping away."[27]

In retrospect, then, the colonial period in Rwanda reformed and reinforced an already well-developed precolonial political system. Colonialism did not create an entirely new administration, nor did it result in a major exogenous disruption. Rather, the main process was a gradual cooption, adaptation, and transformation of preexisting institutions. The core territory was not fabricated but rather consolidated. The net effect is that a preexisting precolonial administration was extended and, in some dimensions, intensified. This gave Rwanda's governing institutions an unusual depth and power, one that would continue into the postcolonial era.

Institutions of Labor Mobilization

Rwanda's precolonial state not only had a well-developed and hierarchical system of governing, but there also were a number of institutions of labor mobilization. Like Rwanda's administrative structure, these institutions were ultimately incorporated into the colonial system, albeit in altered form. The precolonial forms of labor mobilization and their colonial counterparts are precursors of similar institutions in post-genocide Rwanda, such as *umuganda*. The long history of forced labor mobilization in Rwanda also provides further insight into why coercive mass mobilization was so effective during the genocide.

Precolonial Rwanda had a number of informal institutions of labor mobilization. One concerned obligatory military service.[28] Another concerned a mandatory labor practice called *uburetwa*, which usually required that each household provide two days of labor (for every five days) to local chiefs. Typical tasks included keeping watch over a chief's house at night, fetching water for a local authority, and clearing land for cultivation. Poor performance could be severely punished.

27. Rumiya, *Le Rwanda*, 237.
28. See Alexis Kagame, *Les milices du rwanda précolonial* (Brussels: Académie royale des sciences d'outre-mer, 1963); Louis, *Ruanda-Urundi, 1884–1919*, 111–12; Jacques J. Maquet, *The Premise of Inequality in Rwanda: A Study of Political Relations in a Central African Kingdom* (London: Oxford University Press, 1961), 102–3, 109; Ministère des Colonies, *Rapport sur l'administration belge du Ruanda-Urundi pendant l'année 1925*, 59; Ministère des Colonies, *Rapport sur l'administration belge du Ruanda-Urundi pendant l'année 1926*, 51; and Newbury, *The Cohesion of Oppression*, 47–48, 76.

A synonym for *uburetwa* was *"ubunetsi"*: "an obligatory corvée from which a person cannot escape."[29]

Under colonialism, these obligations did not disappear but rather were integrated into the new state and intensified. Belgian authorities recognized that labor mobilization was a sign of power and central to the practice of authority in "traditional" Rwanda.[30] Belgian officers ultimately tried to curb the extent of the labor requisitions. In 1924, they reduced the labor requirement to two days out of seven, and in 1927, they legislated one day out of seven—though the practice changed from a requirement asked of every household to one asked of every person.[31] That said, the changes masked a colonial cooptation of the institution. As the Belgians reduced the days of labor that chiefs could demand of the peasantry, the colonial rulers in turn adopted the idea of free labor for their own statebuilding aims. The principle of labor requisition remained, but its immediate beneficiaries and practices shifted. As one colonial official explained in 1920:

> The native must give his chief two days of work each week; the chiefs use this right to furnish corvées to the king. . . . It is in light of this custom that the means of communication [roads] can be developed without too much expense. We need only make the king and chiefs understand the necessity and utility of the roads so that each among them, within their means, will gratuitously provide labor. The native is moreover habituated to submit to this custom of two days per week and would not consider complaining about something natural.[32]

29. On the latter points, see Newbury, *The Cohesion of Oppression*, 141; and Rumiya, *Le Rwanda*, 65–66. There are many sources for the former, including Lieutenant Defarve, "Elements essentials de l'organisation politique & sociale du Ruanda, au point de vue de notre politique indigene & du développement économique du territoire," Ministry of Foreign Affairs, AI (4370), B.5.A, Brussels, Belgium, 4; Ministère des Colonies, *Rapport sur l'administration belge du Ruanda-Urundi pendant l'année 1922*, 22; and René Lemarchand, "Rwanda," in *African Kingship in Perspective: Political Change and Modernization in Monarchical Settings*, ed. René Lemarchand (London : Frank Cass and Co., 1977), 79.

30. See Ministère des Colonies, *Rapport sur l'administration belge du Ruanda-Urundi pendant l'année 1934*, 69–70, and Ministère des Colonies, *Rapport sur l'administration belge du Ruanda-Urundi pendant l'année 1937*, 70–73.

31. Ministère des Colonies, *Rapport sur l'administration belge du Ruanda-Urundi pendant l'année 1925*, 59; Ministère des Colonies, *Rapport sur l'administration belge du Ruanda-Urundi pendant l'année 1926*, 51; and Ministère des Colonies, *Rapport sur l'administration belge du Ruanda-Urundi pendant l'année 1927*, 38. On the shift from household to individual, see Newbury, *The Cohesion of Oppression*, 112; and Pierre Gravel, *Remera: A Community in Eastern Ruanda* (The Hague: Mouton, 1968), 186.

32. Lieutenant Defarve, "Elements essentials," 4.

Or, as an official year-end colonial report explained:

> There exists prestations and corvées in native custom . . . in Ruanda, a
> prestation of two days per week to the native authorities. . . . The ad-
> ministration succeeded in getting the native authorities to consecrate
> these prestations, which have been reduced, to works of public utility,
> such as road construction, instead of being done, as was the case before,
> for the exclusive benefit of the King and the chiefs.[33]

In short, the Belgians adopted the notion of a "customary" labor requirement as an institution that could be used for the construction
of roads, buildings, portage, and other public works projects. Missionaries did the same. One missionary remarked that constructing a church
would have been "absolutely impossible" without relying on corvées.[34]
Even as late as the 1950s, a UN field investigation found that Rwandans were conscripted to build schools, courthouses, prisons, lodging
for officials, automobile roads, and waterways. The investigation referred to this as unpaid "obligatory work" that should be abolished.[35]

Mandatory labor mobilization was widespread and, by all accounts,
highly exploitative and deeply resented.[36] In a historical review, two
leading scholars of Rwanda concluded that "the colonial state system
in Rwanda was based on coerced labor" requisitioned to Rwandan
and European authorities.[37] One Belgian annual report observed that
the masses in Rwanda were "exploited at will."[38] In his study of the
Rwandan colonial period, scholar Jean Rumiya concluded that:

> The violence that characterized daily life during the colonial period
> could not be better symbolized than by the *chicotte* [a whip used to pun-
> ish disobedience]. Both in and outside his home, adult men were sus-
> ceptible to demands at any instant without the possibility to sneak
> away.[39]

33. Ministère des Colonies, *Rapport sur l'administration belge du Ruanda-Urundi
pendant l'année 1922*, 22.

34. Rumiya, *Le Rwanda*, 17.

35. United Nations Bureau International du Travail, "Rapport du comité spécial du
travail forcé," United Nations Document E/2431, Geneva, 1953, 28.

36. On this point, see Newbury, *The Cohesion of Oppression*, 142; Rumiya, *Le
Rwanda*, 237; and Lemarchand, "Rwanda," 79.

37. Newbury and Newbury, "Bringing the Peasants Back In," 871.

38. The expression in French is "taillable et corvéable à merci." See Ministère des
Colonies, *Rapport sur l'administration du Ruanda-Urundi pendant l'année 1949*, 26.
An administrator serving in southwest Rwanda from 1933 to 1935 used the same ex-
pression. See Newbury, *The Cohesion of Oppression*, 141.

39. Rumiya, *Le Rwanda*, 237.

In short, precolonial and colonial Rwanda had extensive institutions of coercive labor mobilization. The institutions are important precursors to the similar postcolonial practice of *umuganda*, as we shall see. The precolonial and colonial institutions also show that the idea of obligatory, state-enforced labor mobilization has historical depth in Rwanda.

Geography and Demographic Density

We have seen how the contemporary Rwandan state is rooted in a precolonial state, one that was altered but not radically ruptured under colonialism. Moreover, Rwanda's precolonial state was well organized and effective, and it had a number of institutions of labor mobilization that were exploited and intensified under colonialism. These are some of the reasons why authority in Rwanda's contemporary state resonates and why the state is so effective at mobilization. But there is another reason—in fact, two closely related reasons—and they concern Rwanda's population density and topography.

Political scientist Jeffrey Herbst has argued persuasively that one important source of administrative weakness in Africa is that African states have low population densities. African states are often spread out over large swathes of sparsely settled territory and, as a result, struggle to "broadcast power," according to Herbst.[40] Rwanda is here again the exception that proves the rule: it is the African country with the highest population density, and it is effective at broadcasting power.

The high density of the Rwandan settlement is not a new development. The first European explorers at the turn of the twentieth century commented on it.[41] On the eve of independence in 1959, Rwanda averaged 241 persons per square mile—a density ratio that was sixteen times greater than in the Belgian Congo at the time, eight times greater than in South Africa, and marginally greater than in France.[42] Sustained population growth rates in the postcolonial period meant that in 1994 Rwanda still had more people per square mile than any other country in sub-Saharan Africa.

Population concentration contributed to another physical feature of

40. Jeffrey Herbst, *States and Power in Africa: Comparative Lessons in Authority and Control* (Princeton: Princeton University Press, 2000), 3.

41. Louis, *Ruanda-Urundi, 1884–1919*, 108–9.

42. Government of Belgium, *Ruanda-Urundi: Geography and History* (Brussels: Information and Public Relations Office, 1960).

Rwanda: a territory with little open space. With the exception of areas set aside in the colonial and postcolonial times as designated wildlife preserves and forests, Rwanda's landscape is cultivated from one end to the other and, in many cases, right to the top of the country's many hills. Rwanda is like a vast, undulating green garden of worked and inhabited land, where the only undeveloped spaces—besides preserves—are swamps in valleys. Such settlement patterns were true even at the turn of the twentieth century.[43]

Rwanda's topography also matters. The country is primarily composed of rolling hills, as reflected in Rwanda's nickname: "the land of a thousand hills." Rwanda's hills increase the visibility of the population. In contrast to flat, expansive landscapes, hilly territory means that inhabitants are often exposed. The country can feel like a fishbowl. As well-known commentator André Sibomana said, "In Rwanda, in normal times, everyone sees and knows everything immediately."[44]

Population density, intensively settled land, and hilly topography have, following Herbst, implications for the practice of state power. These features of Rwanda's human and physical geography increase the capacity for surveillance, and they limit the opportunities for exit and escape. Rwanda's citizenry is eminently findable. As a result, when ordered to perform a duty, especially when that order is national and when there are powerful actors who seek to enforce the order, Rwandans almost inevitably face a choice between compliance and punishment because they have few opportunities to escape. This contributed to the Rwandan state's capacity to reach peasants before and during the genocide and to win their obedience. *Uburetwa*, as mentioned above, was the nickname for an obligation from which a peasant could not escape.[45]

This analysis takes us full circle to a central theme in Rwandan historiography: the issue of obedience and social docility. Many observers of Rwanda comment on the population's "culture of obedience," as we have seen. Obedience, however, may not stem principally from un-

---

43. Louis, *Ruanda-Urundi, 1884–1919*, 112.

44. André Sibomana, *Hope for Rwanda: Conversations with Laure Guilbert and Hervé Deguine*, trans. Carina Tertsakian (London: Pluto Press, 1997), 68.

45. Note too that traditions of surveillance and spying were common even under the precolonial monarchy. As Jan Vansina describes it: "In the districts, the chiefs of cattle and land mutually spy on one another and were spied upon by the subchief of the royal residence and his wife who ran the residence. The provincial chief was thwarted by all mentioned but was supported by the subchiefs who he named. Finally the Twa everywhere served as the king's spies and police." Vansina, *L'évolution du royaume Rwanda des origines à 1900* (Brussels: Académie royale des sciences d'outre-mer, 2000), 55.

thinking cultural responses—though culture may play a role (see below). Rather, obedience stems from the calculation that—given demographic density, settlement patterns, and territorial visibility—successful evasion of or exit from state demands is highly improbable. In short, Rwanda's human and physical geography contribute to state control.[46]

Political Culture and Continuity

The central issue underlying the discussion in this chapter is to understand how and why Rwanda's state was effective during the genocide—even as national authorities were losing ground to the rebels—and to understand ultimately how and why Rwanda's governing elites succeeded in mobilizing so many men to participate in the killing. Therein lies a historical jump. The period in question is the early 1990s, many years after colonialism's end and after the Rwandan "social revolution," in which the monarchy was overthrown and Tutsi political elites were ousted from power. Thus, to claim that there is an institutional connection between the monarchy and the postcolonial state requires an account of legacy and mechanisms of continuity.

The postcolonial record is not replete with elite claims about continuing the legacy of colonialism or of the monarchy. To the contrary, the independence generation of Rwandan leaders sought to distance themselves from the authorities that preceded them. Yet the institutions did not change dramatically. Many observers of the transition period from colonialism to the revolution argue that Rwanda's new leaders often replicated the political behavior of their predecessors. Just as European authorities based their rule on the monarchy's legitimacy and governing patterns, so too Rwanda's independence leaders based their authority on the preexisting political culture.

The similarities in political behavior between the postcolonial and colonial authorities were apparent from the presidency down to local leaders. A leading scholar of the transition period, René Lemarchand, refers to Rwanda's first republic as a "mwamiship" (or kingship—the "mwami" was the Rwandan king). Lemarchand argues that the president's legitimacy was "inextricably bound up" in the popular mind with the legitimacy of the monarchy, and he notes a similar pattern with prefects, burgomasters, and other local authorities.[47] "The es-

46. This point is also made in passing in Prunier, *The Rwanda Crisis*, 3.
47. René Lemarchand, *Rwanda and Burundi* (London: Pall Mall Press, 1970), 272.

sence of my argument, then," Lemarchand concludes, "is that behind the formal institutional framework of the republic lies a traditional role structure which continues to mould the attitudes and strategies of most political actors."[48] Other observers of postcolonial Rwanda make similar points. Danielle de Lame, for example, argues that "in popular perception, the status of the burgomaster equates to that of a chief in the colonial period."[49]

A striking example of the continuity of political culture from the colonial period to the immediate postcolonial one comes from eastern Rwanda. There, an anthropologist, Pierre Gravel, witnessed the sudden rise of a Hutu man to the position of burgomaster. Though harshly critical of the colonial regime and Tutsi chiefs before him, to gain legitimacy the burgomaster "emulated" his predecessor, a Tutsi chief. After being elected, as recounted by Gravel, the burgomaster traveled his constituency saying, "I am chieftain."[50] When he encountered any objections or resistance, Gravel noted, the burgomaster "would shout that he was the chief."[51]

Imitating colonial chiefs took other forms, such as officials forcing people to attend meetings, requiring people to clap their hands in deference, and spying on each other.[52] After studying two post-independence government reports, scholar Filip Reyntjens observed that the inquiries "provide numerous examples of burgomasters, *préfets*, local and regional party officials arrogating to themselves all the attributes, attitudes and values associated with the functions of chief and sub-chief under the *ancien régime.*"[53] There was, in short, continuity between the colonial and postcolonial regimes in how authorities acted.

Two specific postcolonial institutions bear a family resemblance to ones in precolonial and colonial times, and both institutions are relevant to understanding mass civilian mobilization during the genocide. The first is *umuganda*, the "communal work" program, which was introduced under President Habyarimana in the mid-1970s.[54] *Umu-*

---

48. Lemarchand, *Rwanda and Burundi,* 278. For a longer discussion, see 269–79.

49. Danielle de Lame, *Une Colline entre mille ou le calme avant la tempête* (Tervuren, Belgium: Musée royal de l'Afrique centrale, 1996), 75. See also Jean-Claude Willame, *Aux sources de l'hécatombe rwandaise* (Brussels: CEDAF, 1995), 65–66.

50. Gravel, *Remera,* 192.

51. Gravel, *Remera,* 193.

52. Gravel, *Remera,* 194; and Filip Reyntjens, "Chiefs and Burgomasters in Rwanda: The Unfinished Quest for a Bureaucracy," *Journal of Legal Pluralism and Unofficial Law* 25–26 (1987), 71–97.

53. Reyntjens, "Chiefs and Burgomasters," 91.

54. J. B. Nduhungirehe, "Travaux communitaires de développement UMUGANDA," *Dialogue* 63 (July–August 1977), 26–32.

ganda was not identical to precolonial and colonial labor obligations; the postcolonial version was less exploitative, required less time, and its beneficiaries were usually collectives, not specific chiefs. That said, the practice of a communal labor obligation strongly resembles certain aspects of *uburetwa* and colonial corvées. Government officials who explained the rationale behind *umuganda* claimed that the policy *restored* communal labor as a valuable resource for the country.[55] The president called *umuganda* a "necessary obligation" for all of Rwanda's inhabitants.[56]

The second postcolonial institution is wartime civilian patrols. Less is known about the origins and practice of this institution than about *umuganda*. But in each of Rwanda's two periods of war in the postcolonial era—in 1963–64 and in 1990–94—civilian patrols were instituted in response to an external invasion with internal supporters. Official documentation of these policies is lacking. However, a senior military officer explained in an interview with me that:

> Here in Rwanda, civilian defense is not a characteristic of this war [i.e. the 1990–94 period]. It is a characteristic of all wars we have. Each time there is an armed crisis in Rwanda, the civilian population is mobilized to defend themselves and to defend the country. Some are used for counter-infiltration. Some are used for roadblocks. Others are used to transport military equipment.[57]

This officer was not implicated in the genocide. When pressed to explain why the civilian population was used for military purposes, he said:

> For two reasons. The first is because it was a civil war. All individuals are susceptible of being the enemy. The second is because the conflict could have broken out or acts of sabotage could have been committed in all corners of the country. There were not sufficient military means to cover the entire country. It was a guerrilla war.

---

55. See Nduhungirehe, "Travaux communitaires," 27. The official was the minister of planning at the time. A scholar who studied government justifications of *Umuganda* observed that "this policy was presented as the reestablishment of an institution that had long existed in Rwandan culture but that has been suppressed by the colonial economy" because the practice was monetarized. See Philip Verwimp, "Development Ideology, The Peasantry and Genocide: Rwanda Represented in Habyarimana's Speeches," *Journal of Genocide Research* 2, no. 3 (2000), 344.

56. Verwimp, "Development Ideology," 344.

57. Interviewed in Kigali, Rwanda, July 21, 2002.

It is evident that this officer, like others I interviewed, considered civilian mobilization for state and military projects to be a regular, normal practice, particularly during a guerrilla war. As with other institutions of mobilization, the postcolonial practice resembled precolonial practices. Such continuity is rooted in Rwandan political culture—in what political authorities believe is a legitimate and routine demand on the citizenry, and vice versa: what citizens believe is a legitimate and routine demand from those with power.

Genocide as Obligation

I am now in a position to understand and evaluate the widespread perpetrator claims that participation in the genocide was both authorized and obligatory. Recall how some perpetrators described how authorities and bands of men would travel from house to house, demanding that an adult male from each house join the attacks. Recall how the most active perpetrators readily acknowledged that they expected and demanded—under penalty of death, they said—Hutu men to participate. In fact, intra-Hutu pressure was the most common reason that respondents gave for their participation, as we saw in chapter 5. Attacking Tutsis was like a "law"—and disobedience, claimed both those pressuring and those being pressured, would have carried a heavy price. Testimony excerpted in previous chapters showed this, but here are some further examples:

> After the crash of the president's plane, the soldiers stationed at military positions spread through the countryside. They said, "The president has been killed." They told us the Tutsis killed him and that is how the genocide started. . . . They said, "Every person had to defend himself with whatever weapon he could find because the enemy is the Tutsi." *What did you do?* Afterwards if you found a tree branch, you took it [as a weapon], and if you found a Tutsi, you killed him. *Did you form a group?* Yes, I went with them. *Where did you go?* To the *cellules* where Tutsis lived. . . . It was a law. *How can you hit someone if it is an obligation?* *If it were me, I would try to hide.* Where could you hide in war? *But maybe shove with the stick but not actually hit?* That was not possible. *Why not?* If someone orders you with a gun, how can you fight with someone who has a gun? *Why not hide after the first day?* Where would you hide? *Maybe your house?* They would find you there. (Ruhengeri)

In the excerpt, this perpetrator from Ruhengeri Prefecture shows how soldiers traveled civilian areas and instructed Hutus to kill Tutsis. The orders were like a "law," said the respondent. The testimony also is also noteworthy for the calculation of individual compliance it demonstrates. There was nowhere to hide, the perpetrator explained, and refusal to comply would result in punishment from an authority with a gun. A similar dynamic is found in the following excerpt:

> [A] member of the *cellule* committee came to see me, at my place, while I was working in the banana grove. He obligated me, with the others, to go to the river, and he asked us to throw people in the water. I threw one in, and that is what I explained to the court. *How did the official oblig-ate you?* He was part of an attack; he had a gun; he found us working; he asked why we had not left to look for the Tutsis. The attack had two [Tutsi] children with them. *What did he say precisely?* "Why did you not go to kill the Tutsis?" . . . He had been a policeman, and he con-trolled a part of the *cellule.* He was in charge of security. *Why did the attack come looking for you?* I lived near the road. *Did they look for you or just see you?* The attack looked for me because they knew I had a Tutsi wife. They asked me where my wife was because I was at the time alone with my children. I said she was dead, even though I had hidden her. They asked me who killed her. I explained there was an attack from Ruhengeri that took her, and that I did not know where she had been killed. *What happened?* They took me. We went to the river. When we arrived at the river, they ordered us to throw these children in the river. We threw them in the river, and we went back. *Why did you do it?* It was an order. That's what I explained to the tribunal. It was the law. *Why not refuse?* Anyone who refused paid 3000 FRW [about $22] or a jerrican of beer. I couldn't find that. *Still, why not refuse?* I could be killed my-self. You can't refuse someone who has a gun. (Kigali-Rural)

Here again, we see how violent groups traveled the countryside and pressured civilians to join the killing. Participation was an "obliga-tion"—one coercively enforced—that Hutu men were expected to meet.

One consistent theme in many testimonies is that the costs of dis-obedience intensified in wartime. Judging from the two excerpts just quoted, the war climate seems to have added urgency to the orders. The context of war also increased the risks of refusal. In war, non-compliers could be killed. Thus, as the national authorities lost ground to the RPF in the war, their demands on the Hutu civilian pop-ulation to join the war effort became that much more pressing. The following testimony illustrates the point:

> *When you learned . . . you had to chase the Tutsis why did you go?* Be-cause they were enemies who would kill us. . . . *But why did you kill [a*

particular person]? If a leader says it, you cannot refuse it. If the director [of the prison] came here and said, "You, you, and you come," you
cannot refuse. *What would have happened if you refused?* I would not
have been able to find the money to give him because I would have been
considered an accomplice. *How much?* My whole land! . . . In the period
of the *interahamwe,* if you refused the orders of the authorities, they
would consider you to be an accomplice. . . . Before if someone had
killed someone, he was put in prison and sentenced. But during this period, it was a law. (Gisenyi)

Here we see how a perpetrator shifted between rationalizing killing as
self-defense and as "law" that had to be obeyed. Why did he initially
join attacks? Because, he said, the Tutsis were enemies. Why did he
kill? Because, he said, killing was "the law." Why not refuse? Because,
he said, of the credible threat of punishment: he would have lost his
land, and disobedience carried the risk of being branded an "accomplice," which was equivalent to being called an "enemy" and being
targeted for attack. In short, the excerpt shows how war and law
worked together. This was a period of acute crisis—after the president's assassination, the resumption of war, and the rapid spread of violence; the perceptions of uncertainty and threat led to using violence
to assert power and dominance, as I have argued. But there was also a
clear sense that the authorities had decreed a policy of killing with
which men were expected to comply. War and state power worked si-
multaneously to justify and authorize killing.

Many Rwandans said that they participated in the genocide because
of in-group coercion. Perpetrators may be inclined to diminish their
responsibility by claiming that they were following orders under
duress—even if the respondents had already been convicted. But the
stories of genocidal participation as "law," as "obligation," and as the
less costly alternative to being punished for disobedience are remarkably consistent across respondents. Those who mobilized others also
readily acknowledge that they required collective civilian participation and that they considered such mobilization to be a normal course
of action.

Sometimes those who mobilized others were state officials, sometimes they were not but said that they were acting on state officials'
behalf, and sometimes they had usurped power but then acted as if
they were the legitimate authority. In each case, however, civilian mobilization depended on common expectations about how power and

authority work in Rwanda, about the credible threat of coercion, and about the perceived legitimacy of the practice of mass civilian participation in state projects.

This chapter analyzed the institutional origins of these dynamics. Rwanda's state is not conventionally strong in technocratic or bureaucratic terms. Rwanda is a poor, underdeveloped country. But the Rwandan state has uncommonly strong capacity to gain, sometimes coercively, the compliance of the rural citizenry. The idea of state power is deeply resonant throughout the country, and there exist widespread expectations about mass mobilization as common practice. State power and obligatory labor mobilization go hand in hand: they are expressions of one another and they shaped civilian participation during the genocide.

In this chapter, I have argued that there are four principal sources of state power in Rwanda and mass mobilization. These are: (1) an unusually high degree of institutional and national continuity during the last 100 years; (2) an uncommonly well developed precolonial state with specific institutions of mandatory collective labor mobilization, which in turn persisted in the colonial and postcolonial state; (3) dense human settlement; and (4) visible territory, which, when combined with dense settlement, increases the capacity for surveillance and limits the capacity for exit and evasion; such human and physical geography in turn enhances state power and the credible threat of coercion. Finally, during the genocide, war intensified the perceived costs of disobedience, and noncompliers were in fact punished and occasionally killed. Indeed, leading Hutu opposition figures were among the first killed during the genocide. Taken together, these factors combine to make the state effective in Rwanda and effective in particular at civilian mobilization. Even amid a war and a progressive loss of territory, the Rwandan state continued to be effective at civilian mobilization in areas not yet lost to the rebels.

The analysis in this chapter does not explain the rationale for violence or genocide. Rather, the chapter suspends that question in order to understand further why the killing was so rapid and intensive and to understand why so many ordinary Rwandan citizens took part. Without the backing of the state, ethnic violence likely would have occurred in Rwanda after the president's assassination and resumption of war. But without the state, the violence almost certainly would not have become genocide: it would have ended as a limited massacre, as previous episodes of violence had. Instead, the hardliners wrestled control of the state, eliminated Hutu opponents, and unleashed the full force of the state for the project of destroying the "Tutsi enemy." In Rwanda, that had immediate and devastating effect. In Rwanda, once a state-backed policy crystallizes, that policy has tremendous force, even if government orders are to kill.

Conclusion

To summarize, I find that an intense civil war, state power, and pre-existing ethnic/racial classifications are the three primary factors that drove the Rwandan genocide. Each was essential, but, of the three, war was especially consequential. War legitimized killing and justified extreme measures. Perpetrators claimed that violence was a means to defend against advancing rebels, a rationale with meaning and urgency in the midst of an intense and defensive armed conflict. War and the president's assassination also caused fear, anger, and uncertainty, which in turn led some Rwandans to violence. The perception of danger caused by the war and the assassination also undermined moderates throughout the country.

But war alone did not cause genocide. Rather, genocide happened because Hutu hardliners decided to foment violence against Tutsis and because the hardliners had control of the state. After the president's assassination, the hardliners killed key opposition politicians and installed a new government. The hardliners attacked international peacekeepers, prompting international withdrawal from Rwanda, and the hardliners mobilized their loyal institutions, including elite military units, paramilitary forces, political party networks, and broadcast media. The result was that, even though the hardliners were engaged in a losing war against the rebels, they established dominance in the areas not yet lost to the rebels. The state in Rwanda is a powerful tool for executing decisions and mobilizing citizens. By controlling it, the hardliners had the coercive means to enforce their position nationwide.

Categorizing Tutsis as a unitary ethnic or racial group is the third key factor. But hatred based on identity is not the mechanism. I find little evidence of deep, preexisting antipathy and prejudice toward Tutsis on the part of Hutu perpetrators. Rwanda is a highly integrated country in ethnic terms, far more so than most other countries in Africa. Hutus and Tutsis speak the same language, frequently intermarry, and live side by side, among other commonalities. Perpetrators cooperated on a daily basis with Tutsis before the genocide, and most perpetrators expressed generally good relations with Tutsi neighbors—even if many believed that Hutus and Tutsis were members of different ethnic categories and had different physical attributes. Violence also is not constant across time in Rwanda. Killing in the past has happened, but during particular episodes. Thus, something intervenes to cause individuals to switch from seeing people of another ethnic or racial category as neighbors to seeing them as "enemies" who must be killed.

The two key factors that drive the shift are fear and uncertainty in war, on the one hand, and coercive and social pressure, on the other hand. Tutsis became enemies only in war and only when labeled that way by the state. Thus, *in particular circumstances,* Tutsis stopped being neighbors, friends, and family and became a single category—"the enemy." Many perpetrators recall the central phrase of the genocide as "*Umwanzi ni umwe ni umutusi*" (The enemy is one; it is the Tutsi). Embedded in the phrase is the foundation for genocide. That all Tutsis could become "one" and, more specifically, "one enemy" is what allowed a rationale for war to become a rationale for extermination.

The mechanism at work here is collective ethnic categorization. The category "Tutsi" came to represent all individual Tutsis. That category was not invented during the genocide. Ethnic and racial categories preexisted the genocide, and awareness of those categories was widespread and resonant in Rwandan society. Rwanda's national identity cards listed whether each cardholder was Hutu, Tutsi, or Twa. Ethnicity and race were central political idioms in Rwanda, at least since Belgian colonial rule. But the switch that led many ordinary Rwandans with little apparent preexisting hatred to categorize Tutsis as dangerous "enemies" happened only in war and only after the state made that claim.

In sum, the three main factors that contributed to the genocide are war, state power, and preexisting ethnic/racial classifications. War was critical in legitimizing violence and causing the fear and uncertainty that led some to kill. Without war, I believe genocide would not have happened. State power was also essential. Without the backing of the state and without the Rwandan state's capacity to mobilize civilians, the violence would have been more limited than it was. Instead, the killing took on the force of law, and disobedience, in some cases, became synonymous with treason. Finally, collective ethnic or racial categories underpinned the premise of genocide in Rwanda (that all Tutsis were alike). Without those preexisting categories and without a history of ethnic or racial political ideologies, the call to attack Tutsis would not have resonated, and genocide would not likely have happened.

Was extermination planned in advance, before April 6, 1994? To date, the evidence that the hardliners planned, before the president's assassination, to eliminate *all* Rwandan Tutsis is inconclusive. We know that the hardliners were preparing for the worst; we know that they stockpiled weapons; we know that they were prepared to kill some Tutsi civilians; we know that they had invested in irregular and loyal institutions, such as militias. But did they plan to wipe out the entire Tutsi population of Rwanda before April 6, 1994?

We may never know for certain, but my research shows that the genocide need not have been planned in advance for it to have occurred. This is the case for two principal reasons. First, the violence had momentum. Once the hardliners authorized and ordered the population to fight Tutsis and once coalitions of actors at the local level emerged to heed that call, genocidal killing became the order of the day. Those who participated in turn pressured others to kill. Conformity ruled; open disobedience was punished. In that context—war, state instructions to kill, and violence breeding violence—killing Tutsis took on a force of its own. Second, uncertainty and fear are key mechanisms that drove the violence. Rwandans killed in order to protect themselves and to assert power in a period of confusion, crisis, and war. From the beginning of the genocide to the end, the RPF gained ground on government forces. Thus, the more the RPF advanced and the more the hardliners lost ground, uncertainty and fear increased, which in turn sustained the intensity of killing. In short, extermination need not have been planned in advance for it to have occurred.

The analytical issue at stake here is that an overly static conception of genocide as "meticulously planned" *in advance* misses the ways in which events shape outcomes. The Rwandan genocide emerged from a dynamic of escalation; the president's assassination, the resumption of war, and the rebels' rapid advance all were central to that process of escalation. Hutu hardliners ordered genocide as a desperate measure to win a war that they were losing, and their eroding power was critical to why they fomented extermination.

Nothing here undermines the claim that the hardliners who controlled the state are responsible for genocide. Whether they planned genocide in advance, the hardliners deliberately fomented violence against Tutsis after the president was killed and after the war with the RPF resumed. The hardliners' call to destroy the Tutsi enemy imbued killing with the force of authority. Because the hardliners controlled the balance of power in the country, because they faced little opposition from the international community, and because Rwanda's state is an effective tool of mobilization, the violence that the hardliners urged spread rapidly. The hardliners are thus responsible for genocide—this is a point that must be emphasized.

Comparative and Theoretical Implications

There are a number of comparative and theoretical implications of my study. At a micro level, my study shows that self-protection can be a powerful motivator to commit violence. Many ordinary Rwandans participated in genocide because they feared for their safety in war and because they calculated that committing violence would be less costly than openly disobeying. The desire for self-protection was not fabricated out of thin air. A war was in progress. The president had been assassinated. Rebels were advancing. The state ordered the population to defend the nation. Local elites and aggressive young men traveled communities, demanding that other men comply in the name of the law. Dissenters were punished and sometimes killed. These were no ordinary times. Fear is a commonly cited mechanism for violence.[1] My study does not break new theoretical ground on this score,

---

1. On fear and self-protection as key mechanisms, see David Lake and Donald Rothchild, "Spreading Fear: The Genesis of Transnational Ethnic Conflict," in *The International Spread of Ethnic Conflict: Fear, Diffusion, and Escalation*, ed. David Lake and Donald Rothchild (Princeton: Princeton University Press, 1998), 3–32; Roger Petersen, *Understanding Ethnic Violence: Fear, Hatred, and Resentment in Twentieth-Century Eastern Europe* (Cambridge, UK: Cambridge University Press, 2002); Barry Posen, "The Security Dilemma and Ethnic Conflict," *Survival* 35, no. 1 (1993), 27–47; Jack Snyder and Robert Jervis, "Civil War and the Security Dilemma," in *Civil Wars, Insecurity, and Intervention*, ed. Barbara Walter and Jack Snyder (New York: Columbia University Press, 1999), 15–37.

but the research provides evidence to support the theory and details to show how the process worked. None of this excuses the Rwandans who decided to attack Tutsis. Rwandan *génocidaires* made deliberate choices: they decided to participate in genocide and to harm others. Rwandans who became perpetrators should be held accountable for their decisions; the point of the analysis is thus not to excuse but to understand the dynamics that led ordinary civilians to become perpetrators.

My evidence also shows that situations matter. Particular circumstances can cause people to commit harm that they might not otherwise have been predisposed to commit. The point is not a new one to social psychologists. In the early 1970s, Stanley Milgram showed that ordinary men would administer painful, even death-causing, shocks to a person they did not know and had no reason to hate. Milgram emphasized obedience to a legitimate authority as the main mechanism that allowed men to commit harm. Similarly, Philip Zimbardo showed that college-aged men would, when randomly assigned the role of prison guards, behave brutally to peers randomly assigned to the role of prison inmates. In groups and in particular circumstances, ordinary men can change. They can transgress normal codes of behavior and commit violence. To quote Milgram, "This is, perhaps, the most fundamental lesson of our study: ordinary people, simply doing their jobs, and without any particular hostility on their part, can become agents in a terrible destructive process."[2]

These insights have long influenced studies of genocide perpetrators. Emergencies, authority, group pressure, and opportunity can powerfully change the mental frameworks in which men and women make critical, life-altering decisions. Those who commit violence are often well-adjusted, career-oriented fathers and husbands. They tend not to be rabid ideologues, sadists, or abnormal men. They are representative citizens of their societies who find themselves in particular situations and who, in those situations, commit extraordinary acts of evil.[3] As Robert Jay Lifton concluded in his study of Nazi doctors,

2. Stanley Milgram, *Obedience to Authority: An Experimental View* (New York: Harper and Row, 1974), 6; Phillip Zimbardo et al., "The Psychology of Imprisonment: Privation, Power and Pathology," in *Theory and Research in Abnormal Psychology*, ed. David L. Rosenhan and Perry London, 2nd ed. (New York: Holt, Rinehart and Winston, 1975), 270–87.

3. Christopher Browning, *Ordinary Men: Reserve Police Battalion 101 and the Final Solution in Poland* (New York: HarperCollins, 1992); James Waller, *Becoming Evil: How Ordinary People Commit Genocide and Mass Killing* (New York: Oxford University Press, 2002); Herbert Kelman and V. Lee Hamilton, *Crimes of Obedience: Toward*

"The disturbing psychological truth [is] that participation in mass murder need not require emotions as extreme or demonic as would seem appropriate for such a malignant project. . . . Ordinary people can commit demonic acts."[4] To quote another author who studied Nazi perpetrators:

> [They] were not killers by conviction but by circumstance and opportunity. Instead of matching the image of the paranoiac ideological warriors so often invoked when describing the fieldworkers of Nazi genocide, their background profile far more closely matches that of rather ordinary citizens with a well-developed calculating instinct for their private interests.[5]

My study strongly supports these conclusions.

The previous chapters illustrate a related point: people of one ethnicity or religion need not be predisposed to hate or distrust people of another ethnicity or religion in order to harm them. Nor are strong individually held ideological commitments a prerequisite for killing in the name of the state or an idea. These points follow logically from the previous two paragraphs: in particular circumstances, ordinary men can switch from viewing others as unthreatening neighbors to seeing them as enemies. The argument runs contrary to the common wisdom that individuals commit ethnic violence because they have deep-seated animosity toward ethnic others.[6]

Other cases of genocide, however, yield the same counterintuitive conclusions. The Holocaust is the most studied genocide, and while there is disagreement among scholars about what drove most perpetrators, many claim that German perpetrators were not Jew-haters. Rather, as Hannah Arendt and Christopher Browning found, Nazi perpetrators were often ordinary men with limited imaginations and banal aspirations.[7] Daniel Jonah Goldhagen argues otherwise. Goldhagen claims that German perpetrators were ordinary men, but that

---

a Social Psychology of Authority and Responsibility (New Haven: Yale University Press, 1989).

4. Robert Jay Lifton, *The Nazi Doctors: Medical Killing and the Psychology of Genocide* (New York: HarperCollins, 1986), 5.

5. Dick de Mildt, *In the Name of the People: Perpetrators of Genocide in the Reflection of their Post-War Prosecution in West Germany. The "Euthanasia" and "Aktion Reinhard" Trial Cases* (The Hague: Martinus Nijhoff, 1996), 311.

6. The argument is central to Donald Horowitz, *The Deadly Ethnic Riot* (Berkeley and Los Angeles: University of California Press, 2001).

7. Hannah Arendt, *Eichmann in Jerusalem: A Report on the Banality of Evil*, rev. ed. (New York: Penguin Books, 1965); Browning, *Ordinary Men*.

ordinary Germans subscribed to commonly held beliefs in "elimina-tionist anti-Semitism."[8] His position, however, is a minority one in the scholarship. Most scholars argue that while anti-Semitism cer-tainly existed in pre-Nazi Germany, fervent hatred of the Jews was not widespread within the German population. Passive indifference bet-ter describes German attitudes toward the Jews, even after Nazi per-secution began.[9] Nazi ideology and leaders clearly promoted and encouraged anti-Semitism, but the evidence that Germans initially shared such views is thin.

Studies of violence in the former Yugoslavia show much the same. Marshalling considerable evidence, V. P. Gagnon shows that violence in the Balkans in the early 1990s was not the product of mass hatred or distrust between ethnic groups.[10] Tone Bringa's ethnographic re-search in rural central Bosnia has similar results. Bringa finds that be-fore the war Muslims and Croats were aware of ethnic differences between them. Some families and individuals had close interethnic ties; others did not. And awareness of difference did not in and of it-self precipitate violence or resentment. But Bringa finds that peaceful relations rapidly changed in certain circumstances: "War changes peo-ple in profound ways. It changes their perceptions of themselves and who they are, and it changes their perceptions of others and who they are."[11] Bringa also dramatically captures the change on film. She shows how war can lead lifelong friends and neighbors to stop speak-ing and to become deeply mistrustful.[12]

My findings from rural Rwanda are remarkably similar. Before the genocide, Hutus and Tutsis lived together in the countryside, and most of the time they cooperated. Many were aware of ethnic differ-ences, and many were aware of Rwanda's history of ethnic conflict. But recognition of ethnic difference and a history of ethnic violence did not precipitate violence. The awareness of ethnic difference be-

8. Daniel Jonah Goldhagen, *Hitler's Willing Executioners: Ordinary Germans and the Holocaust* (New York: Random House, 1996).

9. Christopher Browning, *The Origins of the Final Solution: The Evolution of Nazi Jewish Policy* (Lincoln: University of Nebraska Press, 2004), 1–11; Saul Friedlander, *Nazi Germany and the Jews: Volume 1: The Years of Persecution, 1933–1939* (New York: HarperCollins, 1997), 4.

10. V. P. Gagnon Jr., *The Myth of Ethnic War: Serbia and Croatia in the 1990s* (Ithaca: Cornell University Press, 2004).

11. Tone Bringa, *Being Muslim the Bosnian Way: Identity and Community in a Cen-tral Bosnian Village* (Princeton: Princeton University Press, 1995), 5.

12. "We Are all Neighbors: Bosnia," video recording, directed by Debbie Christie, Granada Television, distributed by Films Incorporated, 1993.

came salient and the basis for violence only in particular circumstances—in a context of uncertainty fueled by war and assassination and of state orders to attack Tutsis. Many rural Hutu men made fateful choices in those circumstances: they chose to participate in violence against their Tutsi neighbors because they were afraid and because they felt pressure from other Hutus to do so.

The effect of media propaganda, especially radio broadcasts—a common analytical thread in the literature on the Rwandan genocide—is more difficult to measure. Before the genocide, Rwandan private media often showcased RPF atrocities and emphasized Hutu solidarity. During the genocide, radio broadcasts signaled that war was on, that the hardliners were in control, and that, in some instances, ordinary Hutus had to fight the Tutsis. Undoubtedly, the broadcasts contributed at least indirectly to the idea that Tutsis were dangerous and should be killed.[13] But my evidence does not suggest that radio propaganda in and of itself caused most individuals to commit violence. Most men chose to participate in the killing after face-to-face mobilization and in a real situation of war and crisis. The evidence suggests that radio broadcasts had effects on particular perpetrator populations, in particular local elites and the most aggressive killers. But media effects alone did not drive most participation in the genocide.

My findings also run contrary to claims that deprivation, greed, or a "culture of obedience" drive participation. The theories are common in the general literature on violence and genocide as well as the specific literature on Rwanda. The argument about deprivation is that individuals experience hardship or feel that they should be in a better position than they are. Because of the deprivation, they become frustrated and commit violence, often against out-groups in society. They scapegoat.[14] The argument about greed is that individuals participate in order to gain wealth or simply steal. The argument is common in

13. Indirect causation is the central conclusion of a major international court decision that found three journalists guilty of incitement to genocide. International Criminal Tribunal for Rwanda, "The Prosecutor v. Ferdinand Nahimana, Jean-Bosco Baraygwiza, and Hassan Ngeze," ICTR Case No. 99–52–T, Judgment and Decision, December 3, 2003.

14. On the relationship between relative deprivation and violence, see Ted Robert Gurr, *Why Men Rebel* (Princeton: Princeton University Press, 1970); and, for a critique, James Rule, *Theories of Civil Violence* (Berkeley and Los Angeles: University of California Press, 1988), 200–223. For an argument about how frustration can lead to scapegoating, see Ervin Staub, *The Roots of Evil: The Origins of Genocide and Other Group Violence* (Cambridge, UK: Cambridge University Press, 1989). For an application to Rwanda, see Peter Uvin, *Aiding Violence: The Development Enterprise in Rwanda* (West Hartford, CT: Kumarian Press, 1998).

the Rwandan context.[15] The "culture of obedience" argument is similarly a cliché many reference to explain participation in Rwanda.[16]

The theories may work well to explain participation in other episodes of mass violence, but the arguments are less persuasive in the Rwandan context. Rwandan perpetrators were poor, but they were not on average any poorer than other Rwandans; nor did violence start earliest in the poorest regions. Many Rwandans did steal their deceased neighbors' property, but only rarely in my more than 200 interviews with perpetrators did this motive surface as the principal reason to commit genocide. That said, the theory may work to explain the behavior of the worst perpetrators, if not most perpetrators—as I show in chapter 5. Similarly, many Rwandans obeyed orders, but not because of blind acceptance, because of a "culture of obedience," or because those giving direction were legitimate authorities. Rather, given the density of Rwanda's state, Rwanda's geography and patterns of settlement, and the sometimes lethal consequences of dissent, Rwandans calculated that compliance was less costly than opposition.

At a more macro level, my evidence clearly supports the idea that war and genocide are intricately and causally related. Again, the observation is not a new one for the scholarship on genocide.[17] Some

15. Waller, *Becoming Evil*, 69.

16. For some examples, see Gérard Prunier, *The Rwanda Crisis: History of a Genocide* (New York: Columbia University Press, 1995), 57, 245; Christian Scherrer, *Genocide and Crisis in Central Africa: Conflict Roots, Mass Violence, and Regional War* (Westport, CT: Praeger, 2001), 113; Shaharyar Khan, *The Shallow Graves of Rwanda* (London and New York: I. B. Tauris, 2001), 67; Regine Andersen, "How Multilateral Development Assistance Triggered the Conflict in Rwanda," *Third World Quarterly* 21, no. 3 (2000), 441–56.

17. Robert Gellately, "The Third Reich," in *The Specter of Genocide: Mass Murder in Historical Perspective*, ed. Robert Gellately and Ben Kiernan (New York: Cambridge University Press, 2003), 242, 245; Florence Mazian, *Why Genocide?* (Ames: Iowa State University Press, 1990); Donald E. Miller and Lorna Touryan Miller, *Survivors: An Oral History of the Armenian Genocide* (Berkeley and Los Angeles: University of California Press, 1993), 46; Erik Markusen, "Genocide and Warfare," in *Genocide, War, and Human Survival*, ed. Charles Strozier and Michael Flynn (Lanham, MD: Rowman and Littlefield, 1996), esp. 77–81; Robert Melson, *Revolution and Genocide: On the Origins of the Armenian Genocide and the Holocaust* (Chicago: University of Chicago Press, 1992); Manus Midlarsky, *The Killing Trap: Genocide in the Twentieth Century* (Cambridge: Cambridge University Press, 2005); Samantha Power, *"A Problem from Hell": America and the Age of Genocide* (New York: Basic Books, 2002), 91; Jacques Semelin, "Analysis of a Mass Crime: Ethnic Cleansing in the Former Yugoslavia, 1991–1999," in *The Specter of Genocide: Mass Murder in Historical Perspective*, ed. Robert Gellately and Ben Kiernan (New York: Cambridge University Press, 2003), 356; Martin Shaw, *War and Genocide: Organized Killing in Modern Society* (Oxford: Polity, 2003); and Eric Weitz, "The Modernity of Genocides," in *The Specter of Genocide: Mass Murder in Historical Perspective*, ed. Robert Gellately and Ben Kiernan (New York: Cambridge University Press, 2003), 56–57.

authors contend that war is a "cover" for genocide.[18] Other authors argue that acute crisis and social upheaval, of which war is one example, are essential drivers of genocide.[19] Still other authors emphasize a "security dilemma" as a key dynamic that drives violence. The latter argument derives from international relations theory. Applied to a domestic political arena, the claim runs that when a central authority collapses, social groups become uncertain about their rivals' intentions and thus fear for their security. Groups in turn may commit violence to prevent an adversary from inflicting harm against them. In anarchic situations, in short, individuals attack to preempt being attacked.[20] More broadly, Benjamin Valentino argues that the origins of genocide and mass killing lie in the strategic decisions of leaders. Leaders choose genocide and mass killing to counter a perceived threat, and they make such decisions often in the context of war.[21] In an evocative phrase, Valentino and his coauthors refer to genocide and mass killing as "war by other means."[22]

My study not only provides empirical evidence to support and dis-

---

18. The claim is sometimes made with reference to the Armenian genocide. See, for example, Rouben Paul Adalian, "The Armenian Genocide," in *Century of Genocide: Critical Essays and Eyewitness Accounts*, ed. Samuel Totten, William Parsons, and Israel Charny, 2nd ed. (New York: Routledge, 2004), 60; and Jay Winter, "Under Cover of War: The Armenian Genocide in the Context of Total War," in *The Specter of Genocide: Mass Murder in Historical Perspective*, ed. Robert Gellately and Ben Kiernan (New York: Cambridge University Press, 2003), 189.

19. Barbara Harff, "No Lessons Learned from the Holocaust? Assessing Risks of Genocide and Political Mass Murder since 1955," *American Political Science Review* 97, no. 1 (2003), 62; Barbara Harff, "The Etiology of Genocides," in *Genocide and the Modern Age: Etiology and Case Studies of Mass Death*, ed. Isidor Walliman and Michael Dobkowski (Westport, CT: Greenwood Press, 1987), 41–59; Staub, *The Roots of Evil*; and Matthew Krain, "State Sponsored Mass Murder: The Onset and Severity of Genocides and Politicides," *Journal of Conflict Resolution* 41, no. 3 (1997), 331–61.

20. For references to applications of the security dilemma to ethnic conflict in domestic states, see note 1. For a critique of the approach, see Nelson Kasfir, "Domestic Anarchy, Security Dilemmas and Violent Predation: Causes of Failure," in *When States Fail: Causes and Consequences*, ed. Robert Rotberg (Princeton: Princeton University Press, 2004), 53–76. For an application to Rwanda, see Rui de Figueiredo and Barry Weingast, "The Rationality of Fear: Political Opportunism and Ethnic Conflict," in *Civil Wars, Insecurity, and Intervention*, ed. Barbara Walter and Jack Snyder (New York: Columbia University Press, 1999), 261–302. They argue Hutu elites "gambled for resurrection": after calculating they had lost the civil war, they chose genocide and mass participation to weaken the rebels' future base of support. See also René Lemarchand, "Disconnecting the Threads: Rwanda and the Holocaust Reconsidered," *Idea* 7, no. 1 (2001).

21. Benjamin Valentino, *Final Solutions: Mass Killings and Genocide in the Twentieth Century* (Ithaca: Cornell University Press, 2004).

22. Benjamin Valentino, Paul Huth, and Dylan Balch-Lindsay, "'Draining the Sea': Mass Killing and Guerrilla Warfare," *International Organization* 58, no. 2 (2004), 375–407.

tinguish between these claims but also to specify how war contributes to genocide. To reiterate, I find war to be fundamental to the logic of genocide in Rwanda. War legitimates killing as an acceptable practice. War turns rivals into "enemies" who must be killed. War is also fundamental to the conditions under which ordinary men will kill. War creates fear, anger, and uncertainty, which in turn can cause men to commit violence they might in other circumstances never commit. War is also fundamentally *about* violence. Moreover, war, in particular civil war, leads specialists in violence—soldiers—to enter domestic arenas. In short, war is not tangential to or a "cover" for genocide; war is central.

That said, the application of a security dilemma to Rwanda has problems. The dynamic described in a security dilemma does resonate with the rationales for genocide in Rwanda, as chapter 6 shows. Most perpetrators claim that killing Tutsis was a strategy of self-defense against the advancing rebels and after the rebels (allegedly) assassinated the president. But, in contrast to a security dilemma account, "anarchy" and state collapse do not characterize what happened in Rwanda. In early April, the president was killed, as was the prime minister, and surviving Hutu leaders jockeyed for power. War was on, and the rebels were winning. However, after the assassination and in the context of a defensive war, Hutu hardliners emerged to take control of the Rwandan state. They in turn deployed loyal forces to attack Tutsi civilians, and they authorized general violence against Tutsis. Even though government forces were on the defensive and losing ground to rebels, local state institutions and local perceptions of authority remained intact. In other words, the state did not collapse, and state institutions (and common perceptions of what authorities require of citizens) were fundamental to the rapid mobilization for genocide.

Here I come full circle to a tension that runs throughout the book. The evidence clearly shows that fear, uncertainty, and insecurity in the context of a defensive war and after the president's assassination underpinned the rationale for genocide. In addition, episodes of anti-Tutsi violence before the genocide typically occurred in response to actual attacks, perceived threats, and political transitions. Yet perceptions of state power, preexisting institutions of labor conscription, and the country's geography were critical to the rapid mobilization of men and the rapid spike in violence. In other words, insecurity and uncertainty drove the logic of violence, but the execution of violence depended on enforcement capacity. Genocide in Rwanda was indeed predicated on the idea of "war by other means," but other means were also necessary to carry out genocide.

Empirically, the relationship between war and genocide works for other cases. Ottoman Turks committed the Armenian genocide during World War I, and fears of an alliance between Russia and the Armenians clearly contributed to the violence. The Nazis committed the "Final Solution" during World War II. Detailed studies of that genocide show that the specific decisions that led to the extermination of the Jews were related to war (though analysts differ over whether wartime euphoria, defeat, or defensiveness triggered the escalation).[23]

Further generalizations depend on definitions of genocide. Violence in Bosnia, which an international court found to be "genocide," occurred in wartime; the ethnographic research cited above and other research on the Balkans shows the importance of war.[24] Violence in Darfur, which the United States labeled "genocide," also occurred in response to an armed rebellion.[25] A recent study listed seventeen African cases of genocide and political mass murder since political independence.[26] By my count, all but one occurred in countries at war.[27] In short, the relationship between war and genocide is strong.

Mass killing in communist regimes follows a different, but not unrelated, pattern. The violence is the product of leaders' attempts to socially transform their societies, as Valentino argues.[28] Furthermore, most episodes do not occur during actual wars. That said, communist leaders often framed social transformation as "war." Real and imagined obstacles to revolution in turn became "enemies." Take Cambodia, for example. Khmer Rouge leaders were obsessed with hidden "enemies."[29] In the Soviet Union of Lenin and Stalin, counterrevolu-

23. See, in particular, the highly detailed account in Browning, *Origins of the Final Solution*; for another take, see Doris Bergen, *War and Genocide: A Concise History of the Holocaust* (Lanham, MD: Rowman and Littlefield, 2003), 141–42.

24. On the genocide designation, see International Criminal Tribunal for the former Yugoslavia Appeals Chamber, "Prosecutor v. Radislav Krstic," Judgment, April 19, 2004. On other research on the Balkans that emphasizes war, see Susan Woodward, *Balkan Tragedy: Chaos and Dissolution after the Cold War* (Washington: Brookings Institution, 1995), 353.

25. Scott Straus, "Darfur and the Genocide Debate," *Foreign Affairs* 84, no. 1 (2005), 123–33.

26. The list is compiled from the Political Instability Task Force and is available in Monty Marshall and Ted Robert Gurr, *Peace and Conflict 2005: A Global Survey of Armed Conflicts, Self-Determination Movements, and Democracy*, Center for International Development and Conflict Management, University of Maryland, May 2005.

27. Scott Straus, "Is War Over? Evidence from Africa," paper presented at the American Political Science Association Annual Meetings, Washington, D.C., September 4, 2005.

28. Valentino, *Final Solutions*, ch. 4.

29. For some vivid examples, see David Chandler, *Voices from S-21: Terror and History in Pol Pot's Secret Prison* (Berkeley and Los Angeles: University of California Press, 1999), ch. 3; and Karl Jackson, "The Ideology of Total Revolution," in *Cambodia 1975–*

tionaries became "enemies," as they did in Mao's China.[30] Actual wars increase the likelihood of labeling opponents "enemies," which in turn legitimizes violence and, in some cases, annihilation. The communist cases demonstrate that war itself may not be necessary for mass violence to occur. Rather, the cases show that framing political struggle as "war" and labeling opponents as "enemies" may also trigger rationales for violence and annihilation.

By the same token, not all wars or revolutionary changes framed as "war" lead to genocide. My study is of a single country and is thus not well equipped to answer why some armed conflicts lead to genocide while others do not. Yet my research suggests several testable hypotheses.

First, violence will be more intense in countries where leaders have greater capacity for social control, whether through coercive or non-coercive means. In Rwanda, authorities triggered a set of processes and mechanisms by instructing the population to attack Tutsis. Rwanda's state is dense at the local level—authority resonates in the country-side, and state mobilization of citizens is a regular practice. Further-more, Rwandans had few places to hide. In short, by controlling the state, Hutu hardliners had the capacity to enforce their decisions quickly, which in turn shaped the intensity of violence and the par-ticipation in violence. In countries where leaders lack the ability to carry out decisions nationally or with weak institutions, violence will take longer to materialize, and the possibility of evasion by both po-tential perpetrators and victims alike will increase. The result will be less intense violence.

The argument appears to work for other cases, but it requires fur-ther research and empirical specification. Nazi Germany had strong bureaucratic capacity, and that type of state power increased officials' ability to gain compliance and to execute violence rapidly. The Khmer Rouge governed a destroyed state. However, by collectivizing the so-ciety and eliminating political opponents, the Khmer Rouge created strong coercive capacity to enforce decisions. By contrast, the violence in Darfur is considerably less intense, a "slow-motion Rwanda." The

---

1978: Rendezvous with Death, ed. Karl Jackson (Princeton: Princeton University Press, 1989), 37–78.

30. See, for example, the descriptions in chapter 4 of *Final Solutions* as well as in the chapters on the Soviet Union and China in Stéphane Courtois et al., eds., *The Black Book of Communism: Crimes, Terror, Repression,* trans. Jonathan Murphy and Mark Kramer (Cambridge, MA: Harvard University Press, 1999). I thank Ed Friedman and Ben-jamin Valentino for drawing my attention to the points in this paragraph.

reason may be that the Sudanese state, which is spread out across a large territory, is decentralized and weakly institutionalized. Rwanda's state is more compact and effective at the local level, and the geography and human density make the population easy to control.

Second, genocide is more likely in countries with a history of ethnic nationalism. My study showed that at the micro-level most perpetrators did not kill because they had strong commitments to ethnic nationalism. In fact, for many rural farmers with limited education, the core tenets of ethnic nationalism had little resonance. But the same is not necessarily true for national leaders. By 1994, Rwanda had a well-worn political ideology that equated democracy with Hutu rule. Moreover, some Hutu leaders associated Tutsi rule before and during colonialism with repression. These ideological frameworks clearly existed in Rwanda and, if we can judge from the propaganda before the genocide, were salient among some Hutu elites. Salient ethnic nationalism at the elite level increases the likelihood that, in an acute war, leaders will define the "enemy" as an ethnic category.

The importance of ethnic nationalism is a longstanding observation in studies of other genocides, especially the Holocaust. Though the Nazi leadership was extreme in its commitments to racial purity, fascism in Germany was built on a core of racial nationalism.[31] While communism and Maoism clearly influenced the Khmer Rouge, an ethnic nationalist ideal inflected the political philosophy of Democratic Kampuchea's leaders.[32] Slobodan Milosevic and other Serb hardliners in the former Yugoslavia also advocated ethnic nationalism.[33] Similarly, a vision of Arab-Islamic rule has consistently underpinned the political philosophy of Sudan's northern leaders.[34] In a major new study, Michael Mann emphasizes the critical importance of ethnic nationalism in explaining large-scale ethnic violence and genocide.[35] Similarly, in his analysis of modern genocide, Eric Weitz stresses the importance of utopic ideologies of "race and nation."[36] My study sup-

---

31. This is an important theme of Friedlander, *Nazi Germany and the Jews.*

32. Ben Kiernan, *The Pol Pot Regime: Race, Power, and Genocide in Cambodia under the Khmer Rouge, 1975–79* (New Haven: Yale University Press, 1996).

33. Laura Silber and Allan Little, *Yugoslavia: Death of a Nation,* rev. ed. (New York: Penguin Books, 1997), 31–35.

34. Ann Mosely Lesch, *The Sudan: Contested National Identities* (Bloomington: Indiana University Press, 1998), 21.

35. Michael Mann, *The Dark Side of Democracy: Explaining Murderous Ethnic Cleansing* (New York: Cambridge University Press, 2004).

36. Eric Weitz, *A Century of Genocide: Utopias of Race and Nation* (Princeton: Princeton University Press, 2003).

ports these arguments (if not that of "utopia"). But my study also shows that ethnic nationalism is insufficient; an intense, defensive war and capacity for social control also matter. The testable hypothesis is that a history of ethnic nationalism increases the probability of genocide or, more specifically, increases the probability that leaders in war will identify the "enemy" as an ethnic category.

Third, genocide is more likely where the power of dominant elites is eroded or eroding. In these circumstances, leaders will resort to greater levels of violence and irregular tactics in order to remain dominant. In Rwanda, multiparty politics, fierce *intra*-ethnic political competition, the initial low-grade civil war with Tutsis, and the Arusha peace agreement compromised Habyarimana's ruling party and his inner circle. Hutu elites in turn developed extreme measures and invested in parallel institutions to keep power. Small-scale violence against Tutsis occurred in this period, from 1990 to 1993, but genocide did not. Rather, the Hutu hardliners fomented extermination only after the president's assassination, the resumption of war, and the rebels' steady advance. In sum, when dominant elites believe that their eroded power prevents them from winning conventionally, they turn to irregular and extreme tactics, which under certain circumstances can become genocide.

The idea that genocide is the product of escalation is not new: genocide is not usually the first tactic threatened elites choose.[37] What my study highlights is that compromised power and perceived weakness may drive the escalation. A turn in war may be the source of weakness, as might be a fracturing ruling coalition, or regime transition—or all three, as in Rwanda in 1994. The argument is consistent with theories that stress social upheaval—the upheaval or difficult life conditions may create perceptions of weakened power.[38] At the same time, the hypothesis runs contrary to theories of genocide that stress absolute power.[39] Genocide and mass killing tend to occur when regimes are compromised and weakened. But clearly compromised power is insufficient to cause genocide. Rather, constraint in intensive wars drives extreme measures and—this is counterintuitive—mass violence tends to depend also on remaining capacity for social control (even if elites believe they are in a weak position).

There is a fourth counterintuitive implication: mass ethnic violence

---

37. See in particular Valentino, *Final Solutions,* and Mann, *The Dark Side of Democracy.*
38. On social upheaval and difficult life conditions, see note 19.
39. Irving Louis Horowitz, *Taking Lives: Genocide and State Power* (New Brunswick, NJ: Transaction Books, 1997); and Rudolph Rummel, *Death by Government* (New Brunswick, NJ: Transaction Books, 1994).

is more likely to occur in societies with a high degree of interethnic integration. The claim runs against the idea that deep divisions are an essential precondition for genocide. But the evidence suggests that the worst ethnic violence happens in areas with the least physical distance between ethnic groups. Rwanda shows this dramatically. But so does Bosnia: the republic was the most ethnically integrated in the former Yugoslavia. Sudan is deeply divided between north and south, Muslim and Christian, and Arab and black African. But Darfur is an area of comparatively greater integration. Darfuris are all Muslim, those who identify as Arabs and black Africans live in close proximity, and there is intermarriage between Arabs and Africans. In Germany, Jews were well integrated, more so than in some other European countries.

What is the probable reason why interethnic integration might increase the probability of genocide? I offer two. First, interethnic integration creates the capacity to carry out violence. If ethnic groups live in separate regions, the ability for a state captured by one ethnic group to commit exterminatory violence against another diminishes. Second, if insecurity and uncertainty drive the violence, integration would augment the fear. If groups live far away from one another, there is less to fear. But when in close proximity, fear may intensify. The claim about a relationship between interethnic integration and genocide is speculative and does not appear to have universal application (it does not appear to work for the Armenian case, for example). As with the other testable implications advanced in this section, the hypothesis requires further research.

Practical Implications

Although my focus is how and why genocide occurs, the study has a number of practical and policy implications. I focus in this section on two major issues: first, on the question of international intervention to prevent or stop genocide and, second, on the question of reconstruction and reconciliation after genocide. My research shows that decisive international action to stop the killing once it began likely would have had a major impact and saved probably hundreds of thousands of lives. Based on the findings, I also identify some specific scenarios for when international actors should be concerned about an outbreak of mass violence. On the domestic side, my conclusions create reason for cautious optimism about reconciliation and future peace in Rwanda; however, the findings also lead me to criticize many of the approaches taken thus far.

For many outside observers, Rwanda symbolizes the failure of the

international community to uphold commitments to prevent genocide. Rwanda was the "preventable genocide" from which the international community walked away.[40] International observers had
ample early warnings of brewing ethnic violence. When the genocide
began, the United Nations already had a peacekeeping force on the
ground. The genocide's main weapons were rudimentary. Instead of
intervening, however, major international actors evacuated their nationals, drew down the peacekeeping force, and blocked efforts for a
more robust international response. The common wisdom is to blame
the feckless international response on a lack of political will. Yet there
remains debate about how, when, and whether international actors
could have been effective if they had intervened.[41]

There are two phases in the conflict to consider: "early warning" before genocide broke out and intervention once genocide was under-
way. Many observers malign the United Nations for failing to act
decisively when Roméo Dallaire cabled to UN headquarters in January to say that he had evidence that hardliners were training militias
to kill Tutsi civilians. Dallaire said that he wanted to raid the caches
in Kigali where militias had buried their weapons. However, officials
at UN headquarters in New York opposed the plan, telling Dallaire instead to inform President Habyarimana. Under the circumstances, the
recommendation was spectacularly naïve, given that the hardliners responsible for the militias were the allies of the president. Whether the
militia training was evidence of a full-blown plan for genocide, the evidence *was* incontrovertible proof that dominant elites had developed
extreme and irregular tactics to fight their armed rivals—and that
should have triggered a response.

The point has implications for future cases. Finding clear evidence
of genocide planning before mass violence occurs may be too high a
threshold for effective preventive action. Such evidence is rare. Rather,
international watchdogs should be wary when previously dominant
elites begin to radicalize in response to fears that they will lose power
and when they eschew normal institutional means to confront their

40. Organization of African Unity, *Rwanda: The Preventable Genocide: The Report
of the International Panel of Eminent Personalities to Investigate the 1994 Genocide
Rwanda and the Surrounding Events*, 2000.

41. See articles by Alan Kuperman and Alison Des Forges in *American Foreign Policy: Cases and Choices*, ed. James Hoge and Gideon Rose (New York: Council on Foreign Relations, 2003), 76–106; and Benjamin Valentino, "Still Standing By: Why
America and the International Community Fail to Prevent Genocide and Mass Killing,"
Perspectives on Politics 1, no. 3 (2003), 565–78.

rivals. These are signs that a major conflagration is on the horizon. If international actors have peacekeepers in place to safeguard a peace agreement and these dynamics take hold, international actors should develop contingency plans (and troop strength) for if and when events take a violent turn.

Let me turn now to the question of whether an international intervention would have worked in preventing mass murder. The question here is not whether the political will for the use of force exists or, more specifically, why it often does not. Rather, the question here is, if a decision had been made to intervene, would the intervention have been successful? My arguments and evidence suggest that the answer to that question is yes—provided that international action were swift and decisive.

Why would an intervention have been effective? First, an intervention would have strengthened the hand of moderates who sought to prevent mass violence. My findings show that among Hutu elites at the national and local levels, there was a struggle for dominance. Ultimately, the Hutu hardliners won those struggles and succeeded in marginalizing and overcoming the moderates. The hardliners succeeded because they controlled a balance of power in the country, because they acted first to assassinate the key Hutu politicians, and because the gathering intensity of the war undermined moderates. An international intervention would have helped to tip the balance in the other direction. Instead, when they confronted the hardliners, the moderates had no real external support or means to fight. International backing would have changed that dynamic.

Second, a strong international intervention would have short-circuited some of the dynamics driving the violence. Perpetrators premised the rationale for genocide on security. The perpetrators argued, perversely, that killing Tutsi civilians was self-defense and a way to combat the "enemy." That rationale succeeded only in a period of emergency, confusion, and war. A strong international action would have calmed the situation, thereby allaying the fears and anxieties that were driving the perceptions of insecurity. Decisive action would have thus undermined the hardliners' claims of the necessity of using extreme violence as a means of self-protection. Instead, again, the opposite happened: the international withdrawal of most peacekeepers and nationals only added to the vortex of confusion and crisis.

My study of Giti in chapter 3 provides evidence to support the claim. Giti was the one commune under government control where genocidal violence did not occur. My research shows that once the

RPF entered the area, the dynamics that elsewhere in the country led to genocidal violence stopped. The implication is that had the international community signaled a credible commitment to stabilize Rwanda, genocidal violence would probably have been limited. Undoubtedly, there would have been some violence. Men would have revenged Habyarimana's death by killing Tutsis. But had a stabilizing force asserted control, the violence probably would have been contained.

The absence of large-scale anti-Tutsi violence in Rwanda since the genocide points to the same conclusion. After the RPF won the war and asserted control over Rwanda, there were only isolated attacks against Tutsis (though the RPF has allegedly killed Hutu civilians in Rwanda and the Democratic Republic of Congo). Without the dynamics of acute insecurity and without social pressure to commit violence against Tutsis, Hutu civilians show no inclination to attack Tutsi civilians. Many Hutu men participated in genocide because they feared the negative consequences of open defiance. My prediction is that had Hutus been ordered *not* to commit violence and had there been force to back up the call for moderation, most Hutu men would have complied with the orders for peace.

An effective international response would have required a well-prepared and sizeable fighting force, solid intelligence, and quick decision-making. As I showed in chapter 2, once the violence began, it spiked. There was a window in which to stop the killing, but that window was small. However, none of these elements—training, adequate personnel and equipment, intelligence, or quick decision-making—existed in 1994. The international peacekeepers deployed to Rwanda were not well prepared. Their problems ranged from military coordination to basic logistics, such as feeding troops. The force commander, Dallaire, had very limited knowledge of Rwanda before arriving. UN intelligence-gathering was thin, and key decisions were made thousands of miles away in New York, at UN headquarters.[42]

The lesson here is that if peacekeepers are deployed to a country, they must be prepared logistically and politically to weather a serious crisis. Otherwise, the international community's missteps—and panic, in this case—may unwittingly feed the very dynamics peacekeepers are there to prevent. Whether serious, committed, and well-

---

42. Roméo Dallaire with Brent Beardsley, *Shake Hands with the Devil: The Failure of Humanity in Rwanda* (Toronto: Random House Canada, 2003) and Luc Marchal, *Rwanda: La descente aux enfers: Témoignage d'un peacekeeper Décembre 1993–Avril 1994* (Brussels : Éditions Labor, 2001).

funded international peacekeeping in Africa will ever be a political reality is an open question and not one I seek to answer here. Whether there could have been the political will for decisive action in Rwanda in 1994—only months after the Somalia debacle—is also an issue I do not address. Rather, my study shows (1) that decisive international action could have changed the dynamic that drove the genocide, and (2) why international action would have had that effect.

My study also has important implications for conflict resolution strategies. If the common wisdom is that ethnic hatred and divisions are the main reasons why genocide happened, a logical conflict resolution strategy is to build interethnic ties. In fact, many nongovernmental organizations who have worked in Rwanda since the genocide have based programs on the premise. Similarly, some argue that intercommunal participation in civil society salves violence.[43] My study shows that these strategies probably would not work for cases of extreme violence. Hutus and Tutsis cooperated in Rwanda before the genocide. They shared food and drink regularly. They intermarried. They knew each other intimately. But in particular circumstances, preexisting interethnic ties were not enough to prevent violence. During an intense war and under pressure from other Hutus and the state, many Rwandans chose to kill people they knew and with whom they had previously cooperated. The point is not to discourage projects that seek reconciliation and building intercommunal trust. These are worthwhile goals. But no one should entertain the notion that such ties will stop future violence under particular conditions.

Since taking power in 1994, the RPF has pursued two major strategies for governing post-genocide Rwanda: repression and maximal justice. The first approach is misguided and dangerous. The second arguably is as well, but less so.

The RPF was born a rebel movement, and tactical thinking dominates the leadership. The RPF emphasizes security, which in practice means a strong troop presence countrywide. The former rebels also spearheaded major military interventions in neighboring Democratic Republic of Congo in the name of security. Inside Rwanda, the RPF is allergic to political dissent. Free political expression remains severely limited; the government has frequently shut down the critical press as well as independent civil society organizations, especially those advocating human rights. National presidential and parliamentary elec-

---

43. Ashutosh Varshney, *Ethnic Conflict and Civic Life: Hindus and Muslims in India*, 2nd ed. (New Haven: Yale University Press, 2002).

tions were held in 2003, but the RPF banned the most credible opposition party from contesting and proceeded to win more than 95 percent of the vote. Rwanda's post-genocide regime also has sought to remove references to ethnicity from public discourse. Rwanda is now supposedly a land of Rwandans, not one of Hutus, Tutsis, and Twas. Often the regime justifies repression in the name of ending an "ideology of genocide" and "divisionism," which the new authorities claim drove the genocide.[44]

My study suggests that the authorities are right to concern themselves with stability and security, but they are doing so for the wrong reasons, and their actions may ultimately backfire. I find that an "ideology of genocide" did not drive participation in the genocide. On the whole, war and state authorization did. For the short term, neither is likely in Rwanda. War is not imminent, and the RPF is not likely to authorize the killing of Tutsis. In short, repression is not an effective policy to prevent genocide and likely will breed discontent, which in turn could, over the long run, trigger another round of armed conflict in Rwanda. Given Rwanda's history, there is every reason to expect that another cycle of armed combat will again trigger violence against civilians.

Faced with a population that some in the leadership called criminal, the RPF chose maximal prosecution. The regime arrested anyone accused of taking part in the genocide, including anyone who stole property. Rwanda's prisons rapidly swelled. By 2000, the government had arrested more than 100,000 detainees on genocide charges. Many detainees in turn spent several years in jail without formal charges. A few years later, only a fraction had been tried. The genocide devastated Rwanda's justice system, and detainees on that magnitude would be difficult to process in a poor country like Rwanda's even in normal circumstances. In 2002, facing the reality that finishing the trials could take more than fifty years, Rwanda introduced a system of justice called *Gacaca*, in which the majority of cases would move out of the courtroom and into open-air sessions that community members would adjudicate.[45]

My findings suggest that maximum justice is not the most appro-

44. On political repression in post-genocide Rwanda, see Filip Reyntjens, "Rwanda, Ten Years On: From Genocide to Dictatorship," *African Affairs* 103 (2004), 177–210; Front Line, "Disappearances, Arrests, Threats, Intimidation and Co-option of Human Rights Defenders 2001–2004," Dublin, 2005; Human Rights Watch, "Preparing for Elections: Tightening Control in the Name of Unity," New York, May 8, 2003; and International Crisis Group, "Rwanda at the End of the Transition: A Necessary Political Liberalisation," ICG Africa Report No. 53, November 13, 2002.

45. For good overviews of Rwanda's post-genocide approach to justice, see Alison Des

priate system to account for Rwanda's genocide. Even though many people took part in the genocide, they often did so because of direct state-backed pressure and because they were scared. Maximum justice is not a good fit with this reality. Meaningful accountability should focus on prosecuting the national and local leaders who used their authority and power to order and legitimize killing as well as on the thugs who did the lion's share of killing and mobilization.

Given its slowness, Rwanda's justice system has generated considerable resentment among survivors and their families as well as among detainees and their families. The RPF also excludes general discussion of crimes its soldiers committed in Rwanda and the Democratic Republic of Congo from *Gacaca* hearings. The result is that many Rwandans believe the justice system is unfair: impunity still applies to the victors. That resentment is likely to contribute to long-term instability in Rwanda and to hamper reconciliation. Though the decision might have been a difficult one to make, given the magnitude of the genocide and the scale of participation, the RPF authorities might well have limited their focus to the key leaders and thugs most responsible for initiating and executing the genocide. There are lessons here for other societies trying to rebuild after mass violence.

Final Thoughts

Some of my findings and conclusions are surprising—at any rate, they surprised me. When I went to Rwanda to research the genocide in depth, I expected ethnic antipathy, nationalist beliefs, and radio propaganda to be the factors that drove the killing. I found instead that war, state power, group pressure, and ethnic categorization were the most consequential factors. Surprised, I sought to verify what I found and to make sense of the genocide in light of what I found. The result is this book.

When I discuss my findings with others, I am often asked, "Do you think that everyone is capable of committing genocide? Could it happen anywhere?" The questions are difficult to answer. It may be true that genocide can happen in any society, but a more accurate claim is that genocide tends to happen under particular conditions. In previous chapters, I sought to specify the conditions that mattered in Rwanda

---

Forges and Timothy Longman, "Legal Responses to Genocide in Rwanda," in *My Neighbor, My Enemy: Justice and Community in the Aftermath of Mass Atrocity*, ed. Eric Stover and Harvey Weinstein (New York: Cambridge University Press, 2004), 49–68; and Lars Waldorf, "Mass Justice for Mass Atrocity: Rethinking Local Justice as Transitional Justice," *Temple Law Review*, forthcoming.

in April 1994. In this chapter, I have extended the arguments to other cases. As Tone Bringa notes above and as I have tried to document, war does change people. So does coercive social pressure. The desire to protect oneself and one's family—whether from outsiders or insiders—is a powerful motivation, one that should not be underestimated. After spending six months talking to perpetrators and after nearly a decade of study, I come to the conclusion that successful resistance in the face of direct, wartime pressure to participate in genocide required luck, resources, uncommon savvy, strong moral principle, and great courage—and probably all five. I might wish to promote such factors (at least the latter three), but a better strategy is to work to prevent the conditions in which ordinary people have to face such terrible choices.

Appendix

Appendix table 2.1 Commune-level onset of genocide listed by source[a]

Commune listed by prefecture	Government memorial commission (with page #)	Leave none	Death, despair	ICTR	Author interviews	Other	Onset estimate
Butare							
Ngoma	Apr 19 (5)	Apr 7–11, 19–20[b]	Apr 21 (352)		Apr 10 (2), 14		Apr 18–20
Mugusa	Apr 26 (6–7)	Apr 21?		Apr 22[c]			Apr 21–23
Huye	Apr 22 (8) (503)	Apr 20 (468, 537)			Apr 21		Apr 21–23
Muyaga	Apr 27 (8–9)				Apr 22, 27		Apr 21–23
Gishamvu	Apr 20, 23 (10)	Apr 15–19[d]	Apr 13 (353)				Apr 18–20
Shyanda	Apr 22 (11)	Apr 22 (503)					Apr 21–23
Mbazi	Apr 25 (11)	Apr 25 (467)			Apr 20		Apr 21–23
Kibayi	Apr 19 (12)						Apr 18–20
Muganza	Apr 19 (13)			Apr 19[e]			Apr 18–20
Ruyinya	Apr 21 (14)		Apr 20 (345)				Apr 18–20
Maraba	Apr 15 (15)	Apr 14–16, 17–20[f]					Apr 15–17
Kigembe	Apr 17 (15)	Apr 18 (454) (335)	Apr 21				Apr 18–20
Nyaruhengeri	Apr 21 (16–17)	Apr 18–19 (452–53)					Apr 18–20
Ndora	Apr 20 (18)	Apr 22 (467)					Apr 18–20
Nyabisindu	Apr 21 (18)				Apr 21 (2), 24		Apr 21–23
Rusatira	Apr 22 (19)	Apr 22 (467)					Apr 21–23
Rushashya	Apr 22 (19)						Apr 21–23
Muyira	Apr 22 (20)						Apr 21–23

[a] There are six principal sources for the table: The sources are: (1) a report from a six-member commission appointed by the Rwandan government's Ministry of Higher Education. The report lists major massacre sites and the dates of those massacres in most communes throughout the country. The report makes observations for about two-thirds of the communes in Rwanda but has two major limitations. First, in general, the commission focused on and reported massacre sites and the dates of those massacres, not when the genocide began in a commune. Second, the report does not appear to have a methodology for specifying onset. (2) Alison Des Forges, *Leave None*, which has detailed commune-level information about onset dates for three-quarters of the communes in Butare Prefecture, about half the communes in Gikongoro Prefecture, and for a few other communes in the rest of the country. (3) African Rights, *Death, Despair, and Defiance*, which is primarily a collection of survivor testimony and has information about onset dates for about 30% of the communes in Rwanda where genocide occurred. In most cases, survivors report onset of genocidal violence they witnessed; however, in a significant number of cases, survivors report what they heard in neighboring communities. (4) Various decisions handed down by the International Criminal Tribunal for Rwanda (ICTR), and news coverage of the ICTR. (5) Ruka's *Dictionnaire nominative* (see below). (6) My interviews with 230 perpetrators nationwide.
[b] Note that the first killings from April 7–11 were limited; major killing did not begin until April 19-20; see 68, 472, and 485.
[c] Internews March 15, 2002, Butare Trial.
[d] Note that the first killings from April 15–18 were limited; the first report of a major killing was April 19; see 495 and 463.
[e] Internews November 20, 2001, Butare Trial.
[f] Note that the first killings from April 14–16 were sparse, while the first major reported killings occurred between April 17-20. See 442, 445, and 451.

(continued)

Appendix table 2.1 Continued

Commune listed by prefecture	Government memorial commission (with page #)	Leave none	Death, despair	ICTR	Author interviews	Other	Onset estima
Ntyazo	Apr 24 (21)	Apr 24 (497–98)	Apr 25 (356)				Apr 24+
Nyakizu	Apr 15 (22)	Apr 13–14 (373–76)	Apr 19 (337)				Apr 12–
Byumba							
Kiyombe*g							RPF
Muvumba*							RPF
Cyungo							No date
Kivuye*							RPF
Cyumba*		-					RPF
Mukarange*							RPF
Buyoga					Apr 7, 9 (2), 11	Apr 10h	Apr 9–1
Ngarama							No date
Kinyami							No date
Kibali			Apr 9 (366)				Apr 9
Giti	None (27)						No killi
Muhura	Apr 8 (25)				Apr 8, Apr 10		Apr 9–1
Rutare					Apr 8, 10		Apr 9–1
Bwisge							No date
Gituza							No date
Tumba							No date
Murambi		Apr 7 (209)	Apr 7 (385)		Apr 7		Apr 6–8
Cyangugu							
Kamembe	Apr 19 (30)	Apr 7 (209)	Apr 7–9 (493–503)	Apr 9; Apr 8–9; Apr 10i	Apr 7 (2), 8, 9		Apr 6–8
Cyimbogo	Apr 13 (31)		Apr 7–8 (480)		Apr 10		Apr 6–8
Gisuma	Apr 10, 12–13, 15, 10–21, 19 (36–42)		Apr 7–8 (506, 520, 578)	Apr 8–9j	Apr 7		Apr 6–8
Karengera			Apr 7 (490)				Apr 6–8

gA * indicates incomplete government control as of April 6, 1994, either because the commune was partia or completely in the demilitarized zone or in areas controlled by the RPF. In the absence of a precise bounda I base this estimate on maps found in Alison Des Forges, *Leave None*, 693; Filip Reyntjens, *L'Afrique des gran lacs en crise*, 92; *Guns over Kigali*, 31, and Department of Defense declassified note, 3.

hBased on proceedings in the pilot Gacaca program as monitored by Human Rights Watch, personal commu nication.

iThe April 9 date comes from the Indictment in "Prosecutor vs. Emmanuel Bagambiki and Samuel Ima ishimwe"; the second date comes from the March 1, 2001 and September 19, 2001, Internews reports on the tr proceedings; the third dates comes from the October 23, 2000, Hirondelle report on the trial proceedings.

jICTR, "The Prosecutor v. André Ntagerura, Emmanuel Bagambiki, and Samuel Imanishimwe," Case N ICTR-99-46-T, Judgement and Sentence, February 2004, 114, 117.

(continue

pendix table **2.1** Continued

ommune ted prefecture	Government memorial commission (with page #)	Leave none	Death, despair	ICTR	Author interviews	Other	Onset estimate
Nyakabuye							No date
Gishoma	Apr 14 (47)				Apr 12		Apr 12–14
Bugarama				Apr 7[k]	Apr 7–8, 16		Apr 6–8
Gafunzo			Apr 9 (531)		Apr 7, 8, 9, 10		Apr 9–11
Kagano			Apr 8–9 (457, 464)	Apr 12[l]			Apr 9–11
Gatare	Apr 6–12 (50)		Apr 7–8, 11–12 (450, 512, 518)				Apr 6–8
Kirambo			Apr 9 (457, 468)				Apr 9–11
kongoro							
Nyamagabe							No date
Mudasomwa		Apr 7–8 (311)			Apr 10		Apr 6–8
Mubuga		Apr 10, 14 (313, 442)	Apr 10, 13 (291)				Apr 9–11
Nshili							No date
Kivu		Apr 11–12 (332)	Apr 11 (332)		Apr 9, 10		Apr 9–11
Rwamiko		Apr 7–8 (311)	Apr 7 (293–94, 299, 332)		Apr 13	Apr 6–8	
Karama	Apr 21 (58)		Apr 12 (329)				Apr 12–14
Kinyamakara		Apr 9–12 (332)	Apr 12 (359)	Apr 10, 12			Apr 9–11
Rukondo							No date
Musange					Apr 8, 11		Apr 9–11
Karambo					Apr 10 (2)		Apr 9–11
Muko	Apr 7 (61)	Apr 7–8 (209, 312)	Apr 7 (317, 326)				Apr 6–8
Musebeya		Apr 9–11 (325, 314 319)					Apr 9–11
senyi							
Rubavu		Apr 7 (209)		Apr 7[m]	Apr 7 (3)		Apr 6–8
Mutura				Apr 7[n]			Apr 6–8
Rwerere		Apr 7 (209)	Apr 7 (555)				Apr 6–8

[k] ICTR, "The Prosecutor v. André Ntagerura," 107–8.
[l] See Hirondelle, November 2, 2000 (Cyangugu Trial); ICTR, "The Prosecutor v. André Ntagerura," 9, 157.
[m] International Criminal Tribunal for Rwanda, "The Prosecutor v. Ferdinand Nahimana, Jean-Bosco Barayagwiza, Hassan Ngeze," Case No. ICTR-99-52-T, Judgement and Sentence, December 3, 2003, 239, 285.
[n] ICTR, "The Prosecutor v. Ferdinand Nahimana, Jean-Bosco Barayagwiza, Hassan Ngeze," 247, 249.

(continued)

Appendix table 2.1 Continued

Commune listed by prefecture	Government memorial commission (with page #)	Leave none	Death, despair	ICTR	Author interviews	Other	Onset estimat
Kanama	Apr 7 (209)	Apr 7 (544)					Apr 6–8
Giciye							No date
Gaseke							No date
Kayove					Apr 8 (3), 9		Apr 6–8
Nyamyumba					May		May ?
Karago							No date
Satinsyi	Apr 10 (67)	Apr 7 (209)					Apr 6–8
Ramba							No date
Kibilira	Apr 13 (69)						Unclear
Gitarama							
Rutobwe	Apr 15 (71)						Apr 15–1
Musambira	Apr 14, 20 (72–73)		Apr 14, 18 (363)		Apr 19, 20, 30, end		Apr 18–2
Nyamabuye	Apr 23, 24 (74–75)				Apr 9, 14, end		Apr 21–2
Mukingi	Apr 26 (76)						Apr 24+?
Kayenzi	Apr 19 (76–77)						Apr 18–2
Ntongwe	Apr 21 (77)						Apr 21–2
Mushubati	Apr 20 (78)						Apr 18–2
Bulinga	No date						No date
Nyabikenke	Apr 11 (79)						Apr 9–11
Taba	Apr 19 (79–80)			Apr 19[o]			Apr 18–2
Runda	Apr 15, 17 (80–81)			Apr 18[p]			Apr 15–1
Tambwe	Apr 22, 23 (82–83)						Apr 21–2
Kigoma	Apr 22, 23 (83–84)						Apr 21–2
Masango	Apr 21 (84)						Apr 21–2
Murama	Apr 24 (85)						Apr 24+?
Mugina	Apr 20 (86)					Apr 21[q]	Apr 18–2
Nyakabanda							No date
Kibungo							
Rukara	Apr 7, 12–16 (89)		Apr 7 (389–90)	Apr 9–13	Apr 7		Apr 6–8
Muhazi	Apr 11, 15 (92)		Apr 11–12 (379)				Apr 9–11

[o]ICTR, "The Prosecutor vs. Jean-Paul Akayesu," Case No. ICTR-96-4-T, 42, Pargagraph 1 and 51–53, pa: graphs 67,71, 85, 93. Note however that one witness claimed killings were widespread after April 18; see 4 paragraph 47.

[p]ICTR, "The Prosecutor vs. Jean-Paul Akayesu," Case No. ICTR-96-4-T, 36, paragraph 429.

[q]See "Homage to Courage," African Rights. Note that April 20 was the day the Burgomaster of Mugina w killed for opposing genocidal violence. On this point, see also Alison Des Forges's testimony at the ICTR: Thier Cruvellier, "Résistance et collaboration des bourgmestres pendant le génocide," Diplomatie Judiciare, May 2 1997.

(continue

ppendix table 2.1 Continued

ommune sted v prefecture	Government memorial commission (with page #)	Leave none	Death, despair	ICTR	Author interviews	Other	Onset estimate
Rutonde	Apr 12–20, 7 (103–9)		Apr 7 (388)	Apr 7[r]	Apr 8 (2)		Apr 6–8
Nkungu	Apr 13–14, 12–20, 17, 16–19 (107–10)						Apr 12–14
Kigarama	Apr 7, 7–15, 8, 8 (114–17)				Apr 8, 9		Apr 6–8
Kayonza	Apr 12–19, 12–19, 7 (119–21)				Apr 10		Apr 9–11
Kabarando	Apr 7–13 (123)		Apr 13 (383)		Apr 7		Apr 6–8
Birenga	Apr 14–16, 21–23, 7 (124–36)		Apr 7,9 (382, 377)		Apr 7, 9, 10(2)		Apr 6–8
Mugesera	Apr 12, 11–14, 12 (129–31)		Apr 8–12 (368–69)		Apr 9 (2), Apr 10		Apr 9–11
Sake	Apr 10, 6–8 (130–32)	Apr 7 (209)	Apr 7 (371–74)		Apr 7(3), 8(2), 10		Apr 6–8
Rusomo	Apr, 8, 13, 14, 17 (133)			Apr 9–11			Apr 9–11
Rukira	Apr 14–15 (136)				Apr 14		Apr 12–14
ibuye Gitesi						Ibuka[s]	
	Apr 13, 15, 15 (138–43)		Apr 7 (395)	Apr 9–12[t]	Apr 7, 8, 10, 11, 14, 15	April 6–17?	Apr 6–8
Gishyita	Apr 7, 15, 16 (144)		Apr 8 (452)			April 10–11	Apr 9–11
Gisovu	Apr 16 (150)			Apr 9[u]		April 7–10	Apr 9–11
Rwamatamu	Apr 12–13 (154)		Apr 10 (435)		Apr 8, 10	Apr 10–11	Apr 9–11
Mabanza	Apr 9–14 (155–58)			Apr 9–12; 8–9[v]	Apr	Apr 9–11 9–10	Apr 9–11

[r] Internews, March 13, 2001, Semanza Trial.
[s] The source for Kibuye figures is Ibuka, *Dictionnaire nominatif,* 9–1085.
[t] Note in particular paragraphs 298 and 299 of ICTR, "The Prosecutor vs. Clément Kayishema and Obed Ruzinana," Case No. ICTR-95-I-T, where a witness claims that the atmosphere changed the night of April 9 and the rst witnesses dead in the neighborhood happened on April 12. Witness O claims seeing wounded on April 7, ut under cross-examination this timing is unclear and seems to pertain to Kigali; see paragraph 296.
[u] ICTR, "The Prosecutor vs. Alfred Musema," Case No. ICTR-96-13-A, paragraph 362.
[v] The former date comes from ICTR, "The Prosecutor versus Clement Kayishema," paragraph 304 and the latter from ICTR, "The Prosecutor vs. Ignace Bagilishema," Case No. ICTR-95-1A-T, paragraphs 334, 381.

(*continued*)

Appendix table 2.1 Continued

Commune listed by prefecture	Government memorial commission (with page #)	Leave none	Death, despair	ICTR	Author interviews	Other	Onset estima
Bwakira					Apr 14	Apr 12–13	Apr 12–
Rutsiro	Apr 8–10, 10–26 (158–60)					Apr 7–8	Apr 6–8
Mwendo	Apr 15 (163)					Apr 8	Apr 6–8
Kivumu		Apr 7 (209)	Apr 7, 9 (454, 406)		Apr 8, 14	Apr 10	Apr 9–1
Kigali–Rural							
Rushashi	end Apr (211)						Apr 24+
Musasa	May (212)						Apr 24+
Tare	end Apr– May 1994 (208)						Apr 24+
Kanzenze	Apr 6–15 (169–71)	Apr 7 (209)	Apr 7 (270–71)		Apr 7 (2)		Apr 6–8
Gashora	Apr 7–9 (178)	Apr 7 (209)			Apr 6, 7 (3), 8, 10		Apr 6–8
Ngenda	Apr 7–14 (179–81)	Apr 7 (209)			Apr 7 (5), 8 (2), 10		Apr 6–8
Butamwa	Apr 13–20 (181)					Apr 7^w	Apr 6–8
Kanombe	April 6–8, 9 (183–85)		Apr 6–9 (276–81, 284)				Apr 6–8
Bicumbi	Apr 7, 8–10, 11–20 (186–89)			Apr 7–8^x	Apr 8 (2), 9, 10, 11, 13, 15 (2)		Apr 6–8
Gikoro	Apr 13, 16 (190–91)		Apr 7, 13 (287)	Apr 7–10^y			Apr 6–8
Gikomero	Apr 13–15 (192)			Apr 12; 9–11, 12^z	Apr 10, 12, 14		Apr 9–1
Rubungo	Apr 7–28 (195–201)						Apr 6–8
Rutongo							No date
Mugambazi	Apr 10 (206)						Apr 9–1
Shyorongi	Apr 10 (207)						Apr 9–1
Mbogo	Apr 7 (211)						Apr 6–8

^{w}Kimberlee Acquaro and Peter Landesman, "Out of Madness, A Matriarchy," *Mother Jones* 28, no. 1 (January/February 2003), 59–63.
^{x}ICTR, "The Prosecutor vs. Laurent Semanza," Case No. ICTR-9-20-T, Judgement and Sentence, May 200 paragraphs 174, 215, and 224.
^{y}See ICTR, "The Prosecutor v. Laurent Semanza," paragraphs 9, 150, 161, 174, 194–96
^{z}For the former date, see Hirondelle January 29, 2003, Semanza Trial; for the latter dates, see Internews, Se tember 11, 2001, and September 13, 2001, Semanza Trial.

(continue

ppendix table 2.1 Continued

ommune ted prefecture	Government memorial commission (with page #)	Leave none	Death, despair	ICTR	Author interviews	Other	Onset estimate
gali–City							
Kicukiro	Apr 7 (214–16)		Apr 7 (281)				Apr 6–8
Nyarugenge	Apr 8, 20; June 10 (218–21)	Apr 8 (210)					Apr 6–8
uhengeri							
Kigombe*				Apr 14[aa]	Apr 20		Apr 12–14
Nkuli	Apr 7 (225)			Apr 7, 8[bb]	Apr 7		Apr 6–8
Mukingo		Apr 7 (209)		Apr 7[cc]	Apr 7 (4)		Apr 6–8
Nyakinama							No date
Kinigi*				Apr[dd]			Apr 6–8
Butaro*	RPF						RPF
Nkumba*	DMZ						DMZ
Nyamutera	Apr 4 (230)						No date
Ndusu	Apr 10 (231)				Apr 7, 13, end Apr		Apr 6–8
Gatonde	Apr 12–13 (234)			Apr 12[ee]			Apr 12–14
Nyamugali							No date
Nyaratovu				Apr 8–10[ff]	Apr 7(2), 8		Apr 6–8
Cyabingo	April						No date
Cyeru*	Apr 12 (234–35)						Apr 12–14?
Ruhondo							No date
Kidaho*							RPF

[aa]This date refers to the massacre at the Ruhengeri Court of Appeal. There may also have been attacks in the me commune before the massacre, but I do not have evidence of them. On the date of the massacre, see ICTR, The Prosecutor vs. Juvénal Kajelijeli," 134.
[bb]ICTR, "The Prosecutor vs. Juvénal Kajelijeli," 40–41, 130, 161; Internews, October 3, 2001.
[cc]ICTR, "The Prosecutor vs. Juvénal Kajelijeli," 40–41, 103, 129, 161, and Internews, July 17, 2001, December 6, 2001, and November 22, 2002.
[dd]ICTR, "The Prosecutor v. Juvénal Kajelijeli," 148.
[ee]ICTR, "The Prosecutor vs. Ferdinand Nahimana, Jean-Bosco Barayagwiza, Hassan Ngeze," 211.
[ff]ICTR, "The Prosecutor vs. Ferdinand Nahimana, Jean-Bosco Barayagwiza, Hassan Ngeze," 212.

Appendix table 2.2 Prefecture-level variation in the onset of genocidal violence

Prefecture	Onset dates	Category
Butare	Apr 14–24	Late
Byumba	Apr 7–10	Middle
Cyangugu	Apr 7–11	Middle
Gikongoro	Apr 7–12	Middle
Gisenyi	Apr 7–8	Early
Gitarama	Apr 14–21	Late
Kibungo	Apr 7–12	Middle
Kibuye	Apr 7–12	Middle
Kigali-Rural	Apr 6–30	Early[a]
Kigali-City	Apr 7–8	Early
Ruhengeri	Apr 7–8	Early

Source: Appendix table 2.1

[a]Kigali-Rural deserves comment. Kigali-Rural is the least homogeneous prefecture geographically in Rwanda, wrapping around Kigali-City to the northwest, north, east, and southeast. In all but the northwest area of the prefecture and the commune of Gikomero, genocidal violence began quickly and intensively (in Ngenda, Kanzenze, Gashora, Bicumbi, Kanombe, Gikoro, Gikomero, Butamwa, and Rubongo Communes). However, in the northwest area—Rushashi, Musha, Tare, and Shyorongi Communes—most violence began quite late. On balance, the prefecture is characterized by early onset of violence, but the quite distinct sub-regional variation should be remembered.

Appendix table 2.3 Prefecture-level factors determining genocide onset. (bivariate regression results with onset as the dependent variable [$N = 11$])

Independent variables	Estimated coefficient	Constant	R squared
Wealth	.052 (.081)*	1.123 (.429)	.273
Education I (% literate)	−0.018 (.075)	1.927(.510)	.015
Education II (% finished primary school)	−0.98 (.080)	2.343 (.481)	.144
Education III (% with secondary school and above education)	−0.033 (.106)	1.987 (.591)	.011
Profession (% not engaged in farming, animal raising, fishing, or hunting)	.091 (.08)	1.328 (.486)	.125
Unemployment	.118 (.064)*	1.109 (.436)	.273
Parcel size	−.074 (.082)	2.216 (.498)	.083
Population size	−.027 (.075)	1.982 (.508)	.015
Population density	.045 (.074)	1.545 (.501)	.040
Population growth	.177 (.078)**	.964 (.420)	.366
Youthfulness	.163 (.115)	1.064 (.577)	.181
Percentage of Tutsi in prefecture	−.073 (.071)	2.255 (.485)	.103
Frontline proximity	−.571 (.214)**	2.857 (.428)	.442
Political support for MRND	.778 (.246)***	.333 (.497)	.527
Kigali proximity	.036 (.074)	1.600 (.505)	.026
Presence of refugees/displaced	−.833 (.553)	2.500 (.500)	.202

Note: Significance levels: * = .10; ** = .05; *** = .01. The dependent variable is coded such that earlier onset is a lower number (early onset = 1; middle onset = 2; late onset = 3). Most independent variables are coded such that the greater the rank the lower number. Thus, a positive relationship indicates that an increase in the explanatory variable would lead to earlier onset. For example, all the education variables indicate a negative relationship with onset (though not statistically significant ones), suggesting that the less educated a region, the earlier the onset. By contrast, the relationship between onset and wealth is positive: the wealthier the prefecture, the earlier the onset. See appendix tables 2.4–2.6 for independent variables data.

Appendix table 2.4 Regional socioeconomic variables

Prefecture	Education rank (literacy %)	Education Rank (% finished primary school)	Education rank (% sec. school and above)	Wealth rank (inverse poverty)	Profession on rank[a]	Unemployment level (high = 1)	Parcel size (large = 1)	Onset rank
Butare	4	4	2	7	4	5	6	3
Byumba	10	8	8	3	10	9	3	2
Cyangugu	5	4	6	5	2	4	8	2
Gikongoro	11	7	6	8	7	11	4	2
Gisenyi	7	10	5	4[b]	3	3	9	1
Gitarama	2	2	3	6	6	8	4	3
Kibungo	6	3	8	1	9	7	2	2
Kibuye	8	6	6	9	8	10	5	2
Kigali-Rur.	3	5	4	2[c]	4	2	1	1
Kigali-City	1	1	1	2	1	1	10[d]	1
Ruhengeri	9	9	7	4	5	6	7	1

Sources: République du Rwanda, *Recensement général*, 135 (education rank literacy); 140 (education rank years of education); 108 (Profession Rank); and 99 (unemployment). Fernand Bézy, *Rwanda 1962–1989: bilan socio-economique d'un régime*, Institut d'Études du Développement, Louvain-la-Neuve, January 1990, 43 (parcel size). World Bank, "Rwanda: Poverty Reduction and Sustainable Growth," Report No. 12465-RW, May 16, 1994, 9 (wealth). All data collected in 1991, except wealth (collected 1983–85) and parcel size (collected 1991).

[a] Profession rank is the inverse of those in a prefecture whose primary activity is farming, animal raising, fishing, or hunting.

[b] The World Bank report does not include a figure for Gisenyi in its poverty rankings; however, elsewhere, the report refers to the northwest as a single unit. Thus, I assign the same rank to Gisenyi as that given to Ruhengeri.

[c] The World Bank report does not distinguish between the Kigali-Rural and Kigali-City Prefectures, thus I assign them the same number.

[d] As an urban prefecture, Kigali-City naturally has the smallest average parcel size. Elsewhere average parcel size may be an indicator of relative wealth, though that is not the case for Kigali-City.

Appendix table 2.5 Regional socioeconomic and demographic variables

Prefecture	Population size (high = 1)	Density (high = 1)	Pop. growth (high = 1)	Age rank[a] (young = 1)	Ethnic rank (high Tutsi = 1)	Onset rank
Butare	5	3	8	7	2	3
Byumba	3	10	5	3	10	2
Cyangugu	8	7	4	7	5	2
Gikongoro	10	9	8	6	4	2
Gisenyi	6	6	3	4	9	1
Gitarama	2	4	7	5	6	3
Kibungo	7	11	1	2	8	2
Kibuye	9	8	7	6	3	2
Kigali-Rur.	1	5	2	5	7	1
Kigali-City	11	1[b]	2[c]	1	1	1
Ruhengeri	4	2	6	5	11	1

Sources: République du Rwanda, *Recensement général*, 85–87 (population size and adjusted dependency); 17 (density); 21 (growth rate); 239 (age); and 124 (ethnic rank). All data collected in 1991.

[a]Age data measure mean age of child-bearing women.

[b]Note that the census data lumps Kigali-City and Kigali-Rural together for its Kigali score. Given that Kigali-City has the highest density, I have coded that prefecture as "1" and left Kigali-Rural as is in its ranking.

[c]Note again that the census data does not distinguish between Kigali-City and Kigali-Rural. Because it is not clear that they should be distinguished in terms of their population growth rate, I have left the rankings as is. Growth rate is measured a percentage of growth between 1978 and 1991.

Appendix table 2.6 Regional geographic, military, and political variables

Prefecture	Proximity to Kigali	Proximity to front[a]	Military camp	Internally displaced or Burundi refugees	Political support	Onset rank
Butare	8	Low	Yes	Yes	PSD/MDR	3
Byumba	4	High	Yes	Yes	MRND	2
Cyangugu	11	Low	Yes	Yes	MDR/MRND/CDR	2
Gikongoro	9	Low	No	Yes	PSD/MRND	2
Gisenyi	10	Mid	Yes	No	MRND/CDR	1
Gitarama	3	Low	Yes	No	MDR	3
Kibungo	5	Mid	Yes	Yes	MRND/MDR	2
Kibuye	7	Low	No	No	MRND/MDR	2
Kigali-Rural	2	Mid	Yes	Yes	MRND/MDR/PL	1
Kigali-City	1	High	Yes	Yes	Mixed	1
Ruhengeri	6	High	Yes	Yes	MRND	1

Sources: Author estimations
[a]High = prefectures where RPF troops were stationed; mid = neighboring prefectures to those where RPF were stationed; and low = those prefectures where at least one prefecture separated it from a prefecture where RPF troops were.

Appendix table 4.1 Bivariate regression analyses with participation as the dependent variable[a]

Variable	Estimated coefficient	Constant	R squared
Age	−212 (.057)***	2.046 (.180)	.065
Paternity	−.105 (.037)***	1.712 (.122)	.038
Education	−.073 (.052)	1.547 (.130)	.010
Literate	−.019 (.112)	1.435 (.187)	.000
Civic association	−.022 (.129)	1.405 (.172)	.000
Umuganda	−.041 (.162)	1.467 (.309)	.000
Night patrols	.028 (.111)	1.320 (.159)	.000

Significance levels: * = .10; ** = .05; *** = .01; standard errors reported in parentheses
[a]Participation is ranked here and in subsequent regression analyses on a 1–5 scale, as per the categories listed in table 4.8.

Appendix table 4.2 Multivariate regression with participation as the dependent variable

Variable	Estimated coefficient
Age	−.217 (.086)***
Paternity	.013 (.056)
Education	−.101 (.05)**
Constant	2.234 (.226) ***
R squared	.074

Significance levels: * = .10; ** = .05; *** = .01; standard errors reported in parentheses

Appendix table 5.1 Pre-genocide Rwanda with degree of participation as the dependent variable

	Bivariate regression results		
Variable	*Estimated coefficient*	*Constant*	*R squared*
War change	.050 (.113)	1.336 (.164)	.001
Fear of RPF	.214 (.105)**	1.070 (.166)	.021
Change from multipartyism	.152 (.113)	1.155 (.192)	.009
Affected by changes in Burundi	.157 (.063)***	1.132 (.122)	.031
Opinion of Habyarimana government	−.123 (.070)*	1.651 (.170)	.016
Life conditions	−.227 (.088)***	1.958 (.233)	.035
Vision of the future	−.125 (.073)*	1.672 (.176)	.018

Significance levels: * = .10; ** = .05; *** = .01; standard errors reported in parentheses

Multivariate regression results	
Variable	*Estimated coefficient*
War change	−.075 (.151)
Fear of RPF	.222 (.150)
Change from multipartyism	−.029 (.157)
Affected by changes in Burundi	.138 (.082)*
Opinion of Habyarimana government	−.053 (.084)
Life conditions	−.212 (.109)*
Vision of the future	.008 (.087)
Constant	1.630 (.449)***
R squared	.074

Significance levels: * = .10; ** = .05; *** = .01; standard errors reported in parentheses

Appendix table 5.2 Interethnic relations with degree of participation as the dependent variable (weighted results)

Bivariate regression results			
Variable	Estimated coefficient	Constant	R squared
Tutsi in family[a]	−.345 (.114)***	1.985 (.202)	.046
Relations with Tutsi neighbor[b]	.657 (.121)***	.647 (.149)	.134
Post-1990 change in relations with neighbor	.346 (.085)***	.970 (.120)	.084

Significance levels: * = .10; ** = .05; *** = .01; standard errors reported in parentheses
[a]Note that responses are coded such that "no" = 1 and "yes" = 2, thus a negative coefficient indicates that those who did not have a Tutsi family member were more likely to be more violent than those who did.
[b]This variable was coded from good to bad, such that a positive relationship with degree of violence indicates that those who reported negative feelings were more likely to be more violent than those who reported good relations.

Multivariate regression results	
Variable	Estimated coefficient
Tutsi in family	−.358 (.123)***
Relations with Tutsi neighbor	.396 (.137)***
Post-1990 change in relations with neighbor	.196 (.085)**
Constant	1.313 (.289)***
R squared	.147

Significance levels: * = .10; ** = .05; *** = .01; standard errors reported in parentheses

Appendix table 5.3 Racist ideology and propaganda with degree of participation as the dependent variable

	Bivariate regression results		
Variable	*Estimated coefficient*	*Constant*	*R squared*
Hutu and Tutsi as different *amoko*?	.037 (.057)	1.310 (.142)	.002
Tutsis as Hamites?	.091 (.075)	1.262 (.129)	.008
RPF reinstalling monarchy?	.106 (.067)	1.200 (.127)	.013
Heard of Hutu Ten Commandments?	.859 (.321)***	.519 (.334)	.036
Heard of *rubanda nyamwishi*?	.134 (.073)*	1.155 (.155)	.018
Heard of Hutu *Pawa*?	.128 (.080)	1.157 (.159)	.015
Rwanda as a Hutu nation	.016 (.235)	1.353 (.255)	.000
Do Hutus hate Tutsis?	.241 (.236)	1.124 (.256)	.006

Significance levels: * = .10; ** = .05; *** = .01; standard errors reported in parentheses

Multivariate regression results	
Variable	*Estimated coefficient*
Hutu and Tutsi as different *amoko*?	.005 (.083)
Tutsis as Hamites?	−.197 (.125)
RPF reinstalling monarchy?	.112 (.108)
Heard of Hutu Ten Commandments?	.830 (.359)**
Heard of *rubanda nyamwishi*?	−.019 (.101)
Heard of Hutu *Pawa*?	.126 (.120)
Rwanda as a Hutu nation	.350 (.330)
Do Hutus hate Tutsis?	−.034 (.262)
Constant	.271 (.556)
R squared	.062

Significance levels: * = .10; ** = .05; *** = .01; standard errors reported in parentheses

Appendix table 5.4 Motivation with degree of participation as the dependent variable (bivariate regressions; weighted results)

	Estimated coefficient	Constant	R squared
Primary motivation	.119 (.023)***	1.181 (.066)	.117
Aggregate motivation	.126 (.024)***	1.130 (.087)	.144

Significance levels: * = .10; ** = .05; *** = .01; standard errors reported in parentheses

Appendix table 5.5 Other motivations with degree of participation as the dependent variable (weighted results)

Bivariate regression results			
Variable	Estimated coefficient	Constant	R squared
Did the radio incite?	.384 (.179)**	1.020 (.212)	.026
Looting?	.425 (.137)***	.893 (.177)	.056
Alcohol during killing?	.158 (.205)	1.250 (.247)	.005
Obey authorities?	−.419 (.256)	1.910 (.289)	.023
Work for the country?	.600 (.158)***	.717 (.238)	.112

Significance levels: * = .10; ** = .05; *** = .01; standard errors reported in parentheses

Multivariate regression results	
Variable	Estimated coefficient
Did the radio incite?	.108 (.252)
Looting?	−.284 (.205)
Obey authorities?	−.283 (.261)
Work for the country?	.761 (.202)***
Constant	1.020 (.499)**
R squared	.210

Significance levels: * = .10; ** = .05; *** = .01; standard errors reported in parentheses

Appendix table 5.6 Comprehensive multivariate regression
analysis with degree of participation as the dependent variable

Variable	Estimated coefficient
Age	−.094 (.131)
Education	−.071 (.104)
Fear of RPF	.139 (.185)
Affected by Burundi	.061 (.114)
Life conditions	.001 (.155)
Relations with Tutsis	−.198 (.206)
Tutsi in family?	.261 (.216)
Combined motivation	.094 (.036)***
Radio incitement	.087 (.272)
Work for the country?	.179 (.228)
Constant	1.043 (.939)
R squared	.255

Significance levels: * = .10; ** = .05; *** = .01; standard errors reported in parentheses

Index

Numbers in italics refer to figures and tables.